LIFE IN THE BALANCE

7 Strategies for Making Life Work

Michael Komara
With Karl Nilsson

Elk Lake
PUBLISHING™

www.ElkLakePublishing.com • Elk Rapids, Michigan USA

L I F E   I N   T H E   B A L A N C E

Published by Elk Lake Publishing, Inc.
Copyright ©2013 by Elk Lake Publishing
ISBN: 978-0-9793543-4-2

Additional copies are available at *Amazon.com*. For bulk quantities or group discounts, visit *www.7FLife.com*.

For information on Michael Komara's speaking engagements or to book a 7F Life workshop, go to *www.7FLife.com*.

Jacket design: Evan Jones
Art Direction: Karl Nilsson
Format design: Kevin Stoddard
Illustrations: David Wickman
Printed in the United States of America

To my wife Mary Ann and son Drew.

You have enriched my life with your love and laughter.
I am a better person because of you.

WITH GRATITUDE

I sincerely wish to thank the following people who have made rich deposits into my life…

My business partners: Joe Mackey and John Dankovich, along with our company's Chief Integrator, Nathan Bohannon.

My friends and mentors: Dr. Loren Siffring, Dr. Sharon Tice, Tom and Kay Kenny, Walt and Monica Frankiewicz, Joe and Lori Mejaly, Dr. Howard Hendricks, Steve Andrews, Chuck McLeod, Dave Wilson, Jeff and Gina Petherick, Steve Norman, Rick and Rita Howard, Mark and Dave Nelson, Doug and Kim Clark, Tim and Cathie Brandt, Mike Carnill, Jim Kutnow, Joel Andrus, Dr. Tom Constable, Juno Smalley, Mike Suchowski, Gary Foran, Dr. Jim and Laurie Thames, and Jim Slaughter.

My family: My parents Charlotte and Michael "Mickey" Komara. My sisters Paula, Karen and Jodey. My brothers-in-law Jim, Gary and Frank. My cousins Jim, Frank and Kevin.

My assistants: Lisa Siladke and Brett Busuttil who do an amazing job of managing my schedule, keeping me organized and in general helping me look good (I couldn't do what I do without you guys!).

You have all inspired, encouraged, challenged and cared for me. You've shared your lives and wisdom. Your impact on me will extend to others as they interact with the pages that follow.

ACKNOWLEDGEMENT

Walt Disney constantly challenged his "imagineers" to stretch their abilities when creating new technologies for the Disney brand. When Walt told them to "plus it" he meant to go above and beyond the best they'd already achieved.

In my mind, Karl Nilsson is a master imagineer. By continually refining an idea or concept, he proves there's always room for innovation and improvement.

Karl, you have taken my writing and "plussed it" with additional clarity, depth, interest, humor, color, flow and texture. You possess the unique ability to take lifeless letters on a page and infuse them with energy and animation. Your skills as a wordsmith have enhanced my message and made it sizzle.

I can't imagine writing another book without your involvement. Thanks for being my partner in prose!

C O N T E N T S

SECTION 1

Foundations

Here's to Life

Life should not be a journey to the grave with the intention of arriving safely in a pretty and well-preserved body, but rather to skid in broadside in a cloud of smoke, thoroughly used up, totally worn out, and loudly proclaiming, "Wow! What a ride!"

Hunter S. Thompson, author

Working without a net.

To most of us, the expression means taking a risk in business or finance without a backup plan. It means sticking our neck out. Making a gutsy move that could involve tough consequences if we make a mistake.

To one young man in New York City, it meant risking everything.

In 1928, "The Wallendas" were waiting in the wings of Madison Square Garden, eager to make their U.S. circus debut at the Greatest Show on Earth. Minutes before show time, the German acrobats are told their safety net has been lost in shipping. But instead of cancelling, 23-year-old Karl Wallenda decides to go for it. Despite the danger, his high-wire troupe puts on a spectacular performance, working in midair without a net.

One slip, one small lapse in balance and the family would plunge to their deaths.

Their raw courage that night left the sold-out crowd gasping in awe;

they gave the group a 15-minute standing ovation. Their reputation was sealed with that performance, and the re-named "Flying Wallendas" went on to dominate the high-wire profession for decades – walking blindfolded, riding bikes, even doing somersaults on the tightrope.

But their most dangerous trick of all was yet to come.

In 1947, Karl created the troupe's crowning achievement – the seven-person human pyramid. The feat was so unprecedented, so difficult, it had never been attempted in public.

Picture this: 40 feet above the circus floor, four men standing in line on the high wire, each pair holding a long shoulder bar. On top of these bars stand two more men, again with a shoulder bar between them. On top of that bar is a woman – standing upright on a wooden chair teetering precariously on a pole. Incredibly, they insisted on performing the pyramid with nothing below them but thin air.

Working without a net had become the family's trademark.

It was a death-defying act that gave them top billing around the world. Audiences went wild. And it made the Wallendas justifiably famous for the next 14 years.

Then, in my hometown, it all came crashing down.

In January, 1962, the Shrine Circus was held at the State Fairgrounds in Detroit. At the climax of the show, the unthinkable happened. As always, the seven performers balanced on three levels and began to cross the wire. Suddenly, one of the front men stumbled. Some say his knees buckled. Witnesses claim he yelled out, "I can't hold anymore" and then fell off the wire. Within seconds, the entire pyramid collapsed. Three performers were able to grab the wire, but the audience watched in horror as the rest plummeted to the ground. The music stopped, the crowd gasped as bodies fell to the center ring with a sickening thud. Parents covered their children's eyes.

Two men, including Karl's son-in-law, were killed instantly by the fall; a third, Karl's adopted son Mario, survived but was left paralyzed.

Across the nation, newspaper headlines chronicled the tragedy. But despite suffering the worst fall in circus history, the surviving Wallendas climbed back up the very next night to put on another high-wire performance.

Karl continued his risky career after the accident, but stopped performing the human pyramid. He became best known for his "sky walks" – suspending a tightrope between skyscrapers or across large stadiums. In 1970, 30,000 people watched him cross the spectacular Tallulah Falls Gorge in Georgia. 700 feet in the air, the 65-year-old paused midway to perform two headstands on the wire.

Wallenda never quit taking risks. At age 73, he stretched a wire between two ten-story hotel towers in San Juan. He was halfway across when a sudden gust of wind blew him off the rope and to his death. Today, his grandchildren and great-grandchildren proudly continue the Wallenda circus tradition.

ALL THE REST IS WAITING

What can a man like this teach us about abundant living?

In 1972, Karl appeared on the *Tonight Show with Johnny Carson*. Johnny asked him how he'd been able to carry on after the horrific accident in Detroit nearly wiped out his family. How could he climb back up the following night? Why would he risk everything, knowing the potential for failure?

Seated between Ed McMahon and Johnny, Karl answered the question without hesitation: "Life is when you're on the wire. All the rest is waiting."

That, my friend, is a person committed to living life on his own terms. A person living with reckless abandon, taking risks without excuses and without complaining – all for the joy of feeling truly alive.

You and I might not agree with Wallenda's career choice. And the daily decisions we face are usually not matters of life and death. But we must admire anyone who refuses to let adversity or fear of failure prevent him from doing what he's passionate about. While other men his age were off playing shuffleboard or bingo, Karl was experiencing the adrenalin rush of doing exactly what he was created to do.

Wallenda was committed to being the best, even in a risky environment with zero tolerance for errors. How many of us can say that? Are we so fully committed to something – *to anything* – that we'll lay it all on the line to accomplish it?

If the people or resources we expect don't show up, do we still go on with the show? Or do we sit around waiting for the safety net?

If we stumble or get knocked down, do we get back up and start over again? Or do we sit around making excuses?

According to the late Karl Wallenda, our years on earth are either spent *waiting or living*. The goal of this book is to motivate non-acrobats like you and me to stop hesitating and start pursuing life with passion, focus, joy, and above all, with balance!

Live life so completely that when death comes to you like a thief in the night, there will be nothing left for him to steal.

Anonymous

CHAPTER 1

Cure for the Common Life

For years, I've asked my clients and friends a simple but probing question.

Now, I'm asking *you*: "What 'level of living' are you striving to achieve – survival, success, or significance?"

Your answer largely depends on whether or not you have an over-arching goal or dream that you're moving toward. Scottish historian, Thomas Carlyle, said the man without a purpose is like a ship without a rudder.

Does that describe anyone you know?

So many folks are blown back and forth by the winds of chance and the waves of public opinion. But I'm guessing that's not you. You're reading this book because you want more out of life than just following the crowd.

You want to dream bigger and live larger.

You want to get beyond mere survival – maybe even beyond traditional success – to achieve a life of real, purpose-driven significance.

This book is dedicated to getting you there.

Just make sure that what's motivating you is not peer pressure or outside influences. In the movie, *Out of Africa*, Danish baroness-turned-farmer Karen Blixen (played by Meryl Streep) confesses, "My biggest fear is that I would come to the end of my life and realize I had lived someone else's dream."

Your life *can* be a legitimate expression of your heart's innermost desire. But first we've got to locate that flickering spark of desire and fan it into red hot flames.

Dream as if you'll live forever. Live as if you'll die today.

James Dean, actor

WELL-DRESSED ZOMBIES

Have you ever owned an ant farm?

All day long they scurry and tunnel and toil in frantic, robotic activity. For them, one day is exactly like another. Sometimes I feel like one of those ants, sentenced to repetitive, soul-flattening boredom. Can you relate? Have you ever thought, *There has to be a more fulfilling, adventurous, enjoyable way of living than this?*

I have.

I remember looking out the window as a young boy, watching grown-ups walking around like well-dressed zombies and thinking to myself, *There must be more to life than just sleeping-eating-working and then sleeping-eating-working all over again.*

We live in a time and place blessed with more conveniences, comforts, and opportunities than any generation in history, yet depression, addictions and even suicides continue to rise in all industrialized nations.

Apparently, our happiness is not commensurate with our perks.

In fact, it feels like the opposite might be true: *More stuff, less joy.*

My son, Drew, recently traveled to Iquitos, Peru in the Amazon River basin. People there live in extreme poverty, with multiple families crowded into shacks without electricity, clean water or sanitation. They have virtually no material possessions. No shopping malls. No medical care. And yet Drew was amazed by the amount of joy – spontaneous singing, infectious laughter, makeshift games – they displayed.

How is this contradiction possible?

More to the point, is this carefree state of mind exclusive to the under-resourced residents of developing countries? Or is it attainable right here, right now, where *we* live?

I believe it is.

Sometimes it feels like we're carrying the weight of the world on our shoulders. But don't settle for drudgery. We were designed to dance on this planet, not tote it around on our backs. We were built to feel the satisfaction that comes from living life with intentionality and confidence – from being mentally, physically, emotionally and spiritually fit. Or at least be headed in that direction!

FROM SURVIVING TO THRIVING

Somebody smarter than me once said, "Frame every so-called disaster with these words: *In five years, will this still matter?*"

That's a great perspective. Most of what I worried about five years ago never materialized. There's a great freedom that comes when we stop sweating the small stuff – the tyranny of the urgent – and start pouring ourselves into larger things with longer lasting, multigenerational significance.

In a later section, we'll discuss what those bigger issues are, and how each of us has been given unique abilities to address them. For now, just know that our special talents are not to be hoarded, but shared – to be used not only to improve our own lifestyle, but to help people around us, too.

We're all creating a legacy. And we all have the potential to leave the earth a better place than we found it. With that as a grid, how will our family, co-workers, and the world at large remember us when we're gone? Are we living in such a way that our legacy can be admired – or better yet, imitated?

By actively searching for wisdom and balance in the seven key areas of life, we can begin making a difference now and for future generations.

And in the process, finding our most heroic self.

It's never too late to be who you might have been.

George Eliot, Victorian novelist

○   ○   ○

The average person takes 28,800 breaths a day.

Each of those breaths is a gift. So while we're alive and breathing, let's do more than just take up space.

Let's live life to the fullest.

Let's live by the state motto of New Hampshire: "Live free or die."

That motto was coined by Revolutionary War hero, General John Stark, and his full quote is even more profound: "Live free or die. Death is not the worst of evils."

To a man like Stark – and to freedom fighters worldwide – death is preferable to slavery or tyranny of any kind. Yet in this free country of ours, we often put *ourselves* under a form of bondage that limits us from achieving our full potential.

As human beings, we are meant to be free. Not just free from government control, but free from *self-imposed* limitations, too. We are meant to be free from false guilt, past disappointments, and labels that people use to define us. Free from emotional baggage, free from other's inaccurate assessments of us.

Free from anything that weighs us down.

When you're free inside, you don't let fear and worry hold you back. You take big, hairy, audacious chances that produce big, hairy, audacious results.

When you're free inside, you go for the gusto. You move from Cowardly Lion to King of the Jungle. You stop playing "not to lose" and start *playing to win*.

If you're a sports fan, you recognize the vocabulary of winners.

In baseball, it's "swing for the fences."

In golf, it's "grip it and rip it."

In racing, it's "pedal to the metal."

I'm pumped from just typing those words! I love jock jargon and motivational slogans (even the corny ones on framed posters of eagles and mountain climbers). But how many of us are actually living with the kind of boldness we plaster on our walls?

Do we roll out of bed and see each day as a blank canvas full of potential and possibility? Or do we find life to be more of a burden to bear than a gift to be opened each morning?

If you'd rather pull the blankets over your head than face another 16 hours of *whatever*, you're not alone. And there are plenty of plausible reasons for your reluctance to embrace life.

Maybe you try to carry more burdens than you should.

Maybe you believe a lie that someone in authority (parent, teacher, coach, boss) told you about yourself.

Maybe you look backward more than you look forward.

Lots of us spend more time worrying about the past than we do dreaming about the future. Author Dan Zadra said, "Worry is a misuse of imagination." I agree. We wouldn't dig into last night's garbage for ingredients to make tonight's dinner. But too often we allow yesterday's mental garbage to affect today's experiences.

If that's you, I've got great news. You can change all that. You can affect the quality and direction of your life from this point forward. You can change your trajectory from settling for average to striving for excellence. From one who cautions "don't rock the boat" to one who smashes paradigms.

How do we move from surviving to thriving?

Just as exercising your body can increase the *length* of your life, getting your mind and spirit in shape can increase the *width* and *depth* of your life.

Okay then, what's the workout? How do we retrain the brain?

It begins with implementing a sevenfold vision for the life you desire to create, and a belief that you can make it happen. Learning and applying these seven strategies will equip you to capture the brass ring that eludes most people – a truly abundant life.

If we all did the things we are capable of doing, we would literally astound ourselves.

Thomas A. Edison, inventor

CHAPTER 2

Power of Seven

When I was a kid, adults with bad breath were always stooping down and asking me, "What do you want to be when you grow up?"

Over the years, my answers changed: cowboy, fireman, astronaut, president, golf pro – okay, that one's not going to happen.

Now that we're grown up, what's *your* dream life?

We all have one, stuffed away in the dusty junk drawers of our mind. At one time, the dream used to be right up front, all shiny and new. Unfortunately, somewhere along the way, most of us forget our original goal (like winning the Indy 500) and start settling for less (like surviving rush hour). Little by little, we begin trading the great adventure for the not-so-great humdrum.

Good enough becomes, well… good enough.

It's so easy to fall into a rut – especially a comfortable one – and so hard to escape. Laurence J. Peter said, "A rut is a grave with the ends knocked out." The enemy is complacency. But even when we *do* want to change, we can't seem to lift ourselves out – mostly because we don't have anyone to show us how. That nagging desire to break free is still in the back of our minds, but we're not sure what direction to take.

We need a roadmap, a blueprint for success.

No sane person would start building a house without first having a good set of working plans to follow. You can imagine the mess. Contractors showing up with the wrong materials at the wrong time; masons, carpenters, plumbers – all arguing about how the job should proceed, total chaos. The same is true in building a life. Most of us make it up as we go along. But it's far better to start with a reliable schematic of what we want our future to look like – and the strategy to implement it in writing.

To help you gain control and dictate the terms of your life, I've identified seven key areas, all starting with the letter "F." They are the blueprint, the framework, which will enable you to envision, construct and evaluate your new life.

The seven areas are **Fun**, **Fitness**, **Family**, **Friends**, **Firm** (your work), **Finances**, and **Faith**. These essential slices of life all complement one another. What we do – or don't do – in any one of these areas will affect the other six. Aristotle said, "The whole is greater than the sum of its parts." We need to integrate and harmonize all seven parts if we hope to experience what hipsters used to call "having it all together," and what scientists call *synergy* – the ability of a group of elements working together to outperform any of its individual members.

In my 7F diagram, the space given to each area is approximately the same. But in real life, most people won't experience this level of balance and symmetry, with each element receiving equal time and attention. That's okay. We all go through seasons of life when circumstances require us to focus more time and energy in a certain area. What's important is to be aware of when we're temporarily out of balance, and not get entrenched in an unhealthy pattern – or rut.

If a man loses his reverence for any part of life, he will lose his reverence for all of life.

Albert Schweitzer, humanitarian, Nobel Prize winner

In a balanced diet, you can't just eat more red meat to make up for a lack of vegetables. Likewise, you can't over-emphasize one of the 7Fs to make up for a deficiency in another. Each is essential to the whole, like spokes in a wheel.

I know because I grew up in an out-of-balance home…

o   o   o

My father was a self-made entrepreneur, a "man's man" if ever there was one. Born one of 10 children, he left his home in Gillespie, Illinois, at age 17 and moved to the Motor City to be part of the auto boom. He worked hard, saved every penny he earned at Hamtramck's Dodge Main plant, and in his late twenties, bought his first business. Over the years he built, owned, and operated several more successful businesses with his brother Frank.

For years he worked 13 hours a day, 6 days a week. While the businesses flourished, my parent's marriage did not. Through many peaks and valleys, the disharmony took its toll on our family. My dad's 7F diagram would look like this:

By allowing the Firm (his work) to dominate, my dad prospered financially, but did irreparable damage to his key relationships. By overemphasizing the Firm, he sacrificed his business partner *and* his marriage partner in the process. Sadly for me, there was almost no time in his life for Family, Fun or Friends.

When people indulge in this kind of imbalance for an extended period, a strange thing happens. They become so consumed by the Firm (or Finances or Fitness or any other "F" element) that they're no longer conscious of the other six vital areas – or they simply stop caring about them.

At this point, they can actually become proud of their unhealthy devotion. If you point out their imbalance ("Dude, why don't you just get a cot in your office?"), they take it as a compliment. When you suggest it's destructive, they justify it with a big smile, "I'm just knocking it out to provide nice things for my family." Meanwhile, the family would gladly trade those "nice things" in a heartbeat to get more time with their workaholic breadwinner.

Of course, work isn't the only area that tempts us into imbalance. Each of the 7Fs is susceptible to abuse. Regardless of our age or socio-economic status, we're all prone to overdoing certain things – like a pendulum swinging too far in one direction. We need to be aware of this human tendency and be continuously recalibrating our limits for time, energy and resource usage.

We need to understand that when we say "Yes" to one thing, we're automatically saying "No" to many other things. And vice-versa. Learning to allocate precious, finite commodities like time, energy and resources is critical to living the balanced 7F Life.

Now, think about *your* life in relation to each of the 7Fs. How much time, energy and resources are you allocating to each area? How would your diagram look?

How Do the 7Fs Work?

As I studied the 7Fs and their relationship to each other, I realized that two are *personal* (looking inward to work on ourselves), two are *relational* (looking outward to connect with others), two are *vocational* (leveraging our abilities and managing our resources) and one is *spiritual* (using our guiding values to express the other six Fs appropriately).

Think of the personal, relational, vocational and spiritual aspects of our lives as the four legs of a stool. When all four "legs" are present and sturdy, our lives are stable and secure. If we remove one of the legs, we are less stable but can still probably get by. If we remove two legs, our lives become seriously out of balance. If we try to make it through life on just one leg, we'll fall flat on our faces.

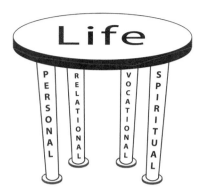

To grasp the pleasure and power of all seven Fs working together, think of a gourmet dining experience. Dining is different from eating. Eating can be scarfing down fast food from a bag. We "eat" to satisfy our hunger. But "dining" is an affirming social experience that takes planning and time. Imagine a seven-course meal so enjoyable, so stimulating to the senses, that it leaves you eagerly anticipating the next course. That's what the 7F Life can be – a way to feast on the best that life has to offer.

Of course, you could skip the appetizers and still feel full. You could probably say no to the soup or ignore the salad and still get by. You might even omit an entrée and you wouldn't starve. But why *would* you? Leaving out any component of our meal would dramatically affect the quality of the experience. So dig into the abundant life, and don't forget dessert!

IT'S NOT ABOUT PERFECTION

More human beings – 24 to be exact – have orbited the moon than have thrown a perfect game in Major League Baseball. Since 1900, only 23 pitchers have achieved perfection on the mound and no one has ever done it twice.

As rare as perfect games are, perfect *people* are even rarer. In all of history, there's only been one, and that was about 2,000 years ago. So unless you can walk across your swimming pool, you're not perfect. Get over it. This book is not for perfect people, it's for ordinary messed up folks like you and me. It's also not about creating a perfect or painless life – sorry, that doesn't exist, at least not on this planet.

A perfect, painless life is impossible because each one of us will inevitably be disappointed and hurt by the selfish acts of others and by the painful consequences of our own poor decisions.

That's the bad news.

Here's the good news: *Those hurts do not have to emotionally immobilize us or define our future.* Please go back and read that again.

Nobody enjoys pain. So I'll warn you up front that if you choose to implement the principles of the 7F Life, you'll need to make some, uh, "uncomfortable" adjustments. Some will be minor. Some will be a struggle. Some will strain your willpower. But realize there is no growth without first identifying what's broken and building it back up.

There's no reward for staying in your rut.

Breakthroughs only come by turning away from old, ineffective habits and toward new, more productive ones. And that can be painful.

Ironically, pain may *also* come from family and friends, people who observe the positive changes in your life and don't want to be left behind. Even loved ones may try to dissuade you or sidetrack you. It's a funny thing about us humans – we don't enjoy seeing others pass us by. Like motorists dueling on a highway, it upsets us at some primeval level. So don't be surprised if others try to block (or belittle) your progress.

Just stick to your game plan, stay focused, and don't listen to static.

o   o   o

Achieving the abundant life will not be a cake walk. Standing out from the crowd makes you a target. Marching to your own drum is tough.

But don't worry. Like everything in life that's worth obtaining, it's the *difficulty* that makes the victory sweet: One night in 1941, a Polish prisoner named Slavomir Rawicz escaped from a Soviet work camp with six other inmates. For the next year, they walked, crawled and climbed across 4,000 miles of wilderness to win their freedom. The emaciated band traveled on foot through the frozen tundra of Siberia, the scorching desert of Mongolia, and finally over the Himalayas into India. They had no maps, no supplies and no equipment. (Their epic journey was told in Rawicz's 1956 book *The Long Walk* and the 2011 film, *The Way Back*.)

During Stalin's reign of terror, approximately five million souls passed through these forced labor camps. No one knows how many of these *gulag* workers died of starvation, torture and freezing. But we do know that at least six hardy souls made it out by cutting the barbed wire and plunging into chest-high snow at minus 20 degrees.

Here's my point – their cellmates *also* wanted freedom, but chose to stay huddled around the camp stove because walking across Siberia (it's 5 million square miles, by the way) seemed harder than accepting the awful status quo.

If it was easy, everyone would have escaped.

Same deal for the abundant life. If it wasn't so doggone hard, everybody would already be experiencing it. Listen up, comrades; you will have to fight for the better life you envision – against complacency, against the demands of others, against the *zeitgeist* of our time. The easy road – the entitlement road – is a fallacy, a mirage. As the old-timers say, the path of least resistance makes both men and rivers crooked.

Don't ever be afraid to take the hard way.

If your ship doesn't come in, swim out to it!

Jonathan Winters, comedian

THE DYNAMIC DUO

In addition to hard work and thick skin, the 7F Life requires two more vital ingredients:

Enthusiasm is the key that unlocks the energy we need to persevere. It's a healthy dose of what fills us up and ignites our passion, the catalyst that energizes and lifts the human spirit. When our willpower falters and our best intentions can't sustain us, enthusiasm can bridge the gap between quitting and winning. Norman Vincent Peale said, "Enthusiasm releases the drive to carry you over obstacles and adds significance to all you do." Simply put, nothing great has ever been achieved without it. Even Dale Carnegie said people rarely succeed unless they have fun in what they are doing.

Sacrifice is saying "No" to *good* things so you can say "Yes" to *great* things. It's about delayed gratification, working behind the scenes, and not caring who gets the credit. Life is not just about getting, it's about giving and making sacrifices for the ones you love – and sometimes for perfect strangers. That's noble. Best-selling author, Mitch Albom, puts it this way, "Sacrifice is a part of life. It's supposed to be. It's not something to regret. It's something to aspire to."

We live in a culture that values fun and leisure. But if life is all pleasure and no pain, our achievements will be superficial and shallow. At some level, we all know that nothing of lasting value is achieved without sacrifice. Struggle is a necessary part of life's equation (ever watch a chick struggle to break out of its eggshell?). Sacrifice and hard work toughen us and build character like nothing else. Nietzsche said it best, "What doesn't kill us makes us stronger."

On the other hand, if life is mostly pain or predominantly sacrifice, we'll lose our joy and zest for living. We won't be much fun to be around. Life will feel like a prison sentence instead of the "get out of jail" card it should be!

That's why we need a healthy balance – a viable, sustainable combination of sacrifice and enthusiasm.

This book is about taking control of the things we can control – our attitude, our choices, our level of effort, and our planning. It's about feeling strong and confident because we know we are living by intent and design rather than by simply reacting to whatever comes our way.

A life of reaction is a life of slavery, intellectually and spiritually. One must fight for a life of action, not reaction.

Rita Mae Brown, author

○　　○　　○

In the Mel Gibson movie *Braveheart*, Scottish rebel William Wallace makes a powerful statement after being captured by the tyrannical English. Bound in chains, with no possibility of escape, the warrior faces his captors. The king's daughter-in-law (who is Wallace's secret lover) begs him to renounce his principles and pledge his allegiance to England. If he doesn't disavow his fight for freedom, he will suffer brutal torture and a humiliating death. Defiant to the end, Wallace looks her in the eye and utters, "All men die. Few men really live."

The 7F Life is for those who want to *really live*.

BEYOND THE HYPOTHETICAL

Today, I went to *Amazon.com* and did a quick search for books under the key words "self-help." The results turned up 246,196 books! According to *Psychology Today*, this massive variety of books on personal transformation proves a couple of points. First, the urge to better ourselves is universal. Second, when we do try to improve, we need lots of reinforcement to make it stick. And according to research, even *more* backup is required to make it a forever habit, an ingrained part of our daily life.

Neuroscientist Dr. David Rock says, "One reason there are so many books on these themes is that we need constant reminders, in different forms, of these ideas."

According to Dr. Rock, "Your brain is more like a forest than a computer." He explains that when it comes to self-help principles, it's a "use it or lose it" proposition. What we don't read and practice daily quickly fades away; all of our good intentions get lost in the trees.

With that woodsy analogy, perhaps you'll forgive me for adding one more self-help book to the unending pile. I hope *Life in the Balance* inspires you to cut the crap, cut the excuses, and use whatever years you have left to rock your world. I'll try to illustrate practical ways to effectively integrate these 7F principles into the daily grind, where the rubber meets the road in our rough and tumble, nitty-gritty existence.

What do I mean by that?

Life can be cruel. People can be thoughtless. Bad things happen to good people. Murphy's Law applies. Roadblocks appear. Common sense is rare. Civility is out of style. Life is not for the timid, and it certainly isn't fair. But in the midst of today's unrest and uncertainty, the 7F principles will give you a decided advantage.

They won't guarantee success, but they will definitely stack the deck.

If life were fair, Elvis would be alive and all the impersonators would be dead.

Johnny Carson, *Tonight Show* host

THE PERSON IN THE MIRROR

Before you begin a diet or a workout program, there's usually a disclaimer: "Check with your physician before starting." Nobody wants you dropping dead on their treadmill or aggravating some unknown pre-existing condition.

Before we start the 7F program, I've got a request, also. If we're going to do an extreme makeover, let's take a quick self-assessment first. What do you value most in life? Financial security? Your reputation? A prized possession?

Kick-start the appraisal with these three scenarios:

1. Imagine your house is on fire. You have only seconds to grab a few treasures and run outside. The kids and pets are safe. What do you rescue? Family photos? Cash box? Diplomas? Heirlooms? Jewelry?

Wedding dress? Hard drive? Little League trophy? What you run outside with is *what you value most*. Jot it down.

2. Imagine your doctor says you only have 30 days to live. How do you spend them? Visiting relatives? Shopping spree? Clubbing? Finishing projects at work? Dream vacation to Hawaii? Religious meditation? Risky behavior? Acts of charity? What you do with your few remaining days is *what you value most*. Jot it down.

3. Imagine you must create a personal time capsule. Your task is to fill up a box with what matters most and seal it shut for 100 years. You can include pictures, DVDs, thumb drives, whatever. You can shove in your childhood teddy bear or your MBA. You can enclose love letters, tax returns, birth announcements, anything that fits. What you put in the box is *what you value most*. Jot it down.

Now, think about your day planner and your checkbook. What did you do this week and what did you buy? Jot it down. Now (drum roll, please), *compare the way you actually spent your time and money with what you just said you value most*.

Do they line up? Or is there a discrepancy between what you esteem and how you behave?

If there's a big fat disconnect, don't beat yourself up over it. Few of us walk the talk 100 percent of the time. It's not because we're evil, greedy, callous people, but because we've got some blind spots.

As we walk through the 7Fs, we'll work on changing our priorities to focus on *what we value most*. And if you'll pardon my directness, you and I may even dump a few things we spend time and money on that we're not so proud of.

At the end of each chapter and in the Appendices, you'll find tools to sustain life change over the long haul, including the Life Balance Assessment. This integration profile can help you recalibrate the 7Fs as your life ebbs and flows over the years. There's even an option to stay plugged in with monthly creative ideas and feedback from the 7F Community. My goal is to keep you connected and growing in the abundant life – however you define it.

When life is firing on all seven "cylinders," it feels like a well-tuned high-performance engine – one that purrs like a Cadillac at idle and roars like a Corvette when you step on the gas.

Let's get revved up!

***

Life isn't about finding yourself. Life is about creating yourself.

George Bernard Shaw, author

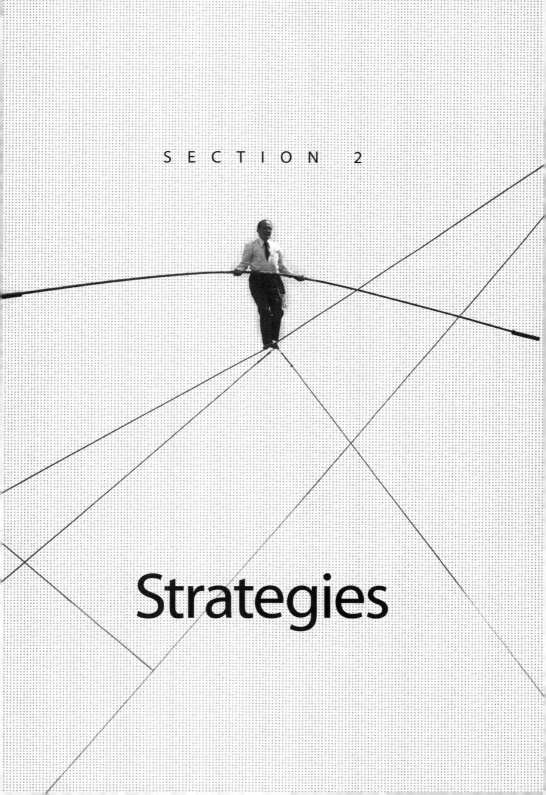

SECTION 2

Strategies

C H A P T E R 3

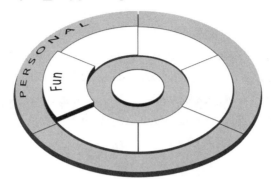

Fun

At the height of laughter, the universe is flung into a kaleidoscope of new possibilities.

Jean Houston, philosopher

A team of FBI agents were conducting a "search and seizure" raid at a San Diego psychiatric hospital under investigation for insurance fraud. With mountains of paperwork to examine, the raid turned into an all-day affair. After long hours of reviewing financial records, the investigators had worked up an appetite. To order a quick dinner for his hungry colleagues, the agent in charge called up a nearby pizzeria...

>Agent: *Hello. I would like to order 19 large pizzas and 67 cans of soda.*
>Pizza Man: *And where would you like them delivered?*
>Agent: *We're over at the psychiatric hospital.*
>Pizza Man: *The psychiatric hospital?*
>Agent: *That's right. I'm an FBI agent.*
>Pizza Man: *You're an FBI agent?*

Agent: *That's correct. Just about everybody here is.*

Pizza Man: *And you're at the psychiatric hospital?*

Agent: *That's correct. When you arrive, don't go to the front doors.*
We keep them locked. You'll have to go around back.

Pizza Man: *And you say you're all FBI agents?*

Agent: *That's right. How soon can you bring the pizzas?*

Pizza Man: *Everyone at the hospital is an FBI agent?*

Agent: *Yes. We've been here all day and we're starving.*

Pizza Man: *How are you going to pay for all this?*

Agent: *I have my checkbook.*

Pizza Man: *I don't think so.*

(*Click.*)

I hope this true story made you laugh. If it did, a number of important psychological and physiological changes just took place in your body and brain. Later in this chapter, we'll look at some of the newly discovered health benefits of humor. But first, let me ask you a question: When's the last time you laughed so hard your face hurt? I mean the kind of laughing out loud that makes your sides ache and your eyes water and ginger ale come out your nose?

If you can't remember, it's probably been too long.

Which is precisely why I chose "Fun" to be the first "F" in the book. Too many of us are like the FBI agents – working hard, skipping lunch, missing the humor that's right in front of our faces (or on the other end of the phone). Oh, incidentally, the agents did get their pizzas – but they had to go pick them up. And if you doubt this far-fetched conversation actually happened, click on *Snopes.com* and search for "FBI pizza."

Now let's see if we can't lighten things up.

○   ○   ○

If your nation's embroiled in an exhausting war effort, what's more powerful, a bomb or a joke? The answer might surprise you.

Winston Churchill is credited with saving civilization from the Nazis. But the man who stood up to Hitler with "blood, sweat and tears" also had a funny side. The humorous exchanges between Churchill and his political rivals – especially with Lady Astor – are legendary. In one heated debate, Lady Astor told Churchill, "If you were my husband, I'd poison your tea," to which he responded, "Madam, if you were my wife, I'd drink it!"

Those few well-chosen words were more effective than a lengthy speech. And the laughter was a welcome relief in the war-weary halls of Parliament. In another purported exchange, Lady Astor accused her archenemy: "Winston, you are drunk." Churchill replied, "And you, madam, are ugly. But I shall be sober in the morning."

The laughter Winston Churchill generated during WWII helped ease the tension and encouraged England to persevere against daunting odds. Poking fun at enemies and allies in the midst of war was a secret weapon Churchill employed with skill. When the U.S. was agonizingly slow in coming to Britain's aid, he quipped: "Americans always do the right thing. After they've tried everything else." Using humor, the venerable Prime Minister skewered Uncle Sam's isolationist policy better than a dozen meetings with FDR.

Will Rogers, Johnny Carson, Jon Stewart – lots of pundits over the years have hit our political funny bone. From Stephen Colbert to Rush Limbaugh, there's no shortage of jokes about government incompetence. And sometimes these comedic observations result in actual policy change. How much better if the politicians (and executives and academics and clergy and all the rest of us, frankly) would laugh at *themselves!*

Maybe a good dose of self-deprecating humor could even break the gridlock in Washington. Back in 1984, then-President Ronald Reagan wowed the crowd at the Conservative Political Action Conference by injecting some of his famously deft humor. "Yes, we have a trade deficit, but this isn't entirely new. The U.S. had a trade deficit in almost all of the years between 1790 and 1875," Reagan said. "I remember them well."

The 73-year-old president paused for the laughter to die down before going in for the kill. "Of course, I was only a boy at the time," he added with perfect comedic timing.

Those who can't laugh at themselves leave the job to others.

Anonymous

○ ○ ○

One dictionary defines fun as "enjoyment or pleasure." Not bad. Another calls it "entertaining amusement." Better. But doesn't the word "fun" deserve a more fun definition? Maybe something like, "the sweet frosting of life."

Have you ever eaten a birthday cake without frosting? It's still edible, but not very tempting! Frosting makes your taste buds do the happy dance. Without it, why bother?

Same for fun. Without it, *why bother?*

Fun is what makes getting out of bed in the morning worthwhile. Fun is what keeps marriages together, keeps employees productive, and keeps society at large from imploding.

Some would disagree. They argue that fun is frivolous or a waste of valuable time. With apologies to The Grinch, Scrooge, and Oscar the Grouch, I submit *they are wrong*. Fun is not optional in a successful, well balanced life. Fun is a unique catalyst that produces essential by-products like better health, heightened awareness, relational attraction, stress relief and much more.

In many situations and occupations, what I call the "fun factor" can mean the difference between success and failure.

Especially in front of a group.

Here's what I mean. The best public speakers invariably use humor to connect with their audience ("If at first you don't succeed, skydiving isn't for you"). By adding laughter to their presentation, even the driest, most boring subject matter becomes palatable ("43 percent of all statistics are made up on the spot"). By adding laughter, they focus the crowd's attention and win them over ("Always remember you're unique, just like everybody else").

Where to start? Jokes are fine for the pros, but for most of us, the best and most comfortable place to find humor for a speech or presentation is from our own personal experience. Think back to an embarrassing moment (maybe one you didn't think was funny at the time). Now that you can laugh at the experience, share it! Good presenters understand the old adage: "Humor is simply tragedy separated by time and space."

Why is that important? Because if people like *you*, they'll usually like what you have to say. And science has found the quickest way to make people *like* you is to make them smile. Psychologists say that laughter synchronizes the brains of speaker and listener so that they are emotionally attuned. Appropriate humor relaxes an audience and makes it feel far more comfortable with you. Having a little fun, especially on the front end, can break down social barriers and preconceived notions so they're more receptive to your ideas.

Pop culture is full of examples.

Consider the difference between two fictional schoolteachers and decide which class you'd rather attend…

In the movie *Ferris Bueller's Day Off*, actor Ben Stein puts his bored students to sleep with his robotic deadpan, "Anyone? Class? The Great Depression – anyone? Class? Anyone?"

In *Dead Poet's Society*, Robin Williams shocks his students by climbing on top of his desk and quoting Thoreau, "The universe is wider than our views of it." This unexpected move demonstrated his point that it's important to see things from different perspectives. In poetry class, he makes another unforgettable point by having his pupils rip a chapter out of their textbooks and throw it away!

I don't know about you, but I've been in both scenarios, and my favorite teachers were always the ones who awakened my brain with some good clean fun.

Fun brings other benefits to our lives, too. In fact, it's a prime motivator for much of human activity. At *Dead Poet's* Welton Academy, it enhanced education by making learning enjoyable. At the same time, it bonded the students to each other and to their mentor, John Keating, in lifelong friendships. When all else failed, taking time off for fun got the stressed-out scholars through academic challenges and tough emotional issues.

Okay, hurrah for Hollywood. But fun's just as potent in *real life* situations. Here's why: Enjoyment invites participation, and participation focuses attention. When you're paying attention, your awareness expands. Increased awareness promotes insight. Insight builds knowledge, which facilitates action. When you take action, you see results. When you get results, you experience pleasure. And when you have pleasure, well, the cycle just continues.

No wonder girls just want to have fun. Boys, too.

George Bernard Shaw said, "We don't stop playing because we grow old; we grow old because we stop playing." Quick, hand me that Frisbee! Or paintball gun, or snow skis, or softball bat, or mountain bike, or fly rod, or rollerblades, whatever hits your fun button.

We can't stop the physical aging process, but we *can* hang onto our childhood sense of wonder. We *can* indulge our yearning for adventure. We *can* cultivate a playful heart. And "playing" can make any season of life a joy to be in.

THE BEST PRESCRIPTION EVER

The old saying "laughter is the best medicine" just might be true.

Laughter can make you feel better, look better and maybe even live longer. But don't take my word for it. Psychologist and nationally-known laugh therapist, Steve Wilson, says, "If people can get more laughter in their lives, they are a lot better off. They might be healthier, too."

That's because we change physiologically when we laugh. In addition to getting a silly grin and squinty eyes, we breathe faster and our pulse quickens, sending more oxygen to our tissues. And because the heart and brain depend on a steady flow of oxygen carried in the blood, anything that improves that delivery system – even temporarily – will improve our quality of life.

Experts are now saying that robust laughter can be like a mild workout, and may offer some of the same advantages. "The effects of laughter and exercise are very similar," says Wilson. "Combining laughter and movement is a great way to boost your heart rate."

A team of researchers at the University of Maryland School of Medicine, led by Dr. Michael Miller, showed that laughter is linked to healthy blood vessels. Based on his study, Dr. Miller suggests we incorporate laughter into our other heart-healthy activities, like eating less, walking more, and reducing our cholesterol. "We could perhaps read something humorous or watch a funny video and try to find ways to take ourselves less seriously," Miller says. "The recommendation for a healthy heart may one day be to exercise, eat right and laugh a few times a day."

Dr. Miller offers a simple prescription that won't bankrupt you and could save your life: "Try 30 minutes of exercise 3 times a week, plus 15 minutes of laughter on a daily basis – it's good for the vascular system."

But what if you were born a sourpuss?

If we're not prone to laughter, Dr. Miller says we should be proactive and find out how fun is done: "The ability to laugh – either naturally or as *learned behavior* – may have important implications in societies where heart disease remains the number one killer." Miller adds, "We know that exercising, not smoking, and eating foods low in saturated fat will reduce the risk of heart disease. Perhaps regular, hearty laughter should be added to the list."

I can just imagine my next doctor visit: "Pop in a Will Ferrell DVD and drink plenty of liquids. If that doesn't work, here's a prescription for some extra-strength *30 Rock*."

Dr. Miller's not alone. According to an article published in *Psychology Today*, indulging your funny bone has a host of measurable benefits:

- Laughing increases productivity and connects people emotionally.
- Giggling reduces pain and allows us to tolerate discomfort.
- Snickering reduces blood sugar levels and lowers stress.
- Chuckling improves job performance, especially work that depends on creativity and solving complex problems.

Which begs the question: What if something really tedious and un-productive like, say, a congressional hearing, was turned into a tickle party?

The ratings on C-SPAN would triple!

If tickling's not your style, plop down in front of Comedy Central and enjoy this newly discovered bonus – laughing *also* boosts our immunity to disease. Watching the Three Stooges throw a pie at somebody (or better yet, tossing one yourself) appears to raise the level of infection-fighting antibodies and increase the number of immune cells on duty. Researcher Arnold Glasow calls it "a tranquilizer with no side effects."

Here's another non-medical benefit: If you're Mr. Fun, you're not only more likely to be healthy; you're more likely to be popular. According to the *Psychology Today* article, "Laughter's role in intimate relationships is vastly underestimated and it really is the glue of good marriages. Laughter establishes – or restores – a positive emotional climate and a sense of connection between two people."

According to the article's author, Hara Marano, some researchers believe the major function of laughter is to *bring people together*. Which is why romantic comedies were invented, right?

Chick flicks aside, Marano's point is nothing to laugh at. If you're not meeting your daily laugh quota, you need to get intentional about it. And because laughter is *social*, you might need to start hanging out with friends and family a lot more often. (Warning: If your last name is Griswold, the "hanging out" part may include Cousin Eddie who lives in his RV.)

Ever watch a comedy in an empty theater? It's not nearly as much fun as a packed house. There's a reason for that. Robert Provine, professor of psychology at the University of Maryland, says that being with friends is essential: "We're 30 times more likely to laugh when we're with other people than when we're alone. People who laugh a lot have a strong connection with those around them. That in itself might have health benefits."

THE JOKE'S ON US

Okay, so fun is vitally important to our well-being.

Important, but *not* automatic.

Fun is a choice. We either embrace it or reject it. Having fun at work or at home or anywhere we find ourselves is largely up to us. It's the disposition, the mindset, that we consciously or unconsciously bring to each situation that makes the difference. Some people have what I call the "Eeyore complex" (named in honor of the dismally gloomy donkey in *Winnie the Pooh*). Folks like that wouldn't crack a smile if they were in the front row at a Seinfeld concert. On the other hand, I know people who can turn a dreadfully dull event into a party. Depending on your outlook, you can have a boring time at Disneyland or an exciting time with your mother-in-law.

It all depends on attitude. And a little secret...

The hidden secret of life is that it's not the *big* decisions that make us or break us. Rather, our happiness and success are the product of the small decisions we make moment by moment. Each day, we make hundreds (if not thousands) of choices. We can choose to get angry at the guy who cuts us off in traffic – or we can choose to let it go and wish him well (you know, give him a wave using *all* your fingers). We can choose to resist a shift in office procedure and pout – or we can choose to willingly embrace the change. We can choose to tell our spouse how much they mean to us – or we can sit there like a bump on a log and watch TV.

All day every day, we can make choices for kindness, generosity, forgiveness, happiness and smiles. Or we can just as easily opt for anger, resentment, jealousy, bitterness and frowns.

And that's true for fun as well.

Often it's right there under our noses, just waiting to be discovered. While we're waiting for our yearly vacation to come around so we can have REALLY BIG fun, we miss countless chances to enjoy mundane little fun. Try it. Look for fun lurking in conversations on the elevator or subway. Get some grins by trying something new at the lunch counter or taking a new route home from work. Don't miss ordinary fun in a quest for epic fun. The little stuff is a blast if you approach it with the right attitude. Like sinking a really tough 3-pointer into the wastebasket. Or hitting the high notes in the shower. Or riding your bike no-handed.

These slivers of intentional fun can make our daily duties a lot more palatable, even memorable. So let's approach tomorrow with a different attitude – more levity, more playfulness, more curiosity.

○   ○   ○

May I get serious for a minute? Maybe you think it's inappropriate to have fun when the world's in such a mess. Perhaps you feel it's disrespectful to have a good laugh when we're surrounded by so much human suffering. If that's you, I can understand why. If I flipped on the news right now, I'd see natural disasters, gruesome crimes and political scandals. I'd hear about murders, layoffs, epidemics, riots, floods, wildfires and terrorist attacks. If I sat there long enough, I'd become depressed, heartbroken, frustrated, angry, and – here's the problem – *imbalanced.*

Let me be clear, life is hard and suffering is real. Bad things happen to good people. Every day a new tragedy pushes yesterday's nightmare off the front page. There are more than enough discouraging issues in this world to keep us all walking around with stoic expressions on our faces. So I'm not suggesting that life be one continuous joke.

But let's keep things in perspective.

If Winston Churchill could crack jokes during the London Blitz, we can lighten up during our tough times, too. No song's ever said it better than the iconic "Smile (Though Your Heart Is Breaking)." The music was written during the Great Depression by Charlie Chaplin for his 1936 movie *Modern Times*. Lyrics were added during the Cold War, as Nat King Cole urged us to forget Khrushchev for a moment and hope for a brighter tomorrow: "Light up your face with gladness, hide every trace of sadness."

Since then, the song's been recorded by most of the human race, including Judy Garland, Dianna Ross, Michael Bolton, Michael Jackson, Barbra Streisand, Tony Bennett, Lyle Lovett, Harry Connick Jr., Eric Clapton, Celine Dion and the entire cast of *Glee*. And boy, did Jerry Lewis love it! As the theme song of his annual telethon, it helped inspire millions of people to contribute $2 billion to fight Muscular Dystrophy every Labor Day weekend from1966 to his last broadcast in 2011.

That's the power of a smile.

ARE WE HAVING FUN YET?

Okay. We need fun, but what *is* it? What exactly is it that makes something funny? Mark Twain once said that dissecting a joke was like dissecting a frog – both die in the process.

With that caveat, let's take a stab at it (bad pun).

Fun can be a "thing," like feathers on your hat or a new woofer for your stereo or the latest issue of *Golf Digest*.

Fun can be an "activity," like hunting for antiques or playing Texas Hold 'Em with the guys or grabbing a latte with your spouse.

Fun can be an "event," like a softball tournament or charity ball or movie premier. It can range from an annual Super Bowl party (planned out like D-Day) to an impromptu family night with the kids (Pixar and popcorn).

Fun can even be a "challenge," like building a deck or mastering the game of chess. Sometimes, taking on a tough, strenuous challenge and seeing it through to the end is the most fun of all. I have friends who train for triathlons, and their idea of fun is a freezing cold 20-mile run at 5:00 a.m. (I have a restraining order on these fellas, just so they don't stop by).

Did you notice that nothing on the fun list – things, activities, challenges – is what you'd necessarily call "hilarious?" Which means you don't need to be a stand-up comic or a practical joker to have fun. And you don't need a small fortune, either! Whatever event or recreation or hobby spells f-u-n for you, just do it more often and don't hold back.

Humorist Erma Bombeck put the role of fun in perspective…

If I had my life to live over I would have eaten less cottage cheese and more ice cream … I would have invited friends over to dinner even if the carpet was stained … I would have taken time to listen to my grandfather ramble about his youth … I would have burnt the pink candle before it melted while being stored … I would have sat on the lawn with my children and never worried about grass stains … I would never have bought anything just because it was practical … but mostly, given another shot at life, I would seize every minute, try it on, live it, exhaust it and never give that minute back until there was nothing left of it.

That's good advice no matter where you are in the game of life – teeing up the first hole, playing the back nine, or heading for the clubhouse. Grab whatever minutes, hours and years you have left and use them up 'til there's nothing left.

○   ○   ○

Fun is a desirable personality trait. It makes you attractive to employers, clients, co-workers, everyone. Are you fun to be with? Do you give off good vibes? If you're not sure, here's a way to check – take a look around. If you're a fun person to be with, there's a good chance you have lots of friends. If your only friend is your pet goldfish, chances are that you're probably not much fun.

All things being equal, people prefer hanging around fun people.

There's just something magnetic about folks who can make us smile.

My wife Mary Ann and I invented the imaginary "Fun Meter" to get a gauge on how we're doing. We'll frequently ask each other, "What's your Fun Meter reading these days?" or, "On a scale of 1 to 10, are we having fun yet?" (Caution: If your query is met with a massive eye roll, just back away.)

FUN METER

Maybe 1 on the meter is a root canal and 8 is a backflip into the pool. Maybe 2 is a tax audit and 9 is watching your son score his first touchdown. Maybe 3 is airport security and 7 is a day at the spa. Anyway, you get the idea. If you're not pegging the needle now and then, start asking why.

Kidding aside, what's *your* meter been reading lately?

The scientific theory I like best is that the rings of Saturn are composed entirely of lost airline luggage.

Mark Russell, comedian

FUNDAMENTALS OF FUN

You don't have to teach children how to have fun. Just turn 'em loose with a garden hose or sidewalk chalk or a new puppy. The smiles come automatically. But it's not so simple with adults. We've forgotten how to let go. And while there's no step-by-step guide for having fun, we can all learn to unleash our inner joker. To help, here are what I call the Top Ten fundamentals of fun:

1. LOOSEN UP

In a candid interview with music journalist Deborah Evans-Price, country superstar Reba McIntire was asked: "If you could write a letter to yourself at age 19, what would you say?"

Reba replied, "Quit taking things and yourself so seriously. Enjoy life! Quit being so stressed out over the little things. It is not worth it. Relax and enjoy life."

That's good advice if you're 19 or 91.

If you could write a letter to *yourself* as a teenager, what would you say? Knowing what you now know about life, what counsel would you give? Take a moment right now and jot down what comes to mind.

How do you feel about what you wrote? Do you need to make any adjustments in your adult life because of what you wrote?

Our friends "down under" have a saying that I think we'd do well to adopt. You'll often hear Australians say, "No worries, mate" at the end of a conversation. The catchy phrase conveys "Everything is under control. It will be okay." It's an expression of confidence implying "Don't sweat it. We can do this."

I've even heard them use "No worries, mate" to *begin* a conversation. Brimming with optimism, they start each personal interaction by proclaiming right up front that things are going to turn out fine. Australians have a positive disposition and a contagious "can do" spirit that I love. They rarely seem to be uptight, and they embody the idea of "hangin' loose."

Does that describe you? Or would people say you take life too seriously? Come on, be honest. I can almost hear you saying, "But you don't know how tough my job is. The workplace is brutal."

Don't feel like the Lone Ranger.

We *all* have responsibilities with varying degrees of importance and anguish – from burned-out hourly workers to anxiety-ridden executives. Each and every job – from delivering newspapers to delivering babies – comes with its own set of worries and frustrations. The grass may look greener in the other guy's gig, but there are plenty of good reasons to feel beaten down and demotivated in any career. Question is, do we allow the weight of our responsibilities to get the best of us?

The solution is deciding where we are going to place our focus…

2. LIVE FOR TODAY

Do you live in the present or the future?

Here's how you can tell: While you're doing whatever you're doing (working, golfing, shopping), is your focus on the *outcome* or on the *process*? In other words, do you have fun while you're *experiencing* something or are you focused only on *completing* it?

Do you focus on the *doing* or the *finishing*?

If you're a goal-oriented Type A person, you want results, baby, and the sooner the better. You can't rest until you reach a goal and cross it off your list. The trouble is, the list never ends and the years go by and you never slow down to have any fun. Then all of sudden, you're in an expensive box six feet under and you're dead without really ever being alive.

Imagine a master gardener who plants and prunes and fertilizes prize-winning roses, but never stops to smell them.

If that sounds like it might be you, ask yourself: What's more important, the end result or enjoying *what* you're doing and *who* you're doing it with?

With the right focus, there's joy in every step of the journey, not just the destination. The existentialist philosophers call this awareness "being here now." Buddha said, "Do not dwell in the past, do not dream of the future, concentrate the mind on the present moment." Of course, we need to learn from the past and we need to prepare ourselves for the future. But don't worry and fret about either. If you do, there's a risk, like Ralph Waldo Emerson said, of "always getting ready to live but never living."

So what about the past? Somebody once said, "You can clutch the past so tightly to your chest that it leaves your arms too full to embrace the present."

And the future? Albert Camus said, "Real generosity toward the future lies in giving all to the present."

Even that philosophical party pooper, Goethe, said, "Nothing is worth more than this day."

So embrace it.

Don't get me wrong, we do need to be productive. We do need to be accountable for our time, decisions, actions and performance. But if our focus is exclusively on the outcome (future), we are going to rob ourselves of the pleasure of the moment (present). Dale Carnegie said, "Today is the only life you are sure of. Make the most of today."

Think about it. Carnegie wrote *How to Win Friends and Influence People* way back in 1936. This man who practically invented leadership training knew the secret to real success is being fully engaged today. He knew the inconvenient truth that you and I need to wrestle down: It is possible to be *efficient* without being *effective*.

Make sure you know the difference.

Life is not measured by the number of breaths we take, but by the moments that take our breath away.

Anonymous

3. SHARPEN YOUR FOCUS

I'm as competitive as they come.

As a result, I've struggled in this area. Here's an example: When I was in my teens, I was a jock. Star athlete. Big man on campus. Despite my swelled head, my high school history teacher took an interest in me and invited me to play racquetball with him. Without hesitation, I said, "Sure!"

My motto was (and is), if you can swing it, throw it, kick it or pass it, count me in. I had never played racquetball before, but it didn't matter; game on!

As we stepped onto the court, I focused like a laser on winning. Nothing else mattered. While I gave my teacher a run for his money, I came up short and lost the match. I was so ticked off about losing (the outcome) that I completely missed out on the fun of playing with him (the experience).

I put the result above the process. Worse yet, I was a sore loser. Instead of being grateful for the chance to have fun playing a new sport, I was sullen and quiet after the game. Frankly, I acted immaturely. I had some growing up to do. Trouble is, many adults never grow past this level!

How about you? If you're playing golf, is it strictly for business purposes? Are you just trying to close a sale? Is it just to lower your handicap? Or can you stop for a moment and enjoy the beautiful landscape you're playing on? Can you fully enjoy the interesting people you have the privilege of golfing with?

I admit that I'm guilty of focusing too much on the future – on the next achievement or the next accomplishment. I get so focused on what lies ahead and what I'm going to do when I get there, that I miss out on the present and all the joy possible in each moment or situation. By living for tomorrow, I often put off happiness and fun to some future time – that may or may not come.

Motivational author Marcia Wieder offers this antidote, "Fill your life with as many moments and experiences of joy and passion as you humanly can." Somebody once said, "Don't grieve over the past or be troubled about the future. Live in the present and make it so beautiful it will be worth remembering."

Good advice. But a lot easier said than done.

I'm a partner in a wealth coaching firm. One of our core competencies is providing investment advice to affluent clients. When I began this book, the S&P 500 Index was down 40 percent year-to-date, and the international markets were in the tank. Large national banks and corporations were failing and others were looking for bailout packages to avoid bankruptcy. On top of that, home and property values cratered. Looked pretty gloomy, didn't it?

So I'm not saying we should ignore serious circumstances and walk around singing "Life Is Just a Bowl of Cherries."

To pretend things are great when they're awful would mean detaching from reality. To ignore disaster or danger would be delusional.

But despite awful circumstances, I *do* have a choice.

I *always* have a choice.

It's up to me to decide what I'm going to zero in on. Am I going to focus on doing the right thing, in the right way, with people I enjoy doing it with? Or am I going to fixate on the negative data splattered across every newscast and newspaper in the country and allow that to affect my demeanor?

Tony Dungy, former head coach of the Indianapolis Colts, shared an important insight on this topic. He said results depend on many things – but most of them are out of our control! For example, your team may be up against a better opponent, your players may be injured, or the ball may not bounce your way. In football and in life, many things that affect our results are beyond our control.

To offset that, the Colts focused on what they *could* control – they spent their time and energy on improving their process. Dungy believed that if they continued to improve their *process*, the *results* would take care of themselves.

Did it work? Dungy was the winningest coach in Colts franchise history. He was also the first head coach to defeat all 32 NFL teams. And he became the first African-American head coach to ever win the Super Bowl, by defeating the Chicago Bears in 2007.

The things that are in our control – the principles and values that guide our life and work – should be our focus, not the outcome. The results will eventually come if we keep doing the right thing, even if it costs us dearly. Coach Dungy said, "It's the journey that matters. Learning is more important than the test. Practice well, and the games will take care of themselves."

Likewise, focus on getting better as a person – start by improving your skills, your character and your relationships – and sooner or later you'll get winning results.

4. ADJUST YOUR ATTITUDE

The attitude we bring to any given situation determines much of what we experience in life – both good and bad. Our attitude is our mental posture or position on an issue, person or circumstance. It's the emotional state *we put ourselves in*. For example, when you walk into work each morning, do you make a conscious decision to have a positive attitude?

You can if you choose to.

The attitude we choose has a tremendous impact on how we view life, how we treat people, and how people treat us. It determines how we respond to negative news or interruptions. It determines whether we see the humorous side of a circumstance or just the potential pitfalls.

One of the best descriptions about the power of attitude was written by pastor and author, Charles R. Swindoll:

> We have a choice every day regarding the attitude we will embrace for that day. We cannot change our past. We cannot change the fact that people will act in a certain way. We cannot change the inevitable. The only thing we can do is play on the one string we have, and that is our attitude. I am convinced that life is 10 percent what happens to me and 90 percent how I react to it ... we are in charge of our attitudes.

It amazes me how different people can experience the same circumstances but display completely different attitudes. Case in point: In January 2009, US Airways flight 1549 crash-landed on the Hudson River after a flock of birds flew into the plane's engines. In one second, all power and thrust was gone. The plane was basically a 100-ton rock falling out of the sky. Incredibly, Captain Sullenberger landed the plane safely on the Hudson River, and all 155 passengers survived.

Pictures of the plane floating in the middle of the icy river with the passengers standing on the wings waiting to be rescued left an indelible impression on all of us.

After everyone was safely brought to land, reporters interviewed the passengers. Most recounted the harrowing experience with words like "terrifying," "frightening," and "scary." But one woman, grinning ear to ear, chuckled that she'd had worse landings on actual runways! Smiling and relaxed, she took the entire event in stride. Amazing, isn't it?

Out of that group of passengers, who is more likely to see difficult circumstances as *challenges* instead of *problems*?

Who will learn and grow from adversity, and who will become paralyzed by it? Who do you think is more likely to get on with their life – and have fun?

I'm betting on the passenger with the sense of humor.

○   ○   ○

In his book, *How I Raised Myself from Failure to Success in Selling*, Frank Bettger writes about his days as a minor league baseball player. He was going nowhere. Things looked bleak. When his manager accused him of being lazy, he explained that he wasn't lazy, just nervous. Bettger thought he could hide his nervousness and his fear of the crowds by appearing to "take it easy." His manager warned him that his strategy wasn't working and that if Frank hoped for a future in baseball he would need to put some enthusiasm into his work.

Frank says although he didn't *feel* enthusiastic, he decided to *act* enthusiastic anyway. "I made up my mind to establish the reputation of being the most enthusiastic ball player they had ever seen. I thought if I could establish such a reputation, I'd have to live up to it." He began to act like a man electrified. He threw the ball around the diamond so fast it almost broke his infielder's hands.

Bettger said his approach worked like magic. By acting enthusiastic, he almost entirely overcame his fear. His nervousness began to work *for* him – he played better than he thought he was capable of. His enthusiasm affected other players and they became energized, too.

Within ten days, his new enthusiasm – having fun with his game – got Frank promoted to a higher level of minor league team. With this transfer he received a 700 percent salary increase, even though, "I didn't know any more about baseball than I did before."

Two years later, Frank was playing for the St. Louis Cardinals and had multiplied his income by 30 times! Changing his attitude literally changed his life.

Unfortunately, some people are so negative that if science found a cure for cancer, baldness and halitosis they'd find something wrong with it. Know anyone like that? You can step outdoors and proclaim, "What a beautiful day!" And this person will frown, "Yes, but clouds could be forming."

Try to limit your time around these "glass half empty" people.

5. DON'T WORRY ABOUT CIRCUMSTANCES

One of the most mistaken (and arrogant) notions we hold is that we are in control of our own lives, that we shape our own destinies. In actual fact, we control very little in this life. Most circumstances bounce our way randomly, like ping pong balls dropped from an airplane. There are only a few things we can control in life – our effort, our affections, our choices, and perhaps the most important of all, our attitude.

In other words, we can't control our circumstances, but we *can* control our reactions to them.

Winston Churchill described the two different outlooks and categories of people in this world succinctly: "The pessimist sees the difficulty in every opportunity; an optimist sees the opportunity in every difficulty."

Which do *you* choose to see? Some people live their lives looking behind them, peering over their shoulder for some disaster coming up to bite them on the butt. Others keep their focus forward, looking past obstacles for new paths of opportunity and adventure. Those are the ones who make this world a better place to live in.

Thomas Edison was a genius... and an optimist. He never let obstacles deter him. In fact, they inspired him. In 1914, Edison's Menlo Park workshop burned to the ground. All of his equipment, experiments in progress, and years of research were gone. His friends attempted to console him, but to their surprise he said, "The fire burned up all our mistakes. Now we can start over."

The indomitable creator went on to earn a total of 1,093 U.S. patents for his inventions. He and his staff worked on up to 40 projects at a time, churning out an average of one patentable invention every two weeks.

Edison understood and practiced an important principle about mistakes and failures long before leadership expert John Maxwell gave us his similar advice, "Every experience can be a success if you can answer one question: *What did you learn from the situation?*"

○　　○　　○

Each day we have a choice about how we will respond to our circumstances. You may be familiar with a short story called "The Street," written by Allan Seager. In the story, two men, both seriously ill, occupy the same hospital room. One man is lying next to the room's only window. The other man lies flat on his back, unable to sit up. Every day, the man by the window describes the beautiful scene outside the window for his roommate. Soon, the man in the other bed begins to live for those descriptions – a few minutes each day when his world is expanded and energized by hearing about the activity, color and beauty outside the window.

One day, the man by the window dies peacefully. The remaining patient asks the nurses to switch him to the bed by the window, only to discover that it faces a brick wall!

Incredulous, the man asks the nurse what could have compelled his deceased roommate to describe such wonderful things outside the window. The nurse responds that the man had been blind and could not even see the wall. She says, "Perhaps he just wanted to encourage you."

This story illustrates that *we see what we want to see* – and we all see things differently. It's our attitude that dictates what we make of our circumstances.

Henry David Thoreau agreed: "It's not what you look at that matters, it's what you see." We can choose to see the good or the not-so-good in our surroundings, in the people we deal with, in the fiscal policy we work under, in the schools we teach at, and so on.

The choice is ours.

The greater part of our happiness or misery depends on our disposition and not our circumstances.

Martha Washington, First Lady

6. LIGHTEN UP!

Did you enjoy the beautiful locations in the *Lord of the Rings* movie trilogy?

Did you know it was all shot in New Zealand?

I had the privilege of traveling there with family and friends recently. It is truly some of the most stunningly beautiful real estate on earth. Typical of tourists, we sped across the country from one interesting city to the next, trying desperately to stay on schedule. To our frustration, the hilly, circuitous roads made our sprint extra challenging. Twisting and turning, strips of tarmac wound up and down the mountains like corkscrews. While the scenery was captivating, the constant change of elevation and the endless switchbacks made me a bit nauseous.

When we arrived in Queenstown, the women split off to visit the quaint shops along The Mall. Thirsty for knowledge, the guys decided to study local culture. By that I mean the nearest pub. We strolled into Chico's Bar & Grill and sat next to a New Zealander named Troy. After we'd exchanged greetings, I said, "I don't think you have a straight and level road in this country," hinting at my challenges with motion sickness. He said, "You're right. But that's not your problem, mate. You need to slow down and enjoy the view. We're in no hurry. The fish will still be there."

I knew he was right. This stranger with the thick accent and a pint of Steinlager Pure in his hand had just imparted a priceless gem of wisdom to me.

If we had only slowed down, we would've experienced more of the richness his amazing country had to offer. We would have enjoyed the people and the places and the pace of life more fully. Because of our self-imposed schedule, we always felt rushed. And for what? Imagine the irony – we were supposed to be on vacation, but we were hurrying so we could slow down and have fun.

In 1976, the Eagles touched a nerve with their hit song, "Life In The Fast Lane." Lyrics hit home for yuppies on the move, "Eager for action, hot for the game, the coming attraction, the drop of a name." Describing a couple burning themselves out, the chorus rightly concludes that life on the edge "surely makes you lose your mind."

Can you relate?

In the 35 years (hard to believe!) since that song was released, the pace of life has increased a hundred times over. Thanks to technology, we're always on the grid, always connected to the entire world and moving at the speed of the internet. Every gadget that was supposed to save time and produce leisure has only forced us to do more work at a faster pace on a tighter deadline.

And it gets worse every day.

That whooshing noise in our ears is the sound of life rushing by us as we struggle to keep up with our responsibilities. Some of these obligations are just part of life. We can't escape them. But there are other aspects of "busy-ness" that we bring upon ourselves. We miss a lot of the beauty and fun life has to offer by voluntarily participating in an endless rat race.

High achievers struggle in this area. They tend to think fun is frivolous. They think that if you're not grinding away at work, if you're not busy producing, then you're wasting your time. If you're not in perpetual motion, you're not adding to your net worth.

What are the symptoms? To a workaholic, it's a badge of honor to be criticized for overworking ("Don't you ever go home? Why don't you just move into the office?"). When someone asks how they're doing, they proudly reply, "Busy, man, swamped. Kickin' it out, makin' it happen."

Workplace bravado is okay now and then or in special crunch times. But it's way too easy to get burning and churning for so long that it becomes difficult to "shut it down" when you need to.

You can also end up with nothing left in your emotional tank.

I think you know what I'm talking about – you drag yourself home after a hard day at work, and you're depleted. Spent. Wiped out. You're sitting on the couch *physically* but you're *emotionally* absent. Technically, your body is in the room, but you're not contributing anything positive to those around you. Your thoughts may be a thousand miles away – or back at the office. As a result, your ability to engage with your friends, spouse or children is diminished. Your ability to be supportive and caring to the people who matter most is gone.

If that frenetic pace continues – draining your emotional tank – the pain of broken relationships will be knocking on your door.

Author Tim Hansel wrote a book called *When I Relax I Feel Guilty*. I love that title. There are many people who fit that description – I'm one of them. If I find myself lying around the house for any length of time, I have guilty thoughts like, "I should be doing something productive."

We would do well to remind ourselves that we are human *beings*, not human *doings*.

Rabbi and philosopher Abraham Heschel said it beautifully: "Just to be is a blessing. Just to live is holy." The word *holy* literally means to be "set apart, distinctive." Who wants to live like everyone else? Not me. I want to be distinctive. If you live like everyone else, you'll get what everyone else gets – a splintered, fragmented life lacking cohesion, energy, clarity... and fun.

Yes, it's great to be productive, it's great to be the rainmaker, but you must balance your drive to succeed with your built-in need for rest and relaxation.

Or else your head explodes.

I never lose sight of the fact that just being is fun.

Katherine Hepburn, actress

7. PUT FUN IN YOUR DAY PLANNER

For lots of Type A personalities, self-worth and personal identity are wrapped up in the work they do. That's a trap. Chris Evans, an entrepreneur in Raleigh, North Carolina, said, "I needed the company to need me. Much of the time I spent at the office was just to help me feel I was important to the company." That's a sobering thought for those of us who enjoy feeling indispensable.

Contrast that way of thinking with this advice from Mother Teresa, "To keep a lamp burning, we have to keep putting oil in it."

Recreation and fun are the oil that keeps us burning.

Pop quiz: What are the things in your life right now that make you feel like you're carrying a 50-pound sandbag over each shoulder?

Now answer these follow-ups: Should *you* be carrying them? Are they *worth* carrying? Have you asked someone *else* to help you? Can you even admit you *need* help?

As my Aussie friends might say, "Let 'em go, mate." You might be surprised to discover there's someone else in your life better equipped to shoulder that load than you are. It's humbling, but sharing the load and delegating could turn your life around.

○   ○   ○

From shopkeepers to soccer moms, we're all cramming more into our schedules than previous generations could even imagine. How's *your* day planner? Running from one meeting or activity to the next? Does your schedule feel tighter than a Victorian corset, making it hard... to... breathe?

Does instant coffee take too long? Does the microwave oven try your patience? Is a Pop-Tart the only breakfast you have time for?

I remember seeing the plate-spinner-guy on the old *Ed Sullivan* TV show. This nutcase could get a dozen plates spinning on sticks at one time. Just when one would slow down and start to wobble and was about to crash, he'd run over and give it a twirl. It was exasperating to watch him tend to so many things at once. But it's a lot like our lives. The struggle to juggle all of life's responsibilities is real and it's a challenge we all face.

Whether you're a work-at-home parent, corporate exec, or blue-collar worker, you know the stress and strain of trying to juggle job, family, friends, finances, spirituality, shopping, exercise, sleep, social obligations, relationships... the list goes on and on.

The key to being able to lighten up is to add *margin* to our lives...

Margin means "an allowance or reservation for contingencies or changes." That means scheduling in some unplanned time, some room for error, some rainy day resources. It's like driving to the airport. If it usually takes 45 minutes to get there on a normal day, what happens if you run into a traffic backup? If you have zero margin, you miss your flight. If you give yourself an extra 20 minutes, you're wheels up right on time.

One of the keys to adding margin to life is organization. Perhaps you could help yourself by structuring your days and activities in a way that puts you back in control and allows you to pace yourself better.

Dan Sullivan of Strategic Coach designed a system of dividing your time into three types of days: Days on which you work, days on which you prepare and plan, and days on which you do nothing work related. We use Dan's system at our office.

On "work days," 80 percent or more of your activities are critical to fulfilling your responsibilities at work (revenue generating) or at home (seeing that your family is cared for).

On "preparation days," you prepare for work days and complete day-to-day administrative or planning activities.

On "no-work days," you do no work at all – not even checking email or voicemail. You are free to be mommy, daddy, husband, wife, friend, teammate, etc. Free to have fun. These days are so important because they re-energize you to pursue your priorities and passions.

Each person has to decide how many of each type of day per week is right for them. It will be different for everyone. The beauty of the system is that it allows you to isolate activities according to their importance. Try it – you just might find time for some fun!

For those of you who think adding structure to your life would be suffocating, try this exercise. Each day, identify what's most important to accomplish on that particular day. Jot down your top two or three priorities – things that will make you feel great if you complete them. At the same time, ask yourself if there are some things you can let go of. Asking a spouse, a friend, or a co-worker for help is *not* a sign of weakness. On the contrary, it's a sign that you are secure in who you are and that you recognize you can't do it all alone. None of us are so important that we can't hand off a few items to someone who could probably do them better.

None of us is Super Parent or Super Boss.

My friend and business mentor Gino Wickman often reminds me, "You have to delegate in order to elevate."

8. USE YOUR GET OUT OF JAIL CARD

There's another area in life where you may need to lighten your load: Is it possible you feel heavy because you're carrying a grudge?

We've all had situations where we've been wronged – often by someone who was clearly irresponsible or negligent. Even worse, we've been wronged by people who have actually tried to hurt or humiliate us *intentionally.* Ouch.

The problem is, when we've been wronged – and that's all of us – there's usually no court of law to try the "guilty party." No legal way to get restitution or enforce a punishment. No legal way to make a careless or rude or hateful person pay us back or apologize. So what do you do when the wrongdoer refuses to make things right? Do you carry your pain and anger around like a sack of bricks? Do you drag your resentment and desire for revenge around like a boat anchor?

Most people do, but if that's you, I'm begging you to let it go.

If you're holding a grudge, the only person who's paying for the crime is *you.* You are the one keeping yourself locked up. Somebody said, "To forgive is to set a prisoner free and discover the prisoner was you."

These awful loads of anger and bitterness keep us from having joy and fun in life. Like Jacob Marley in Dickens' *A Christmas Story,* too many of us are chained to our past. If you recall, the ghost of Marley was draped in chains and padlocks when he appeared to Ebenezer Scrooge. He was there to warn Scrooge that he too was forging an invisible chain – one that would soon be his to wear for eternity. Like Ebenezer's deceased partner, we shuffle around, clanking our heavy chains and lamenting how unfair life is.

If that's you, the key to unlock the chains is right in your own pocket! It's called *forgiveness* and it can set you free anytime you choose to use it.

Nashville's Sandy Posey sang about being "stepped on, lied to, cheated on, and treated like dirt." If that's you, let it go. If you've been offended, overlooked, or manipulated, let it go. If you can drop the grudge and – even better – forgive the wrongdoer, *you* are the winner, not them.

9. BEWARE OF BUZZ KILLS

We have a bug zapper in our backyard. When flying critters get too close to the irresistible blue light, they get electrocuted. Zapped.

Likewise, there are certain things in life that can kill our fun if we get too close. Worry is a primary zapper of vitality and fun. The Greek word for *worry* literally means to vacillate between fear and hope. It means you are trying to focus on two different things at the same time. You get emotionally cross-eyed. An anxious, worried heart weighs a person down like a mountain climber with a grand piano strapped on his back. Someone said worry is like a rocking chair – it will give you something to do, but it won't take you anywhere. Worry zaps our joy, wears us down, and if we're not careful, immobilizes us.

Think I'm exaggerating?

An epidemic of anxiety and depression is robbing our fun (and our finances) at a record clip. According to industry watchdog, IMS Health, annual sales of antidepressants in the U.S. are at $11 billion and rising. Increasing levels of fear are keeping us isolated, distraught, and preoccupied; effectively crippling our potential for success. Author Dan Brown said, "Men go to far greater lengths to avoid what they fear than to obtain what they desire." Fear of failure keeps us so busy trying not to lose that we have no time to win – to pursue with reckless abandon the goals that would bring us joy. When fear causes us to settle for less, we're disappointed in ourselves and the world around us.

And down the black hole we go.

To have any shot at abundant living, you need to release these burdens. If you're struggling with worry, fear, depression, or all three, hang on; we'll explore alternatives to this near-universal malaise in Chapter 9 on Faith.

Debt can certainly put a damper on our fun, too. Whether it's the stress of credit card debt or the lack of discretionary income, money problems destroy marriages, create tension and cause depression. The mental straitjacket of living paycheck to paycheck keeps the majority of Americans uptight and sleepless. Big or small, debt can zap joy and fun quicker than you can say fried mosquitoes. We'll talk about solutions for this all-too-common problem in the Finance chapter.

There's a folksy poem that's been circulating for at least 60 years. In it, an old woman from the hill country of Kentucky describes the healthy and balanced perspective she developed: "If I had my life to live over again, I would dare to make more mistakes. I would relax. I would be sillier. I would take fewer things seriously. If I had to do it over again, I'd *travel lighter*."

There it is. Stay lean. Stay light.

10. LIVE IT UP!

You've probably heard the saying, "Live every day like it's your last, because one day you're going to be right."

It's grim but true. The fatality rate for humans is 100 percent. But before we kick the bucket, let's live a little. What have you always dreamed of doing? What's on your "bucket list?" What would you most love to do, but (for whatever reason) have been putting off?

My friend Tom grabs the gusto. He pilots his own airplane, rides motorcycles and jet boats, drives off-road vehicles, goes deep sea fishing, flies gliders, and has started numerous successful businesses. He says, "If you don't get out in life, it's just one day after another, after another, and after a while they all start to look alike and that's not for me."

That's not for me either, and if you're reading this book it's probably not for you.

The time to change all that is now.

I double-dog-dare you to re-create your life: Learn to play guitar. Or learn to speak Italian. Take flying lessons. Or fly a kite. Or learn to fly fish. Visit your favorite ballparks around the country. Do a fantasy camp. Take a yoga class. Take up line dancing. Go for a walk in the rain. Or go camping in the Grand Canyon. Start a business. Start a rock band. Run a marathon. Run the tables. Go bungee jumping. Or go horseback riding. Water-ski barefoot. Write a song. Write a poem. Write something on a steamed mirror. Make a movie. Plant a garden. Roll down a grassy slope like you did when you were a kid. Go kayaking. Bowling. Sculpting. Start a nonprofit organization. Do random acts of kindness. Climb a tree. Hike a mountain. Bike a mountain. Just *pick something you like and get out there* – you will feel so much better!

Liked kickball as a kid? Contact the World Adult Kickball Association and join a team in your area. Didn't get drafted by the NBA? Call your local Y for an adult basketball league. Or try indoor soccer. Or hockey. Or water aerobics. Be the oldest karate kid or the youngest shuffleboard champ.

Whatever you pick, take Nike's advice and *just do it*.

The man who can't dance thinks the band is no good.

Polish proverb

UP, UP AND AWAY

When we lived outside Philadelphia, I had the opportunity to go on a hot-air balloon ride. The balloon pilot – an adventurer with an international reputation – offered to take me for a unique ride. Part of the flight plan was to lower the balloon into a deep canyon. I thought about his offer briefly but declined because of the heavy workload I was carrying at the time.

I still regret that decision to this day.

Say "Yes" more often than you say "No" to opportunities like that. The work will always be there. The incredible opportunity will not.

Ever see the movie *Wild Hogs*? Actor Tim Allen leads a group of middle-age stuck-in-a-rut guys on a road trip across the county. Hopping on Harleys, they turn their backs on conformity and crank up Steppenwolf's throbbing "Born To Be Wild." The ride officially starts the minute they all throw their cell phones into a fountain (did that image just make you *cringe* or make you *jealous*?). Sounds fun to me! My real-life friend Bob rode his motorcycle to the four corners of the United States. He made it in 38 days, averaging 365 miles per day. Along the way, he met dozens of interesting people. It was a life-changing experience.

That kind of ride may not be for you, but what *have* you been itching to do? Whatever it is, start scratching the itch! If it requires planning, start planning. If it requires money, start saving. Write it down. Plan it out. Then take some risks. Go on an adventure. Do something where you will not be perfectly safe. Something out of your comfort zone. Something with a chance of potential loss, failure or disappointment. Feel the tension. Stick your neck out.

Taking calculated risks makes us feel alive. We don't know what tomorrow will bring, let alone next year. Boycott monotony.

Do one thing every day that scares you.

Eleanor Roosevelt, First Lady

o   o   o

Some guys mark their midlife crisis by buying a Corvette or a Porsche. Me? I bought a dune buggy. Although relatively small, it's definitely the real deal – complete with roll cage, bucket seats, knobby tires, stick shift and halogen lights. Its Briggs & Stratton engine gets the scaled-down buggy cranking up to 50 miles per hour. And because you're sitting just six inches off the ground, it feels like you're going 80! When you get moving that fast in the open air, the wind makes your eyes water and the rippin' exhaust makes your pulse pound.

Stimulating? Totally.

Safe? Well, sort of.

One thing's for sure, it's a blast going off road in the buggy, doing doughnuts in the dirt or figure-eights in the snow. Mostly I just love being able to break out of the straight and narrow lines we drive our cars in (and live our lives in) day after day.

Most smiles per mile? When we use the buggy to give big thrills to little people. My young nieces Sarah, Grace, and Emma love getting rides in the off-roader. They lift their hands in the air like a rollercoaster and yell, "Faster, Uncle Mike, faster!" My next-door neighbor's son Alex also loves the machine. Sometimes I take him to the local school playground and put him behind the the wheel. He heads straight to a bowl-shaped area, floors it, and drifts through the corners as fast as he can fly. Of course, my son Drew is a hero to his pals as they laugh and shriek and let it all hang out. Seeing the expression on these young people's faces – grinning from ear to ear – is priceless fun in itself.

But wait, as Ron Popeil used to say, *there's more!*

After some cajoling, I relented and got a trampoline for the backyard. I had no idea how much fun it could be. There's something exhilarating about leaving the earth's gravitational pull – if only for a few seconds – while bouncing into the air. Yes, even in our early fifties, my wife and I take our turn on the tramp.

We also use the trampoline at night for stargazing. Mary Ann and I lie on our backs and look up at the constellations. We watch for shooting stars, spot satellites, and trace the flight patterns of airplanes, wondering out loud where they're going. Mostly we just enjoy the quiet and solitude, which in itself is a wonderful, different kind of fun. Once in a while, there's even a little hanky-panky going on out there under the moonlight – and under a discrete blanket!

Such is human psychology that if we don't express our joy, we soon cease to feel it.

Lin Yutang, writer & inventor

LAUGHTER IS FOR LOVERS

Speaking of hanky-panky, how's your sex life?

Is it fun? It should be. If you find sex is boring, predictable and uninspired, it's time to invest in your marriage. To the extent that you do, it will pay huge dividends in many other areas. As your sex life goes, so goes the marriage, and as the marriage goes, so goes every other relationship in your life. The joy of sex (or the lack of it) determines the temperature and resilience of your marriage – and the amount of fun you'll get out of life as a couple.

An erratic (not erotic) sex life weakens a marriage. A dynamic sex life strengthens it. If the thrill is gone, there are shelves full of resources available to enhance your time in the bedroom. Or maybe it's time to attend a marriage conference or couple's retreat where you can be taught (or reminded of) the fine art of establishing and maintaining an intimate relationship. Don't be too shy or too proud to sign up for one. These weekend tune-ups can rescue a failing marriage or strengthen a good one.

When it comes to tune-ups, a great way to cement a relationship is by opening up, letting go, and enjoying some playful humor. As we said earlier, laughter can relieve stress by producing a natural tranquilizing effect in an individual. But what it does between *two* people is a double whammy! When husband and wife laugh together often, the result is bonding and friendship. Of course, a passionate, sexy romance is awesome, but that level of intense emotion is hard to sustain. On the other hand, laughter – and the resulting friendship – is enjoyable and deeply satisfying day after day, year after year. Like sex, laughter requires a degree of intimacy and trust, with both sides contributing. But, man, is it worth it! Finding a way to laugh about difficult issues helps couples put mistakes, problems, and shortcomings into better perspective.

Okay, back to sex. Hollywood won't tell you this. Neither will the talk shows. But sex without love and commitment is *just exercise*. If you want to experience real fun in your sex life, become a student of your mate. Learn about his or her hopes, dreams, fears, concerns and aspirations. Someone (Julia Child, perhaps?) said, "Sex begins in the kitchen" and that means paying attention to what your spouse is saying and feeling. We must first learn to connect on an emotional level before we can ever expect to fully connect on a physical level.

Before you get out that Barry White CD and start lighting scented candles, there's one more kind of fun that couples need to know about –

volunteering. That's right. Volunteer your time and skills somewhere and you'll be grinning for weeks. Seriously. If you want to experience a different level of fun, one that leaves lasting feelings of joy and fulfillment, try serving others less fortunate than you. Opportunities abound: Help someone learn to read, become a Big Brother or Big Sister to a child, make sandwiches at a soup kitchen, help a widow winterize her home, work at a blood drive, rake leaves for a senior citizen, whatever.

There are many nonprofits in your area that need help, or ask for ideas at your place of worship. Serving together as a couple is fun that will put a smile on your face – and in your heart – long after the experience has ended. It's the kind of sacrifice that gives back far more than you give away. And if you can volunteer across cultural, economic, or social barriers, the personal rewards are even greater.

LAUGHTER IS A HEALER

Journalist and activist Norman Cousins literally laughed his way out of a crippling disease that most doctors believed irreversible. After a trip to Russia, Norman was stricken with a painful and debilitating disease that defied treatment. He had considerable difficulty moving his limbs or turning over in bed. At his low point, he could barely open his jaws. Medical experts diagnosed it as *ankylosing spondylitis* – inflammatory arthritis caused by the connective tissue in his spine disintegrating. One specialist said Norman had a 1-in-500 chance of recovering; that same doctor had never witnessed even a single recovery from this condition.

Undaunted, Cousins researched the causes of symptoms like his and began thinking about what he had been exposed to while traveling. Norman concluded his illness was caused by adrenal exhaustion. If so, he figured he needed to get his adrenal glands and endocrine system functioning again. He wondered what effect stimulating his body with positive emotions could have. If negative emotions produce negative chemical changes in the body, perhaps positive emotions could produce positive changes.

Was it possible that intangibles like love, hope, faith, laughter, confidence, and the will to live could have therapeutic value?

Norman hatched a plan. He decided he needed to be in a more cheerful environment conducive to a positive outlook on life. He moved out of the hospital to begin a program of intentionally and systematically exercising affirmative emotions to enhance his body's chemistry: "It was easy enough to hope and love and have faith, but what about laughter? Nothing is less funny than being flat on your back with all the bones in your spine and joints hurting."

Norman thought a good way to start was by exposing himself to huge doses of comedy. Without knowing what to expect, he began watching tapes of *Candid Camera* programs and classic Marx Brothers movies.

He was elated. "It worked. I made the joyous discovery that ten minutes of genuine belly laughter had an anesthetic effect and would give me at least two hours of pain-free sleep." When he wasn't watching funny flicks, Cousin had his nurse read out loud from his stash of humor books. In his own book, *Anatomy of an Illness as Perceived by the Patient*, Norman would later write:

> If laughter did in fact have a salutary effect on the body's chemistry, it seemed at least theoretically likely that it would enhance the system's ability to fight inflammation. So we took sedimentation rate readings just before as well as several hours after the laughter episodes. Each time, there was a drop of at least five points. I was greatly elated by the discovery that there is a physiologic basis for the ancient theory that laughter is good medicine.

Along with other measures, the laughter therapy cut heavily into whatever poison was attacking Norman's connective tissue. His fever receded and his pulse stopped racing. After months of these treatments he was able to return to work full time.

Norman suggests his regimen would also benefit those who are not ill, "Laughing is like internal jogging. It provides a pick-up similar to what you feel after a good workout. You feel refreshed and rejuvenated."

Laughter is not a light-weight remedy. It's powerful stuff. It's one of life's essentials to help improve and prolong life. As author Wilfred A. Peterson stated, "Laughter is the best medicine for a long and happy life. He who laughs, lasts."

DON'T FORGET TO PACK THE FUN

Anyone who's been around the block a few times knows the normal pressures of life can put stress on any relationship. When you add in the natural differences between men and women, rich and poor, young and old, you have a recipe for potential conflict. What oil is to your car's engine, laughter can be to relationships. It can play a vital role in keeping normal friction from escalating into a costly breakdown. Permit me one more metaphor: Injecting humor into a tense scenario is like squirting some WD-40 on a squeaky hinge – a drop or two of laughter can quiet an argument and smooth things out. Whether it's between spouses, workers, neighbors or strangers, sharing a good laugh lubricates relationships.

What soup is to the body, laughter is to the soul.

Yiddish proverb

○　　○　　○

Taking time out for a few laughs (like catching the latest comedy together or sharing a funny story) can help create safe space in a strained relationship, allowing for perspective and mending to take place. Victor Borge said, "Laughter is the shortest distance between two people." As a world traveler, I can tell you it's true – the magical power of laughter to connect people works even when there's a language barrier. Or a generation gap or socio-economic differences.

Remember the movie *Office Space*? Frustrated employees at a software company took an obstinate copy machine out to a field and smashed it into tiny bits. That looked like fun to me. And pretty justifiable. Now, I don't advocate trashing your company's copier. But the hilarious scene illustrates my next hypothesis. With a little imagination (and some willing accomplices) you can have fun at perhaps the least likely place of all – work.

Case in point: When my business partners decided it was time to roll out our company's core values, I was asked to communicate them to our teammates in a fun, creative way. For starters, I knew each of our seven values started with the letter "C" – as in character, competence, commitment, etc. And then it happened. A crazy homonym popped into my brain and I decided to use the theme "Sailing the Seven Cs."

For my presentation to the firm, I ditched my Brooks Brothers and dressed from head to toe as Popeye the Sailor Man – complete with a corn cob pipe hanging from my mouth and his signature bulging forearms (I wish they were mine). Yes, blow me down, I even talked in Popeye's distinctive gravelly voice. Everyone had fun laughing at me and I had big fun stepping out of character.

I took a subject that could have been dry and bland and made it fun and (I hope) very memorable. Lesson? Even if you're the boss, it's okay to be undignified at times!

One of the inevitable byproducts of fun is laughter. And with apologies to Popeye, laughter produces more benefits than a can of spinach. As we close this chapter on Fun, let's revisit some of those perks...

MORE FUN THAN A BARREL OF FACTOIDS

Compiling this section was a revelation.

I was surprised to learn the tangible benefits of including smiles and laughter in our day. The new study of humor and the effects of laughter on the human body is called gelotology. Doctors, psychiatrists and other health professionals are increasingly using humor treatments, laughter meditation, even clown therapy (remember *Patch Adams*?).

Memorial Hospital in laugh-a-minute Muncie, Indiana, has compiled helpful info about laughter. Here are their findings:

- Stanford University studies show that a good laugh can provide health benefits equal to ten minutes on a rowing machine. (I'd do just about anything to stay off that torture device.)

- Dr. Lee Burk of Loma Linda University, California, showed that laughter causes a release of endorphins similar to the "high" joggers experience.

- Dr. Michael Miller from the University of Maryland found that laughter can improve circulatory and cardiovascular health.

- Laughter lowers the level of cortisol in the body, which enhances the work of the immune system and may prevent disease.

- Just 15 minutes of laughter may provide the same benefit as two hours of sleep.

- In the 1950s, people laughed an average of 18 minutes per day. Today, we're down to just four to six minutes.

- Fortune 500 companies (IBM, AT&T, Ford, General Electric, Southwest Airlines, Bank of America and others) use humor in the workplace to increase morale and improve their bottom line.

- Here's my favorite stat: University of Chicago studies show that a great sense of humor can add about eight years to your life. That's 2,848 extra sunrises!

Laughter is an instant vacation.

Milton Berle, comedian

o   o   o

7F ACTION STEPS: FUN

- Write a letter – to yourself at age 19. What advice would you give? What would you do differently? What would you do more of? Less of? Then use this letter as a life map going forward.

- Avoid energy-sucking pessimists. Surround yourself with people who have a good sense of humor. Laughter is more contagious than any disease. Look for the humor in everyday situations.

- For big laughs, check out any DVD by clean comics Brian Regan (*www.brianregan.com*) and Jim Gaffigan (*www.jimgaffigan.com*). Unbelievably funny stuff.

- Bored? Go to YouTube (*YouTube.com*) and type in "Japanese game show marshmallow eating contest." Weird and wild!

- Alan Funt's *Candid Camera* ran from 1960 to 1967. Funt's long gone but you still can watch his classic set-ups online (*CandidCamera.com*).

- Watch full episodes of *Wipeout* online (Google "*ABC Wipeout*").

- Rent your next movie from the comedy section. Can I suggest a few titles? (I stay on the clean side): *Dumb & Dumber, Forrest Gump, Monty Python & the Holy Grail, Ghostbusters, Princess Bride, Man Who Knew Too Little, Ground Hog Day, What About Bob?, Rat Race, Annie Hall, Airplane, Bringing Up Baby, Napoleon Dynamite, 50 First Dates, Talladega Nights, Pink Panther, Evan Almighty, Night at the Museum, The Out-of-Towners, Elf*, etc.

- Start a "Naughty Friday" tradition. Once a month (or as often as you dare), leave work early on a Friday afternoon and go have some unscripted fun with a companion.

- Throw a celebrity party. Invite guests to come dressed as their favorite movie stars, singers or political figures. Literally roll out the red carpet down your driveway so guests can walk up. Take their photos as they arrive. Position life-size stand-up cutouts of celebrities around the area.

- Throw a 70's party. Ask everyone to wear vintage clothing and accessories. Imagine the "stunning" polyester bell-bottoms, silk shirts, aviator sunglasses, big gold chains and medallions – yeah, baby, you're stylin'! Sometimes you just need to let your hair (or shag wig) down.
- Check out Mark Gungor's *Laugh Your Way to a Better Marriage* DVD series. Mark's view of life, love and marriage is sidesplitting. Nothing's taboo, and topics include "The Tale of Two Brains," "The Number One Key to Incredible Sex," and "How to Stay Married and Not Kill Anyone."

Life is worth living as long as there's a laugh in it.

L.M. Montgomery, *Anne of Green Gables*

CHAPTER 4

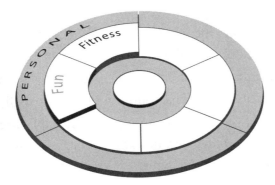

Fitness

Take care of your body. It's the only place you have to live.

Jim Rohn, business philosopher

By late January, people who have shoveled and scraped their way through three months of Michigan winter are ready for a change. For my family, that usually meant thawing out with a quick trip to Florida. But in the coldest days of 2007, things heated up to blowtorch intensity with no help from the Sunshine State...

○ ○ ○

It was a grey, snowy Friday when it all clicked into place.

I'd been working for over six years as a financial advisor at a global brokerage firm, and had achieved considerable success. But despite the comfort level and job security of this position, something gnawed at me, telling me it was time to strike out on my own. My dream was to start my own wealth coaching company, and it consumed me day and night.

After months of planning and preparation, I took one last look around my office, walked down the hall, and handed in my resignation at precisely 4:00 p.m.

That simple move set off a chain reaction. Events unfolded with lightning speed, taking me totally by surprise and teaching me some important lessons about – of all things – fitness.

On Saturday morning, less than 18 hours after resigning, I heard a knock on my front door. It was a courier with an overnight envelope from my former employer's attorneys. In strong, unmistakable language, the letter stated that I was to have no communication whatsoever with my clients.

On Monday, the courier returned with a cease and desist order to stop all business activities in my new company. On Wednesday, I was served with papers stating that my former employer had filed a lawsuit against me in federal court!

In less than a week, my entire plan came screeching to a halt.

All of this was terribly disturbing and totally unexpected. I was especially puzzled because planning for my departure had included conversations with an attorney who specialized in the financial & securities industry. I had hired him specifically to advise me on what was appropriate (and inappropriate) activity when leaving a financial services company. His advice was based on handling dozens of situations like mine and it made good sense. He advised me not to take anything from my office – no client files, no records. Beyond that, he told me to leave my personal computer so they could check it to see that I had not downloaded any confidential information.

To make his point crystal clear, he warned, "Leave the pictures hanging on your wall, the pencils in your drawer, the papers in your files, and the coffee mug on your desk. Hand in your resignation and just walk out. You can go back for your things later."

I followed my lawyer's counsel to the letter and didn't remove so much as a paper clip. On top of that, I was on excellent terms with everyone at my office.

But despite my squeaky clean exit, the lawsuit stated that I had taken client files and proprietary information – the "secret sauce" so to speak. It also claimed that I had violated the non-solicitation agreement, none of which was true. Later on, I realized why my former employer took this aggressive course of action:

1. To buy time to go after my clients – giving them a shot at retaining their business and revenue
2. To prevent me from contacting my clients – delaying the launch of my new company
3. To intimidate future defectors with shock and awe – making anyone else think twice about leaving

As I leafed through the 30-page lawsuit, my mind started racing. Dozens of possible scenarios played out in my brain, all of them ugly: I could lose my new business before it began. I could lose my good reputation in the financial community. I might even lose our home.

Worst of all, I could possibly lose my securities license, making it impossible to work in the industry I loved.

I was devastated. Numb. I was stressed out *emotionally*. At any given moment I was fighting off fear, anxiety and anger. I was challenged *physically*. I lost my appetite, I couldn't sleep and I felt run down. I was vexed *mentally*. I was obsessed with figuring out what could have gone wrong, and weighing my responses to the lawsuit. I was even exhausted *spiritually*. Was "the man upstairs" aware of my dilemma? If so, did he care? As far as I could tell, my prayers were bouncing off the ceiling.

The crush of pending litigation made me question my relationships. Would my friends and colleagues desert me? I wouldn't blame them for backing away to avoid guilt by association. Why go down with a sinking ship? Sometimes at night, I pictured myself standing utterly alone through these trials, and it was chilling.

My lawyer informed me that I had two choices: We could try to settle out of court. Or we could fight the lawsuit to the end. Based on his experience, this would take about a year to litigate and cost approximately $110,000 in legal fees.

I didn't like either option. After all, I was innocent! But I chose what I thought was the lesser of two evils, and agreed to settle out of court. After several weeks we came to a settlement, the details of which – as they say – I am not at liberty to disclose.

I never want to go through an ordeal like that again. But I did gain some valuable insights during those dark days.

One of the lessons I learned is that being "fit" means more than simply keeping the extra pounds off or getting regular check-ups. Being fit means a person has the emotional maturity, intellectual capacity, and physical stamina to respond appropriately in any situation they face.

When life throws you a curveball, unpleasant circumstances can disrupt your peace of mind, stealing the joy from daily activities. But with enough mental toughness, physical strength and spiritual insight, you needn't allow a negative situation to rock your world.

We can pretend it won't happen to us, but sooner or later, we all experience illness or financial misfortune or legal woes. It's inevitable. But it doesn't have to be disastrous. If you're fit, you can be steady and focused in the midst of crisis. You can think clearly and confidently. You can feel balanced and secure. You can see the hope in any situation and spread your optimism to others in the face of challenge.

When you are at *that* level of fitness you are a powerful individual – regardless of your age, physique, income or social status.

WHAT THE BOY SCOUTS KNEW

In the autumn of 1907, a former British army officer named Robert Baden-Powell penned a book he called *Scouting for Boys*. It went on to become the fourth-bestselling book of all time. Over a century later, his original guiding motto can't be improved on: "Be prepared." When you're truly fit, you *are* prepared – prepared to take on a challenge, to hold up under duress, and to make the right choices. You're prepared to follow through in the midst of stiff headwinds, and prepared to sacrifice when necessary.

Real fitness is being prepared for any of life's circumstances.

By that definition, the letters f-i-t could stand for "functional in testing." Simply put, fitness is being *prepared to function*.

Think about it. Why do we work so hard preparing and disciplining our children? So as adults they'll be the best possible spouses, parents and leaders. Why do we encourage young students to study hard? So they'll have the knowledge and skills to make a positive difference in their community. By being *prepared to function* at an early age, they'll be better compensated later in life, better able to financially care for their families and others.

The degree of fitness you need to reach depends on the function you desire to perform. An NFL *coach* needs peak mental fitness. An NFL *player* needs peak physical fitness. On the other hand, the average NFL *viewer* requires almost zero cerebral or muscular preparation to get to the fridge and back to the TV.

Truck driver, barista, cable guy, whatever, we all need a different level of fitness to succeed in our role. But as a parent and husband I know this – being a mother may require the *most* all-around fitness. Athletes training for the decathlon must prepare for ten different events. But things like pole vaulting or tossing a discus seem easy compared to a mom's job: counselor, chef, philosopher, mind reader, driver, teacher, seamstress, banker, mentor, bookkeeper, nurse – and many have outside careers and classes on top of that!

This level of multitasking takes some serious energy. And caffeine can only take you so far. Which is why I recommend getting in shape.

Let's face it. Moms, dads, singles – work/life balance is never easy for any of us. But being physically fit can give us a needed boost of motivation to find a job, start a business, raise a family, or all of the above.

○   ○   ○

Even if your physique is more Pee Wee Herman than Arnold Schwarzenegger, you'll still need to attach your fitness goals to a worthwhile *purpose*. Something nobler than showing off your chiseled pecs in the weight room (or powder room, or worse yet, in the boardroom).

Have you seen guys on TV gushing about their ripped torso? Or girls bragging about their buns of steel? Did it make you run for the barf bag?

Self-absorption is seriously uncool.

Here's what I mean: One day on California's Venice Beach, a bodybuilder was flexing his massive 21-inch biceps. Young girls on rollerblades circled in awe. Tourists snapped photos. High school football jocks asked for tips on bulking up. Basking in the attention, he grinned and posed and oiled himself. Life was good. But when a lesser mortal asked him what he *did* with all those muscles, he looked totally puzzled. He had no response. He didn't get it. The questioner was wondering if this real-life Superman used his strength to do anything constructive or whether it was all just to look good.

Judging by the awkward silence, I guess you could say the question was verbal kryptonite.

Okay, then, what *is* a legit purpose?

First, it's to be **fit for life**.

If we're not fit, we'll miss countless opportunities and worthwhile pursuits. We won't be able to take advantage of windfall situations or impromptu invitations that require mobility or stamina. When we're truly fit, we're prepared to jump into work, play, travel, adventure, and life's challenges of every type.

Second, it's about getting prepared to **serve others**.

I'm a big fan of staying in shape, but it shouldn't be an end in itself. It shouldn't be a narcissistic pastime to make us feel better when we look in the mirror. It is ultimately about having what it takes to serve our families, our communities and our world. It's about having the energy and drive it takes to provide our loved ones (and perhaps total strangers) with food, shelter and safety – regardless of what conditions or calamities the world may bring.

The Four Kinds of Fitness

We've seen that fitness is more than getting buff for a class reunion or losing weight for bikini season. In fact it's not limited to our *physical* health at all. True fitness is holistic and involves our mind and body in equal parts. To get started, let's take a look at the four kinds of fitness – intellectual, emotional, physical and spiritual…

1. INTELLECTUAL FITNESS

You may have heard the story – it's made the email rounds – about a woman in her eighties who enrolls in college. She becomes an icon on campus and is invited to speak at a banquet. In her speech, she tells the younger students to never let go of their dreams. She says anyone can get old, but only those who challenge themselves can truly grow up. She tells them to seize the day, smell the roses, and never take life for granted. The story ends with the octogenarian dying soon after graduating, with her funeral attended by thousands of college students.

The story may be bittersweet, but the lesson it teaches is true: Never stop growing. Never stop learning. Never lose your sense of wonder.

Many people operate with the mistaken notion that because they finished high school or college, they've gathered all the knowledge they'll ever need. The danger with that kind of lazy thinking is that just like the typewriter, the 8-track tape and the floppy disc, you run the risk of becoming obsolete. You will eventually become a spectator in the bleachers instead of a player on the field in the game of life.

It was not so long ago that people thought semiconductors were part-time orchestra leaders and microchips were very, very small snack foods.

Geraldine Ferraro, U.S. Congressperson

According to research, the top ten in-demand jobs in 2013 did not even exist six years ago. That means we're currently preparing students for jobs that may be obsolete by the time they graduate. They will have to figure out (on their own) how to perform in a role that doesn't exist yet, using technologies that haven't been invented yet to solve problems we don't even know are problems yet! Like Einstein said, "We can't solve problems by using the same kind of thinking we used when we created them."

Workers in our father's generation averaged only three jobs between graduation and retirement. The U.S. Department of Labor now estimates that today's college grad will have between ten and fourteen different jobs by age 38.

Can you say "buggy whip industry?"

○　　○　　○

In cyber lingo, a byte is the number of bits it takes to encode one character of text. A single exabyte equals one quintillion bytes. In 2006, 161 exabytes of data were created, which by the way, is 3 million times the information in all the books ever written. Seriously. And now we're crankin' out 1,000 exabytes per year. The amount of new technical info is doubling every 18 months. To handle it, NTT Japan has created a fiber optic cable that pushes 14 trillion bits *per second* down a single strand of fiber.

Compare that with the speed of information distributed by smoke signal, town crier, printing press, telegraph lines, radio signal, even television. How do we stack up with our ancestors? One weekday edition of the *New York Times* is said to contain more information than the average person in seventeenth-century England could access in their entire lifetime.

Science estimates the total of all human knowledge now doubles every ten to fifteen years. But in certain industries with enhanced incentives – like nanotechnology or green technology – knowledge can double every *five* years.

To keep up with this information tsunami, you need to be a dedicated "lifelong learner."

Those who are perpetually learning not only get healthier paychecks, they get healthier brains, too. According to a study published in the journal *Neurology*, people who did mental exercises – like learning new skills – had a lower risk of cognitive impairment and a risk of Alzheimer's almost three times lower than people who did not. Legendary basketball coach, John Wooden, once said, "If I am through learning, I am through."

The *Wall Street Journal* ran an article titled "The Latest in Mental Health: Working Out at the Brain Gym." According to writer Kelly Greene, a growing number of mental calisthenics programs are springing up. Many of these so-called "mental gyms" are stocked with multiple computer stations loaded with mental fitness software, including "neurobics circuits" that purport to stretch the brain. Hopefully minus the Spandex attire.

How is it that our memory is good enough to retain the least triviality that happens to us, but not good enough to remember how often we have told it to the same person?

Francois dela Rochefoucauld, essayist

In southern California, fitness clubs are combining traditional exercise with time in front of computer screens, claiming that mental calisthenics work best after physical exercise. Some spas have added a series of memory programs, which include classes in brain nutrition, genetic workups and cognitive training.

Brain exercise is moving beyond gyms and spas to retailers in major malls. Lindsay Gaskins and her brainy teammates decided to launch a store with "a collection of fun ways to a healthier brain." Called "Marbles: The Brain Store," it debuted in a tiny kiosk in 2008. As of this writing, they have 17 full-size stores and are expanding across the county. Meanwhile, Floridians can enjoy "brain games" and a frappuccino at the Millennium Cognitive Café. And over 700 U.S. retirement communities have added computerized brain fitness centers.

As Kelly Greene reports, this new industry pins its claims for brain exercise on a relatively recent scientific discovery called "neuro-plasticity" – the brain's ability to rewire itself *throughout your entire life* by creating neural connections in response to mental activity.

Dr. Richard Restak, MD, is Clinical Professor of Neurology at George Washington University School of Medicine. This renowned expert on the human brain states, "The science of plasticity is simple" (easy for him to say!).

"When you exercise your brain, you release natural growth factors and influence neurotransmitters, which enhance your brain's level of performance. The efficiency of cell-to-cell communication via chemical messengers increases… as new things are learned, new maps are created and old maps altered. Alternative circuits can be established to compensate for lost or injured areas."

Still with me? Think of brain circuits like friendships: Those that are maintained and enriched will endure; those that are neglected will disappear. Maintenance, novelty, and enriched experiences are like fertilizer for the brain and bring about growth. It's *exercising* these circuits and networks – not the number of nerve cells – that is the key to improved function.

Dr. Restak recommends four specific exercises for your brain. Here's the workout, and don't forget to shower when you're done…

A. VISUAL EXERCISES

For centuries, stage actors have used "sense memory," traditionally practiced with a coffee cup. Give it a try – hold a cup; recognize and memorize its size, color and composition. Study its markings, chips, stains. Now involve your other senses: How does it feel? How heavy is it? How smooth? Is it cool to the touch? Now set it down and close your eyes. When you re-create the cup in your mind, the same brain circuits are involved as when you were actually exploring the real cup. That's why a skilled actor can make the audience "see" a cup that he's not actually holding. Pick any object that interests you, and re-create it mentally by doing a similar exercise.

B. AUDITORY EXERCISES

Movie pioneer Jack Foley created a way to capture live sound effects by using commonly available sources. For instance, he found that crumpling a newspaper sounds like a blazing fire. (Give it a try – close your eyes, put a sheet of newspaper or cellophane to your ear, and crumple it.) Today's "Foley artists" still dub in footsteps, door slams, punches, and gunfire. And like Foley, they're always listening for everyday objects that can be used to create special effects. For instance, the laser blasts in *Star Wars* were made by hitting a high-tension wire with a hammer. And yes, coconut shells still make the best galloping noises! As an auditory exercise, listen to things around you to sharpen your sensitivity. Figure out what sounds might be substituted for others.

C. MOTOR EXERCISES

Activity involving the hand is functionally related to the brain. Fine motor skills are the intricate movements mainly produced by the body's small muscle groups. They're used in everyday tasks like tying a knot, buttoning a shirt or unscrewing a lid, and in more artistic pursuits like painting, sculpting, and playing musical instruments. Developing nimble fingers is a surefire way of improving brain function. To get better, take up juggling or magic or any hobby that requires detail work like model making, knitting, or drawing. If you're musically inclined, get back to that piano or clarinet. Certain sports can also develop fine motor control, like soccer players practicing precise ball handling with their feet. If you're not David Beckham, try shuffling cards or calligraphy.

D. PERI-PERSONAL SPACE EXERCISES

Dr. Restack defines PPS as a bubble of space around us that our brain includes as part of us. It's this "force field" that enables us to avoid walking into people on a crowded sidewalk. Because of PPS, a violinist's bow or a blind person's cane becomes an extension of the human body. With practice, our perception and control can be extended *beyond* what we can reach with our limbs. To improve your PPS, take up a sport that demands awareness of your body boundary and its extensions. Tennis works great, so does golf. This type of exercise enhances your "kinesthetic sense" (it tells the brain where parts of the body are in relation to each other). It's what enables you to close your eyes and touch the tip of your nose – without any info from your five physical senses. To boost it, try dance, martial arts, or the Chinese exercise Tai Chi. Or golf.

Did I mention golf?

MORE MOTIVATION

Need an incentive to keep your brain fit? How about warding off dementia? "By challenging your brain to learn new information throughout your life, you build up cognitive reserve." Dr. Restak explains, "This is analogous to monetary reserve: The more you have accumulated over your lifetime, the less susceptible you will be to deficits in your later years. In general, the more education and knowledge people acquire over their lifetime, the less likely they are in their later years to be diagnosed with dementia."

In other words, use it or lose it.

Many doctors agree. In a groundbreaking 2002 study published in the *Journal of the American Medical Association*, a clinical trial with over 2,800 older adults concluded that cognitive training – such as identifying patterns in a series of letters, shapes, or words – helped *improve* and *preserve* memory and reasoning skills.

People who are mentally fit typically have a positive attitude, and the result is actual physical benefits. If you're the person who sees the glass half full versus half empty, keep thinking that way. Mayo Clinic research shows that people with a positive outlook typically live 19 percent longer than negative people. It could be that optimists are more likely to seek medical help when they're ill. Or it could be their immune systems are actually stronger because of their sunny outlook. Either way, they live longer. Optimists are also less likely to suffer depression and hopelessness than their pessimist counterparts.

○   ○   ○

Did you know that peanuts are one of the ingredients in dynamite? Or that a flock of larks is called an exaltation? Here are ten more scintillating facts you may not know…

- A hummingbird weighs less than a penny.
- Bamboo can grow three feet per day.
- The electric chair was invented by a dentist (it figures).
- An elephant can smell water up to three miles away.
- Over 97 percent of the earth's water is undrinkable.
- William Taft was the last U.S. president with facial hair.
- The longest recorded flight by a chicken is 13 seconds.
- Dolphins sleep with one eye open.
- Adolf Hitler was *Time* magazine's Man of the Year in 1938.
- There are 336 dimples on a regulation golf ball.

What's my point? It's *exhilarating* to learn something new each day. Whether it's silly trivia or serious insights, learning anything that helps you understand yourself or your world better is stimulating to the brain. Whether it's learning how many times we blink (10 million times per year) or discovering a more efficient way of doing something – it's all good. Albert Einstein (who, by the way, lived 76 years, 1 month and 4 days) said it well, "Intellectual growth should commence at birth and cease only at death."

A word of caution: We've all seen insufferable know-it-alls ruin a party with their pontifications. This kind of pinhead thrives on a sense of self-importance and can suck the air out of any conversation by correcting your facts, or quoting some expert verbatim. With footnotes.

Don't be that guy.

If you pursue a path of continual learning, be on guard against feelings of pride and arrogance. As you acquire more knowledge, you'll be tempted to get a wee bit full of yourself. Your desire to tell others everything you know about a subject – whether they want to hear it or not – will increase. So use a filter.

> *Those who think they know it all are very annoying to those of us who actually do.*
>
> Anonymous

Ironically, the most knowledgeable people I know are usually the most humble. Why? Because they realize they're only scratching the surface of what there is to know about their profession or passion. They're fun to be around and a conversation with them usually results in learning something interesting, helpful, or humorous. I always walk away a little smarter, and sometimes a great deal wiser from what they've shared.

○　○　○

I run into basically two kinds of people: boring and not boring.

People in the first category are everywhere. Talking with them is about as interesting as watching your fingernails grow. I picture them as a stagnant pond.

People in the second category are harder to find. Talking with them is a wake-up call to the brain. I picture them as a fresh, bubbling brook.

I've been blessed over the years to associate with a number of the "fresh bubbling brook" (FBB) types. They're invigorating to be around. One of these rare individuals is my dear friend and mentor, Dr. Loren Siffring.

Despite his advanced years, Loren's mind is sharper than ever. He reads voraciously, attends conferences, and listens to books on CD while driving. He is an accomplished painter, gifted poet, and captivating speaker. He participates in community organizations, serves on several boards of directors, and meets with other FBBs for cross-pollination. He is one of the most intellectually fit people I know, and a joy to be with. Every conversation with him challenges, inspires, and – most importantly – encourages me to keep learning.

7F ACTION STEPS: INTELLECTUAL FITNESS

- Ask others to recommend their favorite authors: "What five books most influenced your life?" By reading these same books, you'll benefit from the content, and have additional common ground for conversation.
- Determine your learning style, then use it. By pursuing your intellectual interests according to your natural learning style, you'll most likely stick to it and stay intellectually fit.
  - If you learn best by *hearing*, get podcasts and books on CD in your area of interest and listen in the car, at home, or in the gym.
  - If you learn best by *seeing*, peruse books, blogs, magazines, online journals and DVDs. Attend plays and lectures, too.
  - If you learn by *doing*, find hands-on learning experiences at workshops or seminars designed to get you involved in the process.
- Go to *www.lumosity.com* to custom design a brain fitness program to enhance your memory, attention and creativity.
- Join a mental fitness program. Google "Brain Gym" for a location near you.
- A good workout isn't limited to your body. Playing chess, learning a language, taking up an instrument, doing crosswords,

tackling Sudoku and similar mental activities all have positive health benefits.

2. EMOTIONAL FITNESS

I'm confident my father would have lived to be 100 if he'd taken care of his body.

But he didn't.

Even so, I can't recall a single day growing up when Dad was sick with a cold or flu. He was robust and full of life. Nothing got him down. That all changed when he turned 78. In short order, he had a blocked carotid artery, kidney problems, liver malfunction, and a debilitating stroke.

Within a few months he went from very healthy to seriously ill. His condition rapidly deteriorated until my wife and I could no longer give him the attention he required. With both of us having to work, we had no choice but to find a medical facility that could monitor and treat his complex health issues around the clock.

That didn't go over big with Dad.

Even in his weakened condition he was quick to tell anyone within earshot how dissatisfied he was with his circumstances. He was used to being in control and having things his way, and being incapacitated was a blow to his pride. He was very demanding and often insensitive with his comments. Whenever I visited, he would loudly complain about the staff, the care, the food, the facility – everything: "Mike, you've got to get me out of here. These nurses don't know what the bleep they're doing."

In reality, he had very good nurses. Frankly, I was amazed they continued to care for him considering the verbal abuse they took. He had a list of things he wasn't satisfied with and would unload it on me during every visit.

Dad's illness was a very stressful time. I can remember sitting in the parking lot of the medical facility, trying to work up enough emotional energy to go inside. Walking into the building, I knew full well I'd be bombarded with 60 minutes of him going off about how nobody cared and how unfair it was and how it was up to me to get him out of there.

I would leave each visit emotionally drained. By the time I got home, I had nothing left to give to my family. Because I was emotionally spent, little things would irritate me, and my family would, unfortunately, feel the harsh effects.

Perhaps you've been there? I felt emotionally exhausted the way a runner would feel physically exhausted after a marathon. I was stretched dangerously thin and I couldn't bounce back. My emotional "elasticity" was shot. I could no longer flex to keep from breaking. I needed to become more *emotionally fit*.

EMOTIONS ARE TRICKY THINGS

When functioning within normal range, emotions are very helpful to show compassion, demonstrate concern, express joy, and so on. But when taken to extremes, emotions can be harmful. Allowing them to run wild can put our relationships and our careers in danger. We've all heard the explosive "rant" tapes of Mel Gibson screaming, snarling, and blasting out expletives. His emotional outbursts have damaged the star's credibility and reputation. On the opposite extreme, if we stuff our emotions inside and never let them out – like *Star Trek's* Mr. Spock – we can also cause ourselves physical and psychological damage.

Unchecked emotions can lock us in a vice-like grip that keeps us from dealing with everyday circumstances in a healthy manner. That's why incidents of road rage can be triggered by a seemingly insignificant move or perceived insult. But we are *not* helpless victims of our emotions. We have a role to play, decisions to make. You could say that anger, joy, surprise, love, grief, laughter and pain are like tools in a toolbox – they can be used for bad or good. You can use a hammer to build a house or to hit someone on the head. Likewise, emotions can be constructive or destructive, depending on who's in charge of them.

The choice is ours.

When it comes to emotions, we need to make heads-up, eyes-open choices. Being able to respond with the appropriate reaction requires emotional fitness. Knowing just what our appropriate emotional response should be in any given situation requires *emotional intelligence*.

The importance of emotional intelligence (EI) was brought to public attention with the publication of Daniel Goleman's bestseller, *Emotional Intelligence*. Goleman described a model of EI comprised of four parts: self-awareness, self-management, social awareness and relationship management.

Notice that the first two parts are *personal* (inward) and have to do with our ability to keep our own feelings under control:

A. Self-awareness is our ability to accurately perceive our own emotions and stay aware of them as they happen. Most spikes in our emotions occur when we experience fear, injustice, guilt, a blocked goal, hurt or grief. Understanding *why* we're feeling the way we do, and knowing where we need to be, is a skill that gives us a wonderful advantage in life.

B. Self-management is about controlling and regulating our emotions; that is, being able to stay calm, clear and focused when things do not go as planned. Self-management also involves our ability to take the initiative and to self-motivate.

The second two parts are *social* (outward), and have to do with our ability to manage relationships with others:

C. Social awareness is about discerning emotions in others and understanding how to react. This means understanding what other people are thinking and feeling, even if we don't feel the same way. The developers of the Emotional Intelligence Appraisal add, "We can't expect the emotional experiences of others to be rational or right… we have to take their emotions for what they are, not what we want them to be."

D. Relationship management is about using awareness of our emotions and the emotions of others to manage interactions successfully. It is letting emotional awareness guide clear communication and effective handling of conflict while showing genuine care and concern. Often in conversation with others, our emotions are more influential than the actual words we use.

They may forget what you said, but they will never forget how you made them feel.

Carl W. Buechner, American novelist

If you can raise your emotional intelligence, you'll enjoy better social relationships, develop more diverse friendships, and be more effective at functioning on teams. You'll be better at resolving conflict and keeping relationships intact during the process. And you will be far more likely to ascend to positions of leadership.

Daniel Goleman wrote in the *Harvard Business Review* in 1998, "It's not that IQ and technical skills are irrelevant. They do matter, but mainly as threshold capabilities, that is, they are entry level requirements for executive positions. My research, along with other studies, clearly shows that emotional intelligence is the *sine qua non* of leadership."

o   o   o

Emotional *fitness* is crucial to being able to apply emotional *intelligence*.

Two former professors of mine, Frank Minrith, MD, and Paul Meir, MD, get at the heart of emotional fitness in their book *Introduction to Psychology and Counseling*: "Healthy persons neither avoid situations that arouse strong emotions nor use the mechanisms of isolation and dissociation to keep from feeling. Their emotions are free and not repressed but their behavior is under control."

Notice the key words – *under control*. We have products to keep our acne, dandruff, tartar and perspiration under control. But what about our emotions? Harnessing them is vitally important.

I'm betting you know someone like "Sam." Quite honestly, Sam is a guy I try to avoid. Why? Because I never know which Sam I'm going to bump into. Is he going to be "up" today? Or down in the dumps? Is he going to be intense like a volcanic eruption or laid back like a Jerry Garcia? Sam is on an emotional rollercoaster that I have no interest in riding.

Over the years I've come to appreciate individuals who are able to show effective personal leadership regardless of their own emotional state or of those around them. They've learned to express the appropriate outward emotion at the appropriate time with the appropriate amount of intensity. They are keenly aware of how their emotions affect those around them.

People who can handle the common stresses and challenges of life in a constructive manner have a leg up on those who can't. Those able to keep their composure have a much better chance of solving problems and staying in relationships (even with people they're in conflict with) than people who can't remain calm. People who are emotionally fit keep from harming themselves and others, and will likely rise to positions of leadership.

Laughter through tears is my favorite emotion.

Robert Harling, author of *Steel Magnolias*

---

o   o   o

My friend, Jack Wilson, Ph.D., is the former Director of Counseling and Health Services at Oakland University. He's currently a performance enhancement coach and works with athletes at a national level. Jack explained to me that emotion, by definition, is nonrational. It needs a system to control or contain it. We need to use our thought processes to determine which emotion to use, when to use it, and where to use it. As King Solomon wisely wrote, "Enthusiasm without knowledge is not good. If you act too quickly you might make a mistake."

The danger of acting on raw emotion – without the influence of rational thought – is vividly displayed in the realm of investing. The average investor rides an emotional rollercoaster that follows a pattern like this:

THE INVESTOR'S EMOTIONAL ROLLERCOASTER

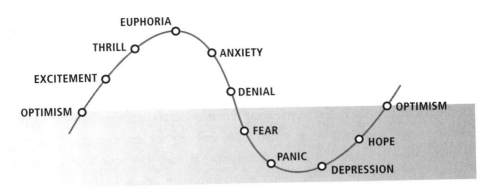

Optimism, excitement, thrills and euphoria (the height of human emotion) are followed by anxiety, denial, fear, panic and depression (the depth of human emotion), which are then followed by the upswing emotion of hope, then optimism … and the pattern repeats itself over and over.

The average investor is ruled by emotion.

The wise investor is ruled by logic.

Here's what I mean: Informed and disciplined investors know that the best time to buy might be when everyone else is despondently selling, and the best time to sell might be when everyone else is euphorically buying.

While it's perfectly natural to experience this range of emotions, it may be harmful or fatal to your brokerage account to base decisions solely on your feelings. Famed investor John Templeton often said, "Bull markets are born on pessimism, grow on skepticism, mature on optimism and die on euphoria."

An emotionally fit person recognizes the emotions they are feeling, interprets the reasons for those feelings, and is able to give an appropriate response based on sound judgment.

The degree of one's emotions varies inversely with one's knowledge of the facts.

Bertrand Russell, philosopher & mathematician

Aristotle was right when he said, "To be angry is easy, but to be angry with the right person, at the proper time, about the proper thing, with the appropriate intensity – that is not within everyone's power and is not easy." The same could be said about all human emotions. The appropriate use of emotion requires thought and maturity.

Doc Childre and Bruce Cryer are founders of HeartMath. They highlight the impact that emotions have on our behavior: "Intelligence capacity is diminished when frustration, anxiety, or inner turmoil operate. Such emotional states cause incoherence in the rhythmic and electrical output of the heart, diminishing neurological efficiency. It's one of the reasons smart people can do stupid things."

And here I always thought it was the tequila.

An emotionally fit person (EFP) knows what they believe and functions from this basis when expressing emotion and making decisions. As a result, these people are able to draw on physical, intellectual, and spiritual resources to express appropriate responses...

EFPs are flexible. They have the ability to adapt to changing situations with self-control and discipline. They are able to "shift gears" quickly and decisively with the demands of crisis or change.

EFPs are empathetic. They are able to see matters from another person's point of view. By mentally "trading places" they are able to be compassionate; demonstrating genuine concern and care for others.

EFPs are secure. They are able to love deeply and to be loved. People who are wrapped up in their own feelings of fear, anger, jealousy, suspicion and inadequacy will have difficulty connecting with others and will likely stick to superficial relationships. An emotionally fit person has enough emotional strength to give to others and still be able to deal with their own challenges or problems.

THE POWER OF POSITIVITY

Ever had a romantic crush?

Ever been cut off by a rude driver?

Ever get scared out of your wits in a movie?

If you answered "Yes" to any of the above, you know emotions can be powerful motivators – both for constructive and destructive behavior. They can inspire us or they can immobilize us. They can help us or harm us. They can inspire us to an act of heroism or send us to prison for a crime of passion. David Burns, professor of psychiatry and behavioral science, writes, "The key to positive emotions is positive, accurate thinking."

This next story illustrates his point.

On New Year's Day, 1929, Georgia Tech played the University of California in the Rose Bowl. In front of a packed-out stadium, Roy Riegels recovered a fumble for California. Somehow, he became confused and started running in the wrong direction. One of his teammates overtook and tackled him 65 yards away, just before he scored for the opposing team!

In the locker room during halftime, Riegels slumped down in a corner and cried. When it was time to head back out for the second half, the coach announced, "The same team that played the first half will start the second." Riegels didn't move. The coach called him by name, but still Riegels didn't move. Finally the coach went right up to Riegels and said, "Roy, didn't you hear me? The same players that played the first half will start the second."

Riegels looked up and said, "I can't do it to save my life. I've ruined you. I've ruined the University of California. I've ruined myself. I couldn't face that crowd in the stadium to save my life."

His coach looked him directly in the eyes. "Son, you made a bad play, but you are not a bad player. Get up and go on back; there is still a second half to play." And he did. The Georgia Tech players said they'd never seen a man play football like Riegels played the second half.

The positive impact that encouragement has on our emotions is hard to overstate. Before his coach's words of affirmation, Roy Riegels allowed his emotions to render his body immobile and useless. But when his coach verbally expressed confidence in him, Riegels' mind and body were rejuvenated to such a degree that he was able to turn in an amazing performance.

The timely and thoughtful words of another can do wonders for our emotions. When you receive a sincere compliment, how does it make you feel – appreciated, valued, inspired, emboldened?

In today's cynical world, people are not always kind to each other. Pats on the back are rare. Because we receive so little in the way of positive feedback, we can literally live off one good compliment for weeks. So why not hand out some kudos? You can always find something positive to say about another person. You may have to look long and hard, but everyone has an admirable quality.

○   ○   ○

People who find it difficult to control their emotions are vulnerable to breakdowns – mentally, socially, even physically. Their marriages, friendships, and careers are often at risk. Conversely, an EFP has a sort of inner gyroscope that keeps them on a healthy, even keel. Because of congruence between their heart (how they feel) and their head (how they think), they have greater resistance to depression, illness and mood swings. As a result, they're inclined to be optimistic and resilient – two proven indicators of psychological health, longer lifespan, and dynamic relationships.

7F ACTION STEPS: EMOTIONAL FITNESS

- Go to *www.talentsmart.com* and take the Emotional Intelligence Appraisal. You'll receive a customized learning program based on your emotional intelligence scores. Your report will indicate your emotional intelligence, reveal your current skill levels, and tell you how to improve.

- Develop an attitude of gratitude. Write down all the things you benefit from every day. Don't forget the basics (do you have clothes to wear, food to eat, transportation, shelter, freedom, employment, friends, family, and health?). Focusing on what you *do* have rather than on what you *don't* will lift your spirits.

- Stop comparing and start caring. If we compare ourselves to those "ahead" of us – bigger homes, better jobs, newer cars or fatter portfolios, we will feel depressed. A better approach to life is sharing whatever you *do* have – including time and talent. Volunteer to serve at a homeless shelter or teach immigrants to read. You'll go in with the intention of helping *others* and leave knowing it was *you* who benefited most.

- If you have difficulty controlling your emotions, seeing a professional counselor or therapist may be the best first step. When you find your emotions controlling you rather than the other way around, it can feel like you are a prisoner in your own body. Don't wait for another outburst, seek professional help.

3. PHYSICAL FITNESS

Would you rather be golfing or reading this book?

Me too.

My business partners and I really love golf. We're not great players, but we enjoy it immensely – for the competition, the social aspect, and the sheer beauty of the course designs. To improve our game, we decided to start working out together with a trainer certified in designing fitness programs for golfers who want to increase their strength, balance and flexibility.

Soon I found myself doing all kinds of unusual exercises that had me panting for breath between sets. To my surprise, I was winded by the vigorous workouts. I was even more surprised when I experienced chest pain. Thinking I may have a clogged artery or the beginning stages of heart disease, I went to my doctor. He ordered a standard stress test along with a new test where radioactive isotopes were injected into my veins. Guess what? Everything checked out normal. Heart rate and blood pressure were normal at stressed levels, arteries were clear.

My clean bill of health was great news – and very humbling. At age 49, I had to face the hard cold fact that I wasn't ill, just woefully out of shape! I discovered that slim doesn't necessarily mean fit. I appeared to be in great shape, but what you see on the outside doesn't always reveal what's happening on the inside.

There's a billboard in San Francisco that reads, "Join This Gym: Look Good Naked." For some, that's a powerful reason to work out. Many view looking good as the primary goal of physical fitness. As we discussed earlier, there's nothing wrong with maintaining our appearance, but physical fitness has to do primarily with *functionality*. As I said, if you are physically fit you are free to engage, respond, lead, endure and succeed.

You've reached middle age when all you exercise is caution.

Anonymous

Physical fitness also has to do with responsibility. If you're fit, you're able to maintain your own well-being, plus help the people around you. You can respond appropriately in any situation – with the ability to do whatever it takes. A friend of mine was walking in New York when a thug came up and snatched his companion's purse. Fortunately, two Marines on furlough witnessed the theft and took off running after the criminal. They quickly caught him and returned the purse. They were able to respond. If you're physically fit and see someone struggling with an attacker, or a child in danger of drowning, you are able to respond. You have the capacity to defend yourself and help others as needed.

Please don't be offended, but if you are functioning below a level that allows you to respond to emergencies, you are not fit.

o   o   o

What if I told you I knew the secret to increasing your longevity and quality of life? What if I could cut your risk of heart disease, diabetes and colon cancer? How about reducing stress and improving your sleep? How about losing weight? What if I knew how you could do *all that* plus increase your attention span and mental sharpness – would you be interested?

Most likely you would.

Of course you already know what I'm driving at. Physical fitness can produce these important health benefits. Amazing, isn't it? You don't need a magic pill to get these results. They are within your reach.

INVEST IN YOUR BODY

Much is said and written about building our social capital, intellectual capital, and financial capital. Isn't it time we started viewing the building of our *health capital* as essential to our daily well-being?

The dividends of exercise are high. But what kind of investment does physical fitness require? More than just joining a health club. In fact, 80 percent of the 40 million Americans paying for gym memberships are not using them. That's $12 billion a year down the drain. They start with great intentions but soon get frustrated and drop out. To stay with it – to achieve the fitness results you want – a busy mom (or dad or single person) *must* have four things in place:

1. Time. The toughest part is choosing to allocate time for fitness. Consider booking a personal trainer, or having an accountability pal, or at the least start putting workouts into your day planner.

2. Energy. Most adults are sleep deprived and nutritionally challenged. We eat plenty, but we consume too much saturated fat and refined sugars. Getting adequate rest and a healthy diet are job one.

3. Goals. I'm never getting six-pack abs. So I'll settle for fitting into my college blue jeans and be thrilled with that. Setting realistic goals and seeing the potential health benefits of being fit are essential.

4. Purpose. Getting fit involves work, sweat, and maybe a little pain. It takes time and sacrifice. Before you begin, be able to answer the question your aching muscles will ask you over and over: "Why am I doing this?"

DESIGNING YOUR PROGRAM

Experts in the health & fitness industry recommend using the acronym F.I.T.T.E. when designing a customized training program. This comprehensive approach encompasses frequency, intensity, type, time, and enjoyment:

Frequency. Decide on the number of days per week you're going to invest in yourself with physical activity. Keep in mind the words of Edward Stanley, Earl of Derby, when considering frequency: "Those who think they don't have time for bodily exercise will sooner or later have to find time for illness."

Intensity. Determine the heart rate you need to sustain during your workouts: Subtract your age from 220. Your workout heart rate should be approximately 75 to 80 percent of the resulting number. Your goals should help determine the intensity of your workouts – are you training for competition, general good health, or something in between?

Type. Consider the kind of activity you'd like to engage in – walking, biking, racquetball, tennis, golf, swimming, pickle ball, whatever. Also, think about the equipment you might use – exercise machines, Bosu balls, stretch bands, free weights or just a pair of comfortable shoes.

Time. How many hours can you consistently devote to your activity (per day, per week, per month?). Check your schedule and figure out the best time of day to work out (first thing in the morning, lunchtime, evenings?). When answering, consider when you feel you're at your peak energy. Be consistent and practical. I normally feel at full strength in the afternoon or early evening, but it's difficult to work out consistently then because of work and family. As a result, I exercise early in the morning.

Enjoyment. What physical activity would you look forward to doing regularly? What type of workout leaves you energized? What exercise makes you feel "pleasantly tired" rather than broken down? Whatever you chose, it shouldn't feel like a chore that you dread doing. You should view this as *your* time. Most of us spend the bulk of our day giving away time and energy to others, which is a great thing. But we need to refuel and recharge if we are going to be any good to others over the long haul.

MOVEMENT IS MEDICINE

Here's your prescription: Take the stairs. Walk the dog. Park farther away. Hide the remote. Shoot some hoops. Boogie to the Wii machine. Make whoopee. You get the idea.

Earlier, we looked at mental training as a way to boost our IQ. But according to columnist Gretchen Reynolds, "There's another easy-to-achieve, scientifically proven way to make yourself smarter. Go for a walk or a swim." In a 2012 *New York Times* article, Reynolds writes about the beneficial relationship between exercise and brain power: "Scientists have discovered that exercise appears to build a brain that resists physical shrinkage and enhance cognitive flexibility. Exercise, the latest neuroscience suggests, does more to bolster thinking than *thinking* does."

That might be the best reason ever to get off the couch.

Reynolds adds, "Why would exercise build brainpower in ways that thinking might not? The brain, like all muscles and organs, is a tissue, and its function declines with underuse and age. Exercise seems to slow or reverse the brain's physical decay, much as it does with muscles."

The human brain represents only 2 percent of total body weight, but requires 25 percent of the oxygen we take in. When muscles contract they produce a protein called "insulin-like growth factor 1" (IGF-1). This protein produces "brain-derived neurotrophic factor" (BDNF). Translation? This stuff is like Miracle-Gro for the body. It builds up over time if you pursue an *ongoing exercise program*, and can help us continue to increase our mental capacity and stave off mental degeneration.

I don't know about you, but I can't afford to lose any more brain cells!

NUTRITION AND WEIGHT

Nutrition is an essential part of any fitness program. Did you know that each cell in your body regenerates every 45 to 60 days? What you ate two months ago is what your body is made of today. All foods consist essentially of proteins, carbohydrates and fats in *differing amounts* and are used by our body to sustain growth, repair damage, and maintain vital processes.

The key phrase is "differing amounts." A carrot is zero percent fat. A bacon strip can be up to 80 percent fat. Despite health warnings and broken zippers, there's an absolute explosion in bacon sales (there's even bacon-flavored tooth paste. I'm not making this up).

What kind of food are you using to fuel your body? Big Macs? Big Buford's? Big Gulps? Processed foods and sugary drinks contain fewer nutrients, more calories, and lots of unpronounceable chemicals that can harm our health. But it's an easy fix if we have the willpower. Example: Researchers at the Harvard School of Public Health estimate that simply replacing the partially hydrogenated fat in the U.S. diet with natural vegetable oils would prevent as many as 100,000 deaths annually – that's an average of 274 deaths per day.

Incidentally, that Big Mac features 29 grams of fat and 550 calories. Add some fries and tally up another 25 grams of fat and 500 calories. Toss back a large soda and, *kaboom* – another 50 grams of sugar and a quick 220 calories. You'd have to run around the equator twice to burn off that lunch. (Ironically, the highest calorie item at McDonalds isn't a burger at all, but the 1,150-calorie Big Breakfast with hotcakes and large biscuit.)

Is it any wonder the USA is the fattest industrialized country in the world? Our obesity rate is the planet's highest at 33 percent, while Japan's is the lowest at 3 percent. That works out to 78 million obese adults and 13 million obese children in America. Plus another third of our population is considered technically "overweight." (Note to self: Check stock prices for plus-size clothing stores.)

Before you think I'm the Debbie Downer of dinner, consider these options to obesity. Kristin Keffeler of Kinetic Enterprise reminds us that people eat for three main reasons: 1) because we're hungry, 2) because we think it's time to eat, or 3) simply because it's there.

As you might guess, two of those reasons aren't very good ones.

Kristin recommends eating only: 1) what your body needs, 2) what you are able to digest well, and 3) what gives your mind its greatest clarity.

When you're tempted to chow down, ask yourself: "Am I actually hungry? Or am I just bored? Am I self-medicating with food? Will I be angry at myself later for eating this now? Can I delay this decision and eat later?"

o   o   o

One of the keys to not overeating is *knowing when to stop*. But here's the problem – it takes our brain about 20 minutes to tell us that we're full. To avoid that overstuffed feeling (and the extra calories), we need to quit eating while we're still a little hungry.

Try it. I can almost guarantee you will feel full and satisfied after hitting the pause button for a short time. Before taking your next bite, place yourself on this 0-10 hunger scale:

0 – You are so hungry that you're not even hungry any more.

1 – You have a massive headache and feel dizzy.

2 – You are grumpy, can't concentrate and feel light-headed.

3 – You are hungry, your stomach is growling.

4 – You are not hungry, but feel like you might be in a couple of hours.

5 – You're satisfied.

6 – You literally feel the food expanding in your stomach.

7 – You feel drowsy; you unbutton your pants and loosen your belt.

8 – You feel sluggish and change into sweat pants.

9 – You are too full to move.

10 – You feel sick and dislike even the thought of food.

I admit, I've been to 10 a few times. But now I try to live in zones 4 and 5. Hit 6 on special occasions only and you'll be healthier and thinner.

o   o   o

Here's the bad news: For some of us, the worse a food is, the more we want it. Just thinking about manly junk food makes me salivate like Pavlov's dog. My favorites? Basically anything that makes my cardiologist wince makes me hungry. And if it's deep fried, I want twice as much.

Here's the good news: We don't have to swear off 100 percent of our guilty pleasures to eat healthier. There are small changes we can make and not have to switch to tofu burgers. When it comes to eating and dieting, Kristin Keffeler believes we just need to strike a balance. On one hand, we don't want to be foolish and dig our own grave with a fork and spoon, as the saying goes. On the other hand, severe calorie-restricting diets can produce bad health – and as we all know by now, they're impossible to sustain.

So enjoy your food and drink, but do it in moderation.

SLEEP AND STRESS

Sleep is a vital part of physical fitness. If you're not too tired, check out this sleep quiz developed by Cornell professor James Maas, author of *Power Sleep*. In his book, he asks four questions:

1. Do you fall asleep the moment your head hits the pillow?
2. Do you feel drowsy when driving?
3. Do you need an alarm to wake up in the morning?
4. Do you feel slow or frustrated by problem solving and creative tasks?

If you answered "Yes" to number 2 or 4 you may be sleep deprived and harming yourself.

In our zoom-zoom culture, we frown upon rest as "downtime" and trivialize the need for a good night's sleep. Our 24-hour society means we sleep up to four hours a night less than previous generations. That's a problem. Sleep deprivation impairs our judgment, social skills and productivity. The more we sleep, the better we perform. Duh. How does it apply to your kids? Surprise! Teens need 8 to 10 hours – it's proven that top performers in school are getting more rest than their lower-scoring peers.

Sleep deprivation has numerous negative effects, including anger issues, loss of coping skills, and reduced immunity. Can't shake those pounds? Sleep deprivation alters the circulating levels of hormones that regulate hunger, causing an increase in appetite and a craving for high calorie, high carb food.

Hence, the all-night Taco Bell.

Sleep is not a luxury. It's critical for memory storage and cognitive warehousing. (Sorry, Leno.) Your brain relies on regular sleep cycles for reorganization, and for the processing of new learning and retention through replenishment of neurotransmitters. (Sorry, Letterman.) The brain and its regenerative function require a minimum of 8 hours of sleep. (Sorry, Jimmy Fallon, Conan O' Brien, Jimmy Kimmel, et al.) Anything less is a health threat – contributing to obesity, heart disease, diabetes, and traffic accidents.

Not to mention crankiness.

o   o   o

Can't get enough sleep at night? Maybe a free and easy solution can be found in the 1986 bestseller, *All I Really Need to Know I Learned in Kindergarten*. Number 12 on author Robert Fulghum's list was "Take a nap every afternoon."

Many famous people would agree this is sound advice. Famous "nappers" include John F. Kennedy, Ronald Reagan, Margaret Thatcher, and Bill Clinton. Other daytime snoozers include Winston Churchill, Albert Einstein, Leonardo Da Vinci, John D. Rockefeller, Ludwig von Beethoven, and Benjamin Franklin.

Sleep expert, Max Hirshkowitz, says, "We're biologically programmed to take a nap in midafternoon. It was the Industrial Revolution that separated us from the siesta, because it was too expensive to shut down big machines in the middle of the day and turn them back on."

Because of our natural "circadian" body rhythms, our alertness drops off around two or three o'clock every afternoon. James Maas of Cornell University coined the phrase "power nap" to describe on-the-job afternoon naps approved by progressive employers. According to Maas, dozing workers aren't loafing; they're recharging their mind and rejuvenating their body.

Forget those ubiquitous energy drinks – quick naps are the *real* pause that refreshes. Best of all, they can actually improve our sleep at night and help offset sleep loss due to travel or late meetings. For fresh ideas and new insights, maybe 40 winks could help your day.

When you can't figure out what to do, it's time for a nap.

Mason Cooley, American literary academic

○   ○   ○

In the movie *Anger Management*, a stressed-out Adam Sandler gets tasered by an air marshal for arguing with a flight attendant. Besides avoiding trouble with the TSA, dealing with stress properly is also critical to a healthy mind and body. There are two primary types of stress – *acute* stress and *chronic* stress:

Acute stress is the healthy type of stress. It's the stress that alerts us to imminent danger, like a reckless driver crossing into your lane or a fire alarm going off. The immediate infusion of adrenaline that comes with acute stress causes us to react quickly in self-defense or self-preservation. This fight-or-flight reaction kept our ancestors alive when a mastodon poked his trunk into the tent. And it can give us modern warriors a boost of energy and clarity that can save our hides, too.

Chronic stress is the unhealthy type. Some define it as what happens when the demands made on a person exceed that person's ability to cope. It comes from continually being under pressure at work, at home, on the freeway, anywhere. It's the type of stress that, over time, wears us down and does far more harm than good. Some chronic stress factors are within our power to reduce or eliminate, like managing our time better or learning to accept things we can't change. But for those non-negotiable situations when we just need to hunker down and plow through a project, we could benefit from taking a 30-second vacation.

Here's how: When you find yourself in a chronic stress situation that won't go away – something urgent that you must deal with – take a short break and breathe deeply for 30 seconds. Breathing deeply is a proven way to decrease your heart rate, lower your blood pressure, increase oxygen to the brain, and decrease production of stress hormones.

Yup, I said *hormones.* Although the saber-toothed tigers are gone, our subconscious response to stress still triggers the release of hormones like adrenalin and cortisol – producing a pounding heartbeat and that embarrassing perspiration. Unfortunately, these abnormal levels usually can't be worked off by running or fighting (at least not in most offices), so they set off a chain reaction of emotional and physical effects like red faces, wet palms, elevated blood pressures, rapid breathing and blinding headaches.

If you can't slay a physical dragon, get moving anyway. "Going for a short walk, doing stretching or breathing exercises, or just getting away from your desk would have a greater impact," says Neil Shah, the director of the Stress Management Society in Britain. Exercise also produces endorphins, the body's natural opiates, legal mood elevators which can temporarily relieve depression.

○   ○   ○

The benefits of protecting your physical health are many. Stay active, sleep well, and control stress – and you just might experience a second honeymoon on your golden wedding anniversary. Or maybe you'll enjoy sitting in the stands watching your grandkids play baseball. Or maybe you'll see the sapling you planted in the backyard grow up to provide shade for a new generation.

If you are not physically fit, it will negatively affect your enjoyment of the other six "Fs." Despite your best efforts, you simply won't have the stamina and strength to fully engage in them.

So get going. You can do it!

7F ACTION STEPS: PHYSICAL FITNESS

- Subscribe to *Fueling Your Fire*, a free health and fitness bi-weekly eZine (electronic magazine) at *www.kineticenterprise.com*.
- If you can work it into your budget, find a personal fitness trainer to custom-design a program according to your interests and needs.
- If hiring a trainer isn't in the cards, use the F.I.T.T.E. guidelines discussed in this section to put a program together for yourself.
- If you're the type who's unlikely to stick to an exercise program on your own, join a class. Water aerobics, yoga and other classes are offered through your local YMCA or fitness centers. If that doesn't work with your budget, invite friends over for an at-home exercise party. Have everyone bring a favorite exercise and lead the group through it. Between the wheezing and the gasping, you'll be able to catch up on what's happening while you have fun working out.

4. SPIRITUAL FITNESS

Most people gain weight when they take an ocean cruise.

I *lost* ten pounds the hard way.

To celebrate completing my master's degree, my parents sent my wife and me on a Caribbean cruise to unwind. We flew to Miami, and boarded one of the largest, most luxurious vessels ever built at that time. While in port, the Norwegian Cruise Line ship was so stable that it felt like a resort hotel – only the nautical furnishings reminded us that we were not on land. The ship was steady and our footing was sure as we walked the hallways.

After throwing off the ropes, we set sail for the high seas – and believe me, the seas did get high. Not long after we got out into the Atlantic, a major storm kicked up. Even though the massive ship was two football fields long,

106 feet wide, and weighed approximately 70,000 tons, it began to roll from side to side like a tiny fishing boat.

I had never experienced conditions like these and it didn't take long before I started to feel sick. Really sick. While the ship tossed back and forth for several stormy hours, the pleasure cruise felt more like a survival course. I remember staggering down the hallway to our cabin and suddenly losing my balance. It was clear that I was not a seasoned sailor with "sea legs." As the ship tilted to starboard (or was that to port?) I couldn't find anything to steady myself with and slammed helplessly into the wall.

When economic, relational, or medical "storms" hit your life – and they will hit us all – what do *you* have to hold on to? What do you reach for to steady yourself? Is whatever you're gripping so tightly with white knuckles stronger than the storm you are facing?

If I had ventured on deck during the violent storm, I could have easily fallen overboard and been lost at sea. Will your faith keep you from being swept away?

This is not a religious book, but with your permission, I'd like to share what I think are three universal principles that can calm the choppy waters of life and bring us balance, safety and strength when we need them.

The three essentials are **faith**, **hope** and **love**.

These spiritual principles can give us meaning and stability in a world of continuous change and rolling seas. They are not exclusive to any one religion – they are the primary components that should be included in whatever "operating system" you make part of your life...

A. FAITH IS A PLACE

Faith is believing something is real even when we cannot see it or prove it. In that sense, it's like the wind – even though it's invisible and we can't touch it, we see its effects: leaves fluttering, hair blowing, windmills turning. That's the way it is with faith; we know it's there because we feel it strengthening us, guiding us, stabilizing us. And because we feel it, we can be sure about the things we hope for, even when our confidence looks foolish to the rest of the world. Dr. Martin Luther King, Jr. said, "Faith is taking the first step even when you don't see the whole staircase."

Faith is not a *physical* location of course; it's a place in your heart where you can go to find inner strength and peace of mind. It's where you can find still waters and green pastures to restore your soul. In my life, it's the quiet place I go to seek wisdom from God and sense his presence... and protection.

If that's too metaphysical, let me share an example.

My wife loves jigsaw puzzles. The tougher the better. One of her puzzles is 1,000 pieces of a blue boat on a blue bay under a blue sky. It seems impossible unless you know the secret – start by building the corners. Having faith is like having the corner pieces of that monochromatic puzzle – it enables us to build the framework we need to put the rest of the pieces together. Without it we are lost in the middle, meandering aimlessly through life. Faith creates a beautiful picture – from 1,000 abstract pieces – of what our lives are capable of becoming. It makes everything we've dreamed of and longed for seem possible.

○　　○　　○

I love progressive rock because the bands touched on some deep subjects. In 1977, the group Kansas recorded their biggest hit, "Dust in the Wind." The band's lead vocalist, Kerry Livgren, penned this song as a meditation on mortality: "All we do crumbles to the ground, though we refuse to see... it slips away... and all your money won't another minute buy... all we are is dust in the wind."

The lyrics struck a chord with anyone who's wrestled with the brevity of life and the inevitability of death. Like the song, existentialist philosophers have long suggested that life is basically meaningless. They believe there is no God to trust in, no higher calling to aspire to, and nothing beyond the grave to hope for. We spend our brief days in useless toil and end in oblivion.

Even Shakespeare intoned, "Life is but a walking shadow, a tale told by an idiot, full of sound and fury, signifying nothing."

But I disagree.

With faith, we *can* live with significance and purpose.

Faith gives dignity to all human beings and profound meaning to our fourscore and ten on this earth. Victor Hugo, the author of *Les Miserable*, said, "Faith is a necessity to man. Woe to him who believes in nothing." More recently, gospel legend Mahalia Jackson said, "Faith and prayer are the vitamins of the soul; man can't live in health without them."

Incidentally, two years after writing "Dust in the Wind," Livgren converted to Christianity. At the peak of the band's fame, Livgren shifted from what he called "the religion of the month club" to a solid faith that he still pursues today.

Like a compass that points us in the right direction, faith-based principles help us navigate the forests – and minefields – of life. They're what we rely on to make hundreds of daily decisions. Over time, these myriad choices ultimately determine the course of our life. Therefore, our faith system should provide solid guidelines for what is right and what is wrong, what is absolute and what is relative, what is truth and what is falsehood.

A functional faith system is our guide for handling highs and lows like success and failure, health and sickness, prosperity and poverty.

In short, our beliefs determine our behaviors – or at least they should.

o   o   o

Simply having faith isn't enough, we need to *exercise* it.

Otherwise we'll be like the circus elephant that was tied to a small wooden stake by a ten-foot rope. Weighing two tons, he was more than powerful enough to escape, but for his entire life he never ventured beyond the ten-foot radius of his rope. Why didn't the mighty giant snap it off and break free? When baby elephants are small and relatively weak, they are tied to an immovable stick in the ground. Later on, no matter how huge an elephant becomes, he continues to believe he can't free himself – he doesn't have the faith to even try. He can't see beyond his own self-imposed limitations. Does that sound like anyone you know? If we exercise it, our faith allows us to break the chains on our life, to uproot the flimsy stakes that hold us down.

It's easy to talk about faith when things are good and life is rosy. But faith is like a rubber band – it isn't very useful until it's stretched. When our faith is "stretched" and tested at the limits of adversity, it makes us more focused on others and more useful to society. It makes us a better listener, a more dependable employee, a more trustworthy friend, a more loving spouse.

It's only when our faith is exercised that we find out what it's made of. Challenging times reveal whether our faith system is real or if we've built our worldview on a faulty foundation. We soon find out whether it crumbles or stands up to the test. Ultimately, it's during a "crisis of faith" that we discover whether the source of our faith is even worth believing in.

Why is that so important?

Because our faith system determines our *ethics and values*.

They in turn determine how we conduct business, fulfill marriage vows, handle relationships, raise kids, pass laws – every aspect of society. Without a faith system that's "fit" enough to guide us, we are susceptible to pitfalls: employees stealing merchandise, bosses ripping off workers, politicians taking bribes from lobbyists, homeowners walking away from mortgages, athletes reneging on contracts, college coaches recruiting illegally, deadbeat dads not paying child support, businesses overcharging… the list goes on.

Believe me, I'm not pointing fingers or judging anyone. I'm just saying look in the mirror. Because it's only when we are confronted with a lucrative, fool-proof opportunity to fudge the truth, bend the rules, turn a blind eye – any dishonest way to advance our own interests – that we suddenly discover the true character of our faith.

Our faith is developed and becomes more useful – not by seeking the smooth and easy path, but by taking the road less traveled, by facing the difficulties and challenges of life head-on. Through adversity our faith is exercised, strengthened, and fortified. It becomes more fit.

○　　○　　○

Believer or atheist, skeptic or agnostic – we all have faith in something.

The question is, *who* or *what* do we believe in? Religion? Science? Human nature? A higher power? A guru? Ourselves? The focus or object of our faith is critical because it either expands or limits the resources we have to draw upon… and the power we can tap into.

To evaluate your faith, run your belief system through this spiritual grid: Does it inspire you to see beyond your present circumstances and pursue a better future? Does it embolden you to take exciting risks? Does it give you confidence to change and become the kind of person you aspire to be? Does it give you calm in the midst of what seems like all hell breaking loose?

Does your faith help you approach each day with confidence? Does it enable you to learn from every situation – regardless of outcome? Is your overall countenance (the look on your face) more smiles than frowns?

If not, you may be short-changing yourself. If that's the case, I respectfully suggest you check out the Faith chapter later in this book.

B. HOPE IS A ROPE

The second spiritual principle that needs regular cultivation is hope.

The Hebrew word for "hope" is *tiqvih*, which is also the root word for "rope." That means hope is the rope – the connection – between the boat (our life) and the anchor (our faith). Without an anchor, we'll be dragged off course, or worse. Out at sea, a ship can't afford to drift into danger. The stronger the anchor rope, the safer the ship is. Likewise, the stronger your hope, the more secure you are in your faith.

Faith is based on believing in something you *cannot* see. But hope is based on believing in something you *can* see – the actions and character of a person, organization or cause that you know and respect. The stronger the character, the stronger the hope. When the British saw Winston Churchill's iron will and determination, they grew hopeful for victory. When the Italians saw Mussolini's corruption and ineptitude, they grew discouraged and knew defeat was inevitable.

If you've ever gone scuba diving, you'll appreciate this analogy: Hope is like the breathing tube that passes oxygen from the person, organization or cause we believe in (our air tank) to us. And we depend on that oxygen tube for dear life. If that tube gets cut or crimped, the "oxygen" flow is hindered. We'll start to feel faint, grow weary and even consider giving up.

Are your co-workers or employees less productive and innovative than you might wish for? It could be because they've lost hope in your company's future. Hope is critically important to the way we view the *present* as well as the *future*. Leadership expert Dr. John Maxwell writes, "Hope in the future has a dramatic impact on your thinking today. Your thinking today determines your performance today, and your performance today has a direct bearing on your future."

Those without hope for today lack the tenacity it takes to pursue the dreams they have for the future. But those with hope will continue to chase their dream even when the pursuit is an uphill journey.

Where hope grows, miracles blossom.

Elna Rae, inspirational author

o   o   o

Hope is critical to the quality (and length) of our existence – both on a personal and national level. For example, our country is in economic distress today because many people have simply lost hope. We've lost hope in our political and business leaders, in the stability of our corporations, and in our financial and banking systems. Skepticism and mistrust run rampant.

Consumer confidence is down. Trust in Congress is almost nonexistent. The hope that our past prosperity will continue has diminished widely. For the first time, younger generations do not believe they will achieve – let alone exceed – the financial success of their parent's generation.

Is it any wonder?

It seems like we hear about a new scandal or rip-off almost weekly – whether it's Bernard Madoff's multi-billion dollar Ponzi scheme, or politician Tom Daschle's six-figure tax evasion. It's no longer shocking to hear atrocities like AIG's corporate leaders spending the government's bailout money on lavish parties, or investment firms setting up Swiss bank accounts so their U.S. clients can avoid taxes. Even as I write this, a financier stands accused of lying to regulators about tens of millions of dollars. He admitted to committing fraud in a suicide note. His suicide attempt was unsuccessful, but his fatally-injured company filed for bankruptcy... and the list goes on.

When hope is lost, we're in trouble.

I admit, a quick look at today's newscast or market reports can dash just about anyone's hopes – *unless* they have a solid spiritual foundation.

And that foundation can be a powerful reason for optimism...

BITTER OR BETTER

When a person possesses unswerving hope, they can endure very difficult circumstances and still hang on to the belief that things will get better.

Even when the diagnosis is cancer.

Case in point: A couple of years ago, my wife was diagnosed with breast cancer. That kind of news stops you in your tracks and sobers you up fast. Life as we knew it immediately changed. The assumption that we would grow old together could no longer be counted on. The assumption that our schedules were ours to plan evaporated. Research to find a vacation destination changed to research on finding a respected breast surgeon, plastic surgeon, and oncology team.

As a man, I can't begin to imagine what women must feel when thinking about having a part of their body removed and discarded.

But that is exactly what needed to happen.

Mary Ann had three hours of mastectomy surgery. About six weeks later, her chemotherapy treatments began. I'll never forget her first round of chemo. While the nurse was inserting the IV line, I noticed her index finger was heavily wrapped with gauze. I asked, "What happened to your finger?" She said, "Oh, I was mixing up the chemo drugs and a drop fell on my finger."

I thought to myself, *Seriously? A tiny amount fell on your finger and it damaged your skin? And now you're going to drain six liters of that stuff into my wife's body?* That was unnerving.

Mary Ann endured four half-day chemotherapy treatments, with three weeks between sessions. Soon after the second treatment, her long blond hair started to fall out in large clumps. Waking up each morning and finding big handfuls of hair on her pillow was a regular occurrence. Eventually, that routine became too much to endure. She decided it would be better to have her head completely shaved and get it over with. My son and I went with her to the salon, and it was a very difficult emotional experience. Bald, but still very beautiful, she began wearing a wig in public to make it easier on herself and less noticeable to others.

On the first day following her chemotherapy, my wife would feel tired. The second day after was like the lull before the storm. The third and fourth days after were unbearable. She felt like hell. Literally. And I don't use the word lightly. In between her treatments she endured countless blood draws to check her white blood cell count. After her chemo treatments were completed, she had to tolerate numerous plastic surgeries. In the months and years that followed her surgery, she had to be on several medications, including tomaxifin and aromasin, to deter the cancer from returning. To this day, her joints still ache from the chemo treatments.

But she never gave up hope.

While Mary Ann was receiving treatments, another woman around her age would often be seated right next to her. She was undergoing chemo as well, but evidently lacked hope in a good outcome. She would come to each session looking worn and haggard. Her face was drawn, her eyes were lifeless. She would tell us how she couldn't sleep and was racked with worry. Although Mary Ann tried to encourage this fellow patient, her hope grew weaker and her expression grew sadder with each visit.

The strength of our hope makes a huge difference in how we approach each situation.

Over and above the pressure of Mary Ann's doctor appointments, surgeries and treatments, nagging doubts crept in: *Did they get all the cancer? Will it ever resurface?* Through it all, Mary Ann remained hopeful. She clung to the living hope that she would get better, that her medical team was capable, that someone bigger, stronger and wiser was in control and would help her through it all – regardless of the outcome.

In the face of adversity, my wife maintained a resilient and unrelenting spirit. She told me she had a choice: She could become *bitter* or *better*.

With every cell in her body, she chose "better."

Mountaintops inspire us but valleys mature us.

J. Philip Everson, inspirational author

I pray you never have to endure the pain and nausea of cancer treatments. Yet we will all face challenges that we'll find difficult, if not insurmountable...

You may be trapped in a marriage that feels as confining as a prison cell. You may believe the relationship can never be restored – *but there is hope.*

You may be unemployed and weary from searching for meaningful work. You might feel like you can't take another rejection – *but there is hope.*

You may think the economy will never pick up. You may feel like your retirement nest egg is gone forever – *but there is hope*.

Or you may feel like your family has abandoned you and the wound in your heart will never heal – but take courage; *there is hope*.

Whatever the case may be, as long as you are alive, there is hope. Things can change if we don't give up. The Roman philosopher Cicero put it best, *"Dum spiro, spero."* In Latin it means: "While I breathe I hope."

○　　○　　○

John Johnson was the publisher of *Ebony* magazine and winner of countless awards, including the Presidential Medal of Honor. Johnson literally went from rags (a poor boy from rural Arkansas) to riches (one of the 400 wealthiest Americans). This grandson of slaves said, "Men and women are limited not by the place of their birth, not by the color of their skin, but by the size of their hope."

Maybe you think your hope is undersized.

If you don't feel like a self-assured, confident overcomer, don't be surprised. We seldom do. But you must hope as an act of your will (even if you don't feel like it). You must decide to say, "I will be hopeful, despite what I see all around me."

I enjoy flying on cloudy days. I know that sounds a little strange, but let me explain. When the plane takes off and we are blanketed by a thick layer of clouds overhead, the view outside is dreary and dim. But as the plane continues to climb, we rise up through the cloud cover and suddenly break into this beautiful, blue, almost heaven-like sphere. It is crystal clear and bright, and we can see for miles. It reminds me that even if it's cloudy on the ground, even if I'm unsure about my circumstances, even if the situation appears bleak and gray – there's blue sky somewhere.

I just haven't broken through the clouds yet.

So keep hoping, keep reaching, keep climbing; you may not be far from slicing through the haze.

C. LOVE IS A GLOVE

Love is the third spiritual principle, and it's the one that energizes the other two, faith and hope.

In romance novels, love is dainty and pretty like a debutante's white glove. But in real life, it's dirty and stained like a workman's glove. Love is an *action* verb and it's not afraid to get sweaty and grimy while lending a hand or mending a relationship or clearing a path for a friend.

Depending on the circumstance, the "glove" may need to reach out firmly to grab the hand of someone who is stumbling, or boldly to help someone who is afraid, or knowingly to guide someone who has lost their way.

There is a wide variety of gloves for a wide variety of tasks – boxing, skiing, cleaning, golfing, welding, you name it. Likewise, love takes many forms. A friend of mine, Kevin, was on his way home from work one evening. Tired and eager to be enjoying dinner with his family, he was thinking about them as he drove his normal route. Unfortunately, he didn't make it home for another 16 weeks. While motoring through rush hour traffic, he noticed a woman stranded on the side of the road. Her car had a flat tire. Kevin pulled over and offered to help change the woman's tire. She was extremely grateful.

While Kevin was removing the left rear tire, a passing car hit him at full speed. The next thing he remembered was waking up in the hospital. As he regained consciousness, the doctors told him his left leg had been so badly crushed that they were forced to amputate it below the knee.

What causes someone like Kevin to change his plans, take time out of his busy schedule and stop to help someone in need? Love.

What motivates someone like my friend Brian to move from the comfort and safety of his suburban neighborhood to the inner city to be a part of the racial reconciliation that's so desperately needed? Love.

What energized my friend Ron to give his time and energy to a program that helps at-risk kids learn to read? Love.

Love is often described as an emotion. But at the root of real love is *action* – the willingness to extend ourselves for others financially, relationally, or vocationally. You know real love is present and active in your life when you desire good for others even to the point of personal sacrifice.

The Beatles sang "all you need is love," but that's incomplete – it has to have a tangible expression; it can't be just thoughts or feelings. It has to be functional. A love that improves the quality of life for others cannot be theoretical or platonic – it has to include action.

If you are spiritually fit, you are a person who is able to receive and express love. That explains why Kevin, Brian, and Ron took action. Love is a powerful stimulus. It has the ability to move us out of our routines and comfort zones and into the messy lives of others who are hurting.

Love is the immortal flow of energy that nourishes, extends and preserves. Its eternal goal is life.

Smiley Blanton, American psychoanalyst

○   ○   ○

Only love has the amazing power to move us away from a self-centered perspective. A life that's focused inward is a life that is shriveling up and dying. Think of the people around you. Those who are *contracting* (losing their influence and ability to make positive contributions) are usually focused on self and what others can do for them. Those who are *expanding* (becoming emotionally healthier by serving and sharing) are focused on others, and view their resources as tools to help those with less assets or opportunities.

These "other-centered" people get tons of pleasure from sacrificial giving and are a blast to be around. Those who live and love this way generally achieve great success and are always in demand by employers and friends alike.

There are three aspects to this other-centered love:

First, a spiritually fit love *enriches*. It's a contagious love that makes even shy people feel confident and capable and motivated to succeed. It speaks the truth lovingly and it inspires others to maximize their potential.

Second, a spiritually fit love *builds up*. It doesn't puff up our own ego with how smart we are or much we've acquired. On the contrary, it humbles us to the point where we desire to use our skills and resources to improve the lives of others around us.

Third, a spiritually fit love *endures*. This kind of love never gives up. It is not conditional. It's given whether or not it is appreciated or returned. This love returns good for evil, blessings for insults, and doesn't keep score.

So where does this kind of selfless, unconditional love come from? We can't make it, fake it, or buy it. But it is offered to us at no charge. It's free, but it's up to us to receive it. Details on how are in Chapter 9.

I have found the paradox, that if you love until it hurts, there can be no more hurt, only more love.

Mother Teresa, humanitarian

STRENGTHEN YOUR CORE

If you're familiar with physical fitness programs, you know "core training" works primarily on your midsection. It focuses on your middle because all body movements are either enhanced or inhibited by the strength of the core. When your physical core is strong, your posture is better, your golf swing improves (at least in theory), and you can play with your kids without being rushed to the ER.

But we also need to work on our *spiritual* core.

The triad of faith, hope and love we looked at in this chapter represents a human being's spiritual midsection – the basis for all of our spiritual fitness.

When your spiritual core is strong, you're ready to experience abundant living. You are an engaging person to be with; a source of strength to others. You have a resilient spirit. You're able to sleep at night. You're not rattled and you don't fall to pieces when the unexpected hits. Worry and fear don't consume you; uncertainty does not stress you out.

Boxing trainers work mercilessly on their fighter's core strength. They know it's essential to his survival in the ring. Likewise, with a tough enough spiritual core, you can take a punch in the gut and not go down for the count.

A friend of mine had *his* core tested in the worst possible way...

Without warning or explanation, his son committed suicide. To make it even more horrific, my friend was the one who found his son's lifeless body. I can't imagine the pain he and his wife must have felt. While dealing with the grief, my friend was racked with questions. He agonized over and over about what he might have done differently to prevent the death.

But it only led to deeper despair.

Healing could not and did not begin until he shifted his focus away from trying to answer "Why us?" to "What now?"

By that I mean, "What should my response be in light of this situation? What can I learn from this tragedy that can benefit others?"

By relying on the strength of his spiritual core, he was able to begin moving forward. When he allowed his faith to guide him – instead of his raw emotions – he was able to begin the recovery process.

Your ability to rebound from life's disappointments, tragedies and losses is in direct proportion to your spiritual core fitness. The more fit we are, the greater the likelihood is we'll handle life's setbacks constructively. Here's an acid test of where you're at in this area. Ask yourself these questions:

- How do I react when the unexpected happens?
- How do I respond when things don't go my way?
- Do I take secret pleasure when someone I dislike (or envy) fails?
- Am I ready to instantly share my resources with those in need?

If you're not satisfied with any or all of your answers, roll up your sleeves! Developing your spiritual fitness is "core training" that will pay huge dividends.

7F ACTION STEPS: SPIRITUAL FITNESS

- Write down what you really believe and why.
- Have a candid, no-holds-barred discussion about spiritual things with a close friend. Ask tough questions and challenge each other, then reflect on it all with an open mind.
- Find an organization in your community whose charitable work lines up with your spiritual beliefs and get involved.

A WORD ABOUT FUN AND FITNESS

Now that we've concluded the Personal segment of the 7Fs, we've seen a powerful symbiotic relationship: The better we take care of our physical, emotional and spiritual natures, the better we'll look, feel, think, create, and excel at life… plus the more of this earth we'll be able to see and marvel at.

Remember the old science fiction stories of brains kept alive in glass jars? Who'd want to "live" that way? Not me. I want to breathe fresh air, swim in the oceans and run across green fields. Which means fitness is *not* a luxury for me – it's an essential asset. Until robotics make some giant strides, our current flesh-and-blood bodies are the only instrument we have to fulfill our dreams and our destinies.

Scientists like Raymond Kurzweil figure that by 2045 we'll achieve "singularity," a level of artificial intelligence and biotechnology so advanced that we'll transfer our minds into computers – thereby becoming functionally immortal. But until the day you can scan your consciousness into a hard drive, keep eating those vegetables and *keep using that treadmill*.

Seriously, I don't know if we'll ever reach singularity or not. But I do know this – by achieving and maintaining fitness today, we'll have more to give and longer to live.

○   ○   ○

You may recall from the 7F Life diagram (in the introduction) that Fun and Fitness have primarily a *Personal* focus. In other words, no one can do these things for you. You can't delegate them. Only you are in control of your attitude and your time. Which means you can have fun or you can be boring. You can be fit or you can be flabby. You can use your time to exercise your mind, body and spirit – or you can ignore these vital areas and join the increasing number of people content to be under-achievers and over-complainers.

We live in an age where personal responsibility is being replaced by victimhood, passing the buck, and making excuses. But that won't cut it in the 7F Life. We have to take responsibility and exert leadership over our own personal lives, particularly over our minds. The 7F Life requires us to stop being mentally lazy and to actively take control of our thoughts. If we don't, someone (or something) else will – which may not turn out well for us.

Now let's move on to the *Relational* aspects of the 7F Life.

CHAPTER 5

Family

Our most basic instinct is not for survival but for family.

Paul Pearsall, speaker & author

Somebody has described pro football as 22 superbly conditioned athletes on the field watched by 50 million out-of-shape viewers on the couch.

I was part of that TV audience and proud of it.

And why not? My beloved Detroit Lions had a commanding lead over the Bears and we were finally headed to the Super Bowl. Okay, I made that part up. But it was a great game anyway, and I was enjoying a Sunday off from work and responsibility.

With my feet up on pillows, my toughest decision was what to scoop with my Doritos. *Onion dip?* No high pressure meetings. *Salsa?* No high stress deals. *Guacamole?* No worries.

I'd been out of town on a speaking engagement and I was dog tired and ready for home. On the long trip back, I told my wife how much I was looking forward to just flopping out on the sofa and watching a little football.

I had just sat down to relax when the phone rang.

The caller identified herself as the director of a crisis pregnancy center in Des Moines. I hit mute on the TV remote and asked, "How did you get my name?"

Evidently, she'd spoken with a friend of mine three years before, kept my name for some reason, and had finally tracked me down.

"How can I help you?" I asked.

Her reply changed the course of my day and my life forever: "We have a young couple who are going to give their child up for adoption and I want to know if you are interested."

For several years, my wife and I had been trying to adopt and we'd been through conversations like this before. Each one had ended badly when the birth mother or a grandparent changed their mind about giving up the child. Each false start, each set of dashed hopes made us more eager, but more cautious, too.

"We may be interested," I said, trying to sound calm. "When is she expected to give birth?"

"Soon," she replied.

"How soon? Like two or three months from now?"

"No, sooner," came the response.

"Two or three *weeks* from now?"

"No, sooner."

Frustrated by her lack of direct response, I pushed, "Well, how soon then?"

Silence. Then, "Any day now."

My wife, Mary Ann, stood listening in the doorway of our family room. From watching my facial expressions, she knew this was no ordinary conversation. Pausing for what seemed an eternity, I swallowed hard and asked the mystery woman on the line, "When do you need to know if we're interested?"

Her words caught me off guard: "By eight o'clock tonight." I glanced at my watch. It was 3:30 in the afternoon.

Faking composure, I said, "Obviously I'll need to talk this over with my wife and get back with you."

Four hours later, we called her back and agreed to be the adoptive parents.

Our son was born the next day.

○   ○   ○

I soon learned why it takes nine months for a child to develop in its mother's womb. It takes that long to prepare the house, purchase supplies, and (most of all) get used to the idea of a brand new person moving in. Biological parents get approximately 270 days to mentally adjust to having another human life added to their family – a life that will instantly become the center of all activity for years to come.

We had approximately, okay, let's do the math – less than one day.

If you saw Julia Robert's movie, *Eat Pray Love*, you may recall her friend explaining to her just how serious parenting is: "Having a baby is like getting a tattoo on your face. You kind of wanna be fully committed."

That's an understatement!

We threw some clothes in a bag and flew to Iowa the next morning. We met with the crisis center director at her office. She wanted to brief us on what we should and should not reveal about ourselves, for confidentiality reasons. She told us that the birth mother had been only 13 years old when she became pregnant and had recently turned 14. The birth father was the ripe old age of 16.

From the crisis center we drove to Des Moines General Hospital. On the way there, I felt my heart beat faster as my mind raced, thinking about what we were getting ourselves into. When we arrived at the hospital, we went up to the maternity ward and were told to wait outside the room where the birth parents were.

It was totally surreal.

Leaving us in the hallway, the crisis center director went into the room to brief the teenage parents about their communication with us.

I vividly remember leaning my back against the wall and thinking, *What am I doing? I know nothing about these people – these children – who just gave birth to this baby. I don't know if these kids are pot heads, meth heads, boozers.* I'd heard all about crack moms giving birth to addicted babies, and alcohol fetal syndrome, and all the scary implications of unplanned pregnancies.

My nervous thoughts raced: *What kind of homes did they come from? Were they neglected or abused themselves? I'm agreeing to take on full responsibility for this child and care for his every possible need… I don't know what these people look like, how tall they are –*

I was interrupted by the door opening.

We stood up and were invited in. Some of my fears subsided when I saw the young couple. They were both attractive, intelligent, with-it kids who had just gotten carried away. They asked Mary Ann if she would like to hold our son and placed him in her arms. Immediately, my wife began to cry. Or more accurately, she began raining on the baby. Not a sprinkle, a flood. She cried so much that she had to use a blanket to wipe the baby's face because he was drenched with tears.

Then it was my turn. More water. More wiping. It was at that moment, holding an eight-pound bundle of life, that I realized there was much, much more to the concept of family than I had ever understood. Cooing and kissing, it became clear to me that "family" meant more than just sharing the same DNA, or having similar facial features, or living under the same roof.

My wife and I were from the other side of the country and had no prior contact with this child, yet we felt an immediate, undeniable bond. We were not part of the procreation process, but we had an instant, unexplainable love for him.

Eventually we stopped crying, named him Drew, and took him home. We cried again when he left for college last year, but we wouldn't trade him for anything!

WHAT IS FAMILY?

Have you ever heard the expression, "He's like family to me"?

Anyone who's watched *The Godfather* knows loyalty and ties to a non-biological family can run deep. Six feet deep in some cases.

Apart from the nuclear family – where "membership" is most often established by bloodlines – family can have a much larger definition. In a broader and deeper sense, family encompasses those who share **connectedness**, **commitment** and **cause**. Just because someone has a biological family doesn't mean they will automatically experience the *benefits* of family. If you've ever endured the Thanksgiving dinner from hell, you know there can be a variety of factors and dysfunctions at home that keep someone from experiencing the benefits of family.

Who do you think of when *you* think of family? Whoever comes to mind, they do so because you likely feel a connection to them – you share a commitment and a cause. *Time* magazine recently asked veteran activist, Gloria Steinem: "If you knew you had just two years to live, how would you spend them?" She replied, "Mainly by seeing friends, my chosen family."

The bond that links your true family is not one of blood, but of respect and joy in each other's life. Rarely do members of one's family grow up under the same roof.

Richard Bach, author of *Illusions*

So, what *is* a family?

According to the U.S. Census Bureau, a family is "a group of two or more people who reside together and who are related by birth, marriage, or adoption." That narrow definition has pretty much been kicked to the curb. On the other side of the debate, some say that a family is simply anyone in your life that you hold dear and would accept no matter what they do. According to them, if someone makes you feel warm and fuzzy and you'd loan them your last dime, that's a family. Regardless of whether they are single, married, same sex, different sex, living together, kids, no kids, pets, just friends, friends with benefits, whatever – any imaginable grouping can now call themselves a family.

The Three Pillars of a Healthy Family

The debate over what defines an actual family will likely rage on for many years to come. There are tons of political advantages to be gained by both sides in this hot-button debate. But for our purposes, I simply want to focus on what I believe are the three principles that must be present in all well-adjusted, functional families in order to survive and thrive…

PILLAR NUMBER 1: CONNECTEDNESS

Secretly or openly, everyone wants to be connected.

We have a near-universal need to belong. At the heart of every viable family is an unspoken feeling of connection that transcends ordinary friendships.

Behavioral science supports this, but the best evidence might be the success of TV shows like *Cheers*. For 11 seasons, millions around the world watched a "family" of unforgettable characters interact at Ted Danson's (excuse me, I meant Sam Malone's) imaginary pub in Boston. Like any normal family, they squabbled and apologized and laughed and cried. They shared stories, jokes, hugs and lots of adult beverages. With just seven memorable words, the show's theme song reflected a universal craving for *a place where everybody knows your name*.

We particularly desire to interact with families – you could call them tribes – who exude a sense that "we're all in this together." So much so that we're even fascinated with fictitious versions, from the Waltons (traditional) to the Bradys (blended) to the Partridges (single parent) to the Cosbys (minority)… all the way to today's extremely diverse *Modern Family*. This desire for belonging to a family group – even vicariously – is not an emotion, it's an instinct. The craving runs so deep it shows up in everything from a college sorority to a motorcycle gang to a Brownie troop.

This familial need to belong even shows up as allegiance to our alma maters. Class rings (guilty), imprinted coffee cups (mea culpa), and bumper stickers (not yet) continue to identify us with our college experience, decades after graduation. On game days, some of us (guilty again) even fly big flags outside our homes with the colors of our university proudly displayed.

If you're a sports fan you know this! Just look around any stadium and see full-grown men and women wearing the jerseys and headgear of the local team in an effort to connect with "their" guys. To display full loyalty, some even paint their faces with the colors of "their" team.

What's more tribal than putting on war paint?

According to business author Seth Godin, a tribe is "any group of people, large or small, who are connected to one another, a leader, and an idea." In his book, *Tribes*, Godin explains that for thousands of years, humans have joined tribes. Tribes can be religious, ethnic, or political. There are even musical tribes – think Jimmy Buffet's margarita-totin' Parrotheads or the Grateful Dead's hemp-lovin' Deadheads. Devoted fans (tribe members) passionately follow their favorite rock stars (tribal leaders) around the country for concerts (tribal gatherings).

Godin claims this banding together is part of our DNA, and instead of fading away, it's getting bigger and more influential with modern technology: "It's our nature. Now the internet has eliminated the barriers of geography, cost, and time. All those blogs and social networking sites are helping existing tribes get bigger and enabling new tribes to be born – groups of ten or ten million who care about a political campaign, or a new way to fight global warming."

How strong is this need for connectedness?

Clues can be found in the way we punish people – from our own children to hardened criminals. From preschool to prison, separation from the tribe or family is often the height of punishment. We tell children who misbehave to go sit in the corner or go to their room. In the penitentiary, we put the worst offenders in solitary confinement. Isolation – removing the privilege of being with others – is a severe form of punishment in any social environment.

In the movie *Castaway*, a plane crash survivor played by Tom Hanks was marooned for four years on a tropical island. He was able to find plenty of food and water, but the loneliness was so painful that he tried (unsuccessfully) to kill himself. Finally, he created an imaginary friend by drawing a face on a volleyball. He named him Wilson, and had lengthy conversations with his silent partner.

Speaking of islands, way back in 1624, poet John Donne declared, "No man is an island." People are naturally and irrevocably drawn to relationships. Even behind bars, the need for connection survives. Prisoners form families and some humongous guy with no neck gets designated as "Big Daddy."

When kids in urban environments are deprived of normal family ties, they join street gangs to satisfy this longing. These young gangsters have their own code of honor, and the highest tenet is loyalty to the family – to never snitch, to never leave the group, and to always have each other's back, often under penalty of death. Graffiti marks the family's physical boundaries, and gang tattoos mark each member's lifetime affiliation.

○   ○   ○

As critical as connection is, there are many forces in this world seeking to separate and isolate us. Deterrents to connectedness can be as simple as over-scheduling or as complex as human emotions:

Pride. Macho types (male or female variety) exhibit an exaggerated spirit of independence: "I can do this totally on my own – I don't need anyone's help."

Jealousy. Isolation causes hurt feelings that trigger retaliation: "If I can't belong to that tribe, I'll make sure that you can't either."

Arrogance. Overestimating our own intelligence and abilities can separate us: "You can't teach me anything – I already know how to do this."

Fear. People avoid the risk of being hurt by refusing to be vulnerable: "I prefer not having friends to being disappointed by them."

Simon & Garfunkel described our epic battle between the pain of loneliness and the fear of rejection in their classic, "I Am a Rock." You can feel the ache for connection in the subtext of Simon's lyrics, "I've built walls that none may penetrate. I have no need for friendship; friendship causes pain… If I never loved I never would have cried."

These barriers to connectedness ("I touch no one and no one touches me") can also include misplaced priorities, weak people skills, and character flaws like lying, cheating, growing a mullet – the list goes on. Which means it's not always easy to become connected. There will always be challenges and obstacles. But family and connectedness are worth pursuing. The benefits are numerous and may keep you from ending up like the Maytag repair man staring at a phone that never rings.

This desire for connectedness runs deep within us, so deep that we will avidly pursue a variety of relationships until we find it – sports teams, country clubs, fraternities, churches, political parties, civic groups, book clubs, even the neighborhood bar. But whatever our particular tribe looks like, there is one common denominator – when we're with the other people in our group, we feel like we are "home."

Why else would *Cheers* have been nominated for a staggering 117 Emmy awards? The enduring popularity of make-believe family members like Woody (the bartender), Cliff (the mailman) and Frasier Crane (the psychiatrist) prove that above all else *we are social beings.*

Even when we outwardly deny it.

Fact is, introverts often desire the benefits of family even more than extroverts because it's within that context of tribe that they feel safe and secure. Because they prefer environments that aren't over-stimulating, they love to spend time conversing with family at dinner instead of mingling with strangers at a crowded party or club scene. They prefer to focus their energy on a small, trusted circle of tribal members – friends and family.

○   ○   ○

What happens if family is absent during our formative years? When kids are neglected, does society suffer? Back in 1986, Pope John Paul II told the *London Observer*, "As the family goes, so goes the nation and so goes the whole world in which we live."

Maybe we're already seeing that downward spiral played out in America. Today, over 1 in 100 adults in the United States is in prison or jail. When you add in those on probation or parole, over 1 in 31 adults is under correctional supervision.

Here's another way to read the results of absentee parenting: America has 5 percent of the world's population, but 25 percent of the world's prisoners.

That's a parenting disaster. But some children *can* beat the odds.

One of my business partners was, for all practical purposes, abandoned by his parents during childhood. Each of his five fathers (you read that right – he had five different "dads") all left the family. His mother was an alcoholic who would often disappear without warning. She eventually committed suicide. With this kind of horrific background, he seemed destined for failure and almost certain incarceration.

Instead, he became a model citizen.

What made the difference? Fortunately, kind neighbors and a caring athletic coach took an interest in him and filled the gap left by his MIA parents. With love and concern, this surrogate family modeled functionality and character. They enabled him to grow up alongside their kids, extend his reach through education, and cultivate a desire to pursue worthy causes. They graciously included him in their activities, they made deposits of quality time, and they nurtured him. Because he received and valued their gifts, he is one of the healthiest people – in the full sense of the word – that I've ever met.

The only rock I know that stays steady, the only institution I know that works is the family.

Lee Iacocca, former CEO of Chrysler Corporation

○   ○   ○

Flourishing families all share similar characteristics, whether they are biological or social groupings. In his book, *Tribes*, Seth Godin lists some common denominators of tribes that also apply to any healthy family:

- A tribe is comprised of like-minded people
- A tribe has active members who do more than just "show up"
- Membership is voluntary, not created by converting people
- Tribes aren't closed off or isolated
- People can belong to more than one tribe
- Every tribe is different

In addition to these markers, attributes like acts of kindness, protection, and service are expressed consistently and willingly. Stronger members of the family assist weaker ones. Interdependence is assumed and demonstrated. There is a high degree of trust among members. Each family member knows they can depend on the others in times of need. Finally, members adhere to an agreed-upon, recognized set of common values and ethics.

These ethics and values are not inherited genetically or imparted automatically; they are a *learned behavior*. Family is where we learn (or at least, should learn) basic morality and important concepts like respect, dignity, selflessness, honor, leadership, courage – and it is within the family that we pass them on to others. In fact, if it doesn't happen there, it usually doesn't happen at all. Billy Graham said, "A child who is allowed to be disrespectful to his parents will never have true respect for anyone else."

It's hard to believe, but this traditional inculcation of right and wrong has become controversial, and family values once taken for granted have become targets of criticism.

Sadly, the term "family values" has been so misunderstood and misused that today it has a negative connotation. This perception dates back to a 1992 speech by Vice President Dan Quayle. In it, Quayle connected the devastating Los Angeles riots (53 dead, $1 billion in property loss) to a breakdown of moral values and family structure in American society.

Two things happened immediately after the speech: Rodney King became a sort of folk hero. And Dan Quayle became a sort of human piñata.

Undaunted, Quayle caught even more flak for suggesting TV's *Murphy Brown* was setting a bad example: "It doesn't help when primetime television has a character (Candace Bergen) who epitomizes today's intelligent, highly paid, professional woman mocking the importance of fathers, bearing a child alone, and calling it 'just another lifestyle choice.'"

The candidate was universally ridiculed by the press and late-night talk show hosts for his concern over "moral poverty" in media. If you're a political junkie, you probably know that his controversial statement might have cost the Republicans the election. But most folks *don't* know this ironic twist – after her show was cancelled, Candace Bergen told an interviewer that she actually agreed with Quayle!

The Vatican has long declared the family to be the "first school of social virtues" needed by all peoples. In 2009, the Pontifical Council on the Family declared that it was inside the family unit that "people develop fundamental values indispensable for the formation of free, honest and responsible citizens – truth, justice, solidarity, helping the weak, love of others, tolerance, etc."

Regardless of your religious or political persuasion, that statement should ring true. It's only common sense that without the successful transmission of family values, any nation will have moral decline, societal confusion, and ultimately, anarchy.

There are simply not enough police or jails in the world to protect a society who rejects values and ethics.

Under any system of society, the family holds the future in its bosom.

Charles Franklin Thwing, American educator

○   ○   ○

Winning sports teams often describe their level of cooperation and respect for each other as "being a family." Don Mattingly, former All-Star first baseman and New York Yankee captain, had lots to say about being a team player. You could easily substitute "family member" for "team player" as Mattingly describes the importance of teamwork: "I learned I could impact my team by caring first and foremost about the team's success and not my own ... I mean care, really care about the team, about 'us.' When I gave up *me*, I became more."

As Mattingly demonstrated, family is not just about genetics.

It's about relationships.

And in any family, *relationships* are more important than *roles*. Roles change – who pays the bills, who mows the lawn, who runs errands, who burns dinner, etc. In the course of a marriage, husbands and wives may exchange roles as primary breadwinner or care provider or interior decorator, whatever. But their relationship survives their shifting job descriptions. That's because roles adjust and adapt with circumstances, but healthy relationships persevere.

An important key to making relationships work in your family – whatever kind of family that may be – is to work on *yourself.* Forget about trying to change others; that's an exercise in futility. You and I don't have the power to change anyone else. But we can improve ourselves. Tolstoy said, "Everyone thinks of changing the world, but no one thinks of changing himself." Ouch. Are you willing to change yourself? What kind of person are you willing to become for the benefit of your family?

○   ○   ○

We've all seen images of newly-elected leaders hugging their proud spouses in front of adoring crowds. And sadly, we've also seen disgraced politicians standing awkwardly with their shell-shocked spouses. But this kind of dependence on family is not reserved for celebrities.

To prove it, let's take a quiz: If you're going to receive a big award at the company banquet, who do you want with you? If you're going in for a risky surgery, who do you want in the pre-op? If you're on trial, who do you want in the courtroom? When you celebrate life's victories or face life's defeats, who do you most want by your side?

If you answered "family" to each question, congratulations, you are a human being!

Why family? Because they understand you, they know you. You can be real with them and they can be real with you. There's no need to put on a certain face or act a certain way. You are free to be you. Free to let down your guard. You can let it all hang out, let it all go, and they won't think less of you. Professional golfer Anthony Kim said, "My friends *are* my family, they understand me."

Celebrating with someone you are connected to increases the depth of your celebration. A joy shared is a joy multiplied. Conversely, a problem shared is a problem diminished. Strangers cannot fully share your joy, and they cannot fully share your pain. Those moments are reserved for family.

There is an interconnectedness among members that bonds the family, much like mountain climbers who rope themselves together so that if someone should slip or need support, he's held up by the others until he regains his footing.

"Dr. Phil" McGraw, author of *Family First*

o   o   o

You can't push a rope. But you can pull it. Same is true for connection. You can't push it, but if you give it a gentle tug it will probably follow along.

Genuine connectedness is created by *mutual* acceptance – a partnership that's freely offered and freely received. That's why so many blended families and merged corporations have a tough time – "connection" was pushed on the kids and the employees. False connection that is mandatory or forced upon us is inherently weak and usually short-lived.

Being forced into a group that's a bad fit is pretty much doomed to fail. But when there's the freedom to choose (for both the newcomer and the existing family group), a connection occurs and the potential for great things is ignited. That's true for a platoon of soldiers receiving a new recruit, a hockey team embracing a new rookie, or a family adopting a new child into their home...

Don and Melissa had four kids by natural birth.

Then they adopted three more.

But they still weren't through.

With seven children in the house, why would they adopt a pair of orphaned brothers from Ethiopia? Because they understood that "family" is the key to virtually everything good in life. In her book, *No Biking in the House Without a Helmet*, Melissa Fay Greene shares how she transformed a mixed bag of strangers from vastly different backgrounds into a loving, unified family. The wisdom she discovered applies to any group, team, or tribe in need of conflict resolution: "Each fight, each glitch, each mini-tragedy, offered a moment for family introspection, discovery, and repair. Each offered us a chance to emerge at a slightly better, closer level."

Greene's advice to her nine kids rings true for members of *any* family: "A life guided by friendliness, patience, and forgiveness is happier than a life warped by resentments, a sense of victimization, and a desire for revenge."

o   o   o

Question: What can cause more anxiety and sweaty palms than an upcoming class reunion?

Answer: A tax audit and a root canal on the same day. Maybe.

Why does the prospect of seeing former classmates make women go on crash diets, make men get hair plugs, and make rentals of luxury cars go way up? Because shared experiences – like high school – enhance connectedness. That's why we *have* class reunions (that and to prove that we're wildly more successful than the yearbook editors predicted).

Having "shared experiences" is why combat veterans stay close for decades after their last deployment. It's why retired cops or pro athletes or airline pilots flock together. And it's why family trips and adventures are so important. Building memories and then passing them on through storytelling is essential to any tribe. In most primitive societies, telling stories around a campfire is an art form. In many cultures, learning these family stories is required as a rite of passage into adulthood.

As social animals seeking connection, we love to share our experiences with others. That's why it's so stimulating to discuss movies you've seen or countries you've visited with others who've had a similar experience. We can enjoy it all over again by talking about it. In fact, hearing oft-repeated stories about something can be almost as fun as actually doing it!

So if telling stories is such a great way to keep a family together and thriving, why don't we do more of it?

Blame it on the golden arches.

Americans now eat out an average of five times a week. And much of it takes place in fast food restaurants. When it comes to dining out, we prefer to satisfy our hunger in ten minute or less – even though the food is high in fat, salt and cholesterol. Besides good nutrition, what else have we lost? Experts say we are losing the art of conversation. Drive-through eating has largely replaced the traditional family dinner table and its roundtable discussions. Busy schedules mean eating on the run or behind the wheel and we're losing touch with each other's lives.

But there is a solution.

According to a University of Minnesota study, more conversation around the dinner table with family members can have a huge impact. Among American teenagers, there is a strong association between regular family meals and academic success, psychological adjustment, and lower rates of substance abuse. There's even a reduction in early sexual behavior and suicide risk! It's around the dinner table that stories are told, retold and passed on from one generation to the next.

If you're tired of asking a family member, "How was your day?" and getting the same robotic response, see the Action Steps at the end of this chapter. There's a practical resource to jump-start meaningful conversations at your next sit-down meal.

Serving together is another great way to establish connectedness. If you've ever helped on a Habitat for Humanity project, worked at a rescue mission, or volunteered to deliver meals, you've undoubtedly experienced a strong connection with the people you served with. While working side by side, you form a bond that helps you understand yourself and others better. Mahatma Gandhi said, "The best way to find yourself is to lose yourself in serving others."

○   ○   ○

Rose Kennedy was the matriarch of America's most famous political family. She knew that having a connection to your family's history is essential. Rose often told her grandchildren, "Remember, you're a Kennedy." As you know, there were great advantages, expectations, and challenges to being a Kennedy – as there are with any family relationship. We send an important message to those in our family when we say, "Remember, you're a Thompson" (or a Navy Seal, or an Eagle Scout, or a Rotarian) – now go out and act like one."

These admonitions are a reminder that your particular family subscribes to a certain set of standards and values. Your family follows a particular way of treating others and living life. This reminder reinforces the fact that our actions affect the other members of our family. Today, the conduct of a single United States Marine in Guantanamo or Afghanistan can impact the honor of an entire institution that dates back to 1775!

Establishing family traditions – again, in whatever form your family takes – also enhances our feelings of connectedness. Every spring, I get out of town for an annual golf outing with a group of 12 guys. For three days, we golf, play cards and shoot pool together. And of course, we tell stories from previous outings that seem to evolve into taller (and funnier) tales with each passing year. It makes us all feel connected and it's one of my favorite rituals. But even seemingly "small" traditions are important. At our house, Friday is family night, which means scarfing down pizza from our favorite parlor and watching a movie together. We allow very little to interrupt that schedule. We also vacation each year with a certain group of friends. Taking trips together and experiencing new countries and cultures adds "glue" to the relationships and makes us feel even more like family.

Family traditions counter alienation and confusion. They help us define who we are; they provide something steady, reliable and safe in a confusing world.
Susan Lieberman, author of *New Traditions*

So far so good. But can that family feeling transfer to the *workplace*? Probably not if you work at Dunder Mifflin Paper Company.

Or if your boss in any way resembles Michael Scott.

But for the rest of us the news is better. Much better. Businesses that create an environment that allows people working there to feel like family are typically more productive, provide better service to customers, and are more profitable. As you might expect, they also experience less employee turnover.

One of our company's seven core values is "community." That means we want to do business in the context of authentic, healthy relationships. We take a collaborative approach where each team member's input is sought and expected. We not only arrive at better solutions as a family, we have way more fun doing business. To stay on track, we select someone on our team to champion each of our seven core values. The person in charge of "community" organizes experiences and events throughout the year to connect our employees with each other, with our clients, and even with the other tenants in our office building.

PILLAR NUMBER 2: COMMITMENT

If you travel through Florence, Italy, you'll be surrounded by famous palaces and monuments. Millions flock to this "cradle of the Renaissance" to marvel at sites like the Santa Maria del Fiore cathedral – topped by a dome that towers 375 feet in the air! Completed in 1436, this eye-popping marvel was designed by Brunellesschi to dominate a Tuscan skyline of cream-colored buildings and terra cotta roofs. Almost 600 years later, it's still the largest masonry dome ever built. But what made the biggest impression on me was something much smaller and closer to the ground...

Members of a vibrant family must have an unwavering commitment to each other. This private, unseen obligation is a standing order, ready to be called upon at a moment's notice. This level of commitment sounds good in theory. But here's where it gets sticky – the promise is to be honored even when it's *not* convenient or comfortable.

A real pledge of honor is not a flippant, superficial commitment you mumble at some ceremony. The pledge I'm talking about develops a rock-solid sense of confidence between a family's members.

I discovered a concrete example of this while exploring Florence on foot. In addition to its wonderful museums and fountains, the ancient city is known for its bridges crisscrossing the River Arno. While wandering alone through a maze of cobblestone streets, I started across the historic Ponte Vecchio built in 1345. I literally felt like I was walking back in time.

Strolling over this picturesque bridge, I spotted a large steel ring, approximately 12 inches in diameter, attached to one of the stone towers. Stepping up for a closer look, I noticed that hundreds of keys were hanging on this mysterious ring.

Curious, I started asking around to find out what it meant.

Days later, over a bowl of pasta carbonaro, I discovered that it is customary for newlyweds in Florence to go to this medieval bridge for a very special tradition. They start by standing in the middle of the span with an open padlock in their hands. Together they close the lock, symbolizing their complete and permanent commitment. They then throw the lock into the middle of the river and hang their key on the ring fastened to the bridge. Forever after, their key serves as a visual reminder of the commitment they made to each other for life.

That kind of "locked in" commitment is the backbone of any cohesive, influential family. The spirit of shared commitment enables people to do the uncommon – whether it's the Medici family of Florence or the Soprano family of New Jersey.

An overlooked aspect of commitment that is necessary for families to function is *accountability*. It simply means you willingly agree to be responsible for your actions – and it's the opposite of blaming, making excuses or ducking for cover when things go wrong. Keeping a commitment (big or small) is best supported by being answerable to someone else. That's why folks in a 12-step program are accountable to a buddy (sponsor) who backs them up when they're tempted or picks them up when they fall.

There are different types of accountability, here are three:

Safety accountability. This is when one family member tells another where they'll be traveling, when they'll be arriving, who they're staying with, etc. None of us can sleep well until we know for sure that our family unit is as secure as possible.

Progress accountability. At my office we assign specific seven-day goals. If you get one, you commit to accomplishing it within a week. Family members do not willingly let their teammates down – we're all counting on each other.

Truth-telling accountability. When one family member observes hurtful or destructive behavior in the life of another, he is obligated to lovingly bring attention to that matter for the purpose of healing, growing, or restoring a relationship.

When commitment is backed up by accountability, there is a willingness to make personal sacrifices for the well-being of others in the family. Instead of a "me first" mentality, truly committed family members have a "you first" mentality. If members must put themselves in harm's way to protect another family member, they do it. A healthy family has members who understand there is a cost to being a part of this close-knit group. It may cost them significant amounts of time, energy, financial resources and more.

General Harold Moore – recipient of the Distinguished Service Cross – was a man who was fully committed to his "family."

Made famous in the movie *We Were Soldiers*, Moore commanded the 1st Battalion, 7th Calvary Regiment in Vietnam. This excellent film accurately portrays the battle of the Ia Drang Valley, the first significant encounter between American and Viet Cong soldiers. During 48 hours of continuous combat in November 1965, a few hundred Americans held off an assault by 4,000 North Vietnamese. Under Moore's leadership, the 7th Calvary prevailed, losing 78 men while inflicting over *four times* that many deaths on the enemy.

This true story of battlefield heroism is amazing. But the secret to this unit's success began way back in the States. Before leaving for Vietnam, Moore delivered a moving speech to his men – a speech that literally defines the mission of a family:

> Look around you. In the 7th Cavalry we've got Japanese, Chinese, Blacks, Hispanics, Cherokee Indians, Jews and Gentiles – all American. Now here in the States some men in this unit may experience discrimination because of race or creed, but for you and me now, all that is gone. We're moving into the valley of the shadow of death, where you will watch the back of the man next to you, as he will watch yours, and you won't care what color he is or by what name he calls God. Let us understand the situation; we're going into battle against a tough and determined enemy. I can't promise you that I will bring you all home alive, but this I swear, before you and before Almighty God: When we go into battle, I will be the

first one to set foot on the field, and I will be the last to step off. And I will leave no one behind. Dead or alive, we will all come home together. So help me God.

General Moore kept his promise. He was first in and last out. He brought his men back to their loved ones. He stood in harm's way in the heaviest fighting and was ready to give his last full measure of devotion for his family. He inspired his men to go over and above the call of duty and make their mark in history.

That's the kind of family I want to be in.

When everything goes to hell, the people who stand by you without flinching – they are your family.

Jim Butcher, American author

PILLAR NUMBER 3: CAUSE

Ever seen pictures of tourists bobbing around in Israel's Dead Sea?

It's easy to float in it because the water's salt concentration is 33 percent! That's nine times saltier than the ocean. The brine is great for buoyancy, but toxic to all aquatic life. My editor, Karl Nilsson, was there recently and tells me the Dead Sea is, and I quote, "deader than disco." No fish, no crabs, no turtles, nothing. There's no life in it because it's completely landlocked – no fresh water flowing through to flush it out or renew it.

That reminds me of people who are closed off to the world.

A family that focuses exclusively inward, caring only for its own members, is a family undergoing atrophy, whether they recognize it or not. Like a body of water that has no outlet or source of fresh water, it will eventually become stagnant and any life in it will shrivel up.

All healthy families need a *mission, cause or purpose* that is bigger than they are, something outside of the tribe. This movement solidifies the group and gives focus to the family's energy and resources so it can make a positive difference. Nothing enhances the health and vitality of a family more than sharing a common altruistic goal.

When we think of families with a mission, we may be tempted to think of millionaire philanthropists who can donate huge sums of money to charity. But a "family mission" can start out as small as a single little boy with a big heart...

On a freezing cold December night in 1983, 11-year-old Trevor Ferrell was sitting with his family in their warm suburban home. Then, Trevor saw a TV newscast about people living on the streets of Philadelphia. Those images stirred something deep within his heart. Right on the spot, he asked his parents to drive him downtown so he could give his blanket and pillow to the first homeless person they saw. Being a strong, loving family unit, the parents dropped everything and "just did it." Over the next weeks and months, Trevor and his family made nightly trips into Philadelphia's inner city to distribute food, clothing and blankets to the needy.

Soon classmates and neighbors joined in along with hundreds of generous citizens and businesses. Starting with the gift of Trevor's single blanket, this family's mission, cause and purpose soon grew into an entire array of services for the homeless – including shelters, food and training for self-sufficiency. The dream of one family focusing outside of their personal needs took on a life of its own and today is an integral lifeline to the over 13,000 homeless people of Philadelphia.

In my own backyard, another kind of "family" gave us something to cheer about...

It's no secret that the state of Michigan has gone through tough economic times, particularly the city of Detroit, with nation-leading unemployment, an auto industry fighting to survive, and plummeting home values. The Michigan State Spartans basketball team – a tight-knit family – was well aware of the challenges their home state faced. As they entered the NCAA tournament in 2011, they knew that their actions, on and off the court, could inspire a discouraged and struggling state. With a unified mission, cause and purpose, Coach Tom Izzo's determined team rode the emotion and support of countless Michigan residents all the way to the Final Four.

Yes, the Spartans wanted to win a championship, but they also saw an opportunity to give local people something to be proud of, to demonstrate that opposition can be overcome, that working together can accomplish great things.

The result? The entire state was electrified by their performance.

Another Michigan "family" that inspires and encourages is based in the town of Rochester. Founded in 1939, it's called Leader Dogs for the Blind and it provides guide dogs to people who are visually impaired. The president and her team – paid staff, volunteers and supporters – work together like a family to provide independence and safety to their clients *free of charge*. Each year, scores of students are paired with a guide dog. All those aligned with the organization's mission, cause and purpose gladly give their time, energy and resources.

Whenever I see a leader dog guiding someone safely through a crowded mall or busy intersection, I marvel again at the positive impact a "family" can make.

Wherever you live, there are groups of people in churches, synagogues and mosques across this country who have adopted a variety of causes. These groups, functioning like families, assist widows with home repairs, help children in need, run inner city camps for at-risk kids, visit nursing homes and so on. If you're going to be in a family, it's best to be in an *outwardly* focused family – one based on fulfilling a worthwhile mission, cause or purpose.

Look for a family that's making a corner of this world a better place, and jump in!

Call it a clan, call it a network, call it a tribe, call it a family. Whatever you call it, whoever you are, you need one.

Jane Howard, novelist

○   ○   ○

Connectedness + Commitment + Cause = Community

We've just looked at the three pillars of a successful family. Each virtue is well worth pursuing on its own. But when you mix the three *together* you create a powerful chain reaction – you create *community*. The tremendous exponential byproduct of being in a family where there is connectedness, commitment and cause is that a vibrant community forms. Full of life and energy, that community becomes a hub of activity and a source of inspiration and strength. It's where dreams are born and nurtured, where members are defended, and where care for non-members emanates.

It's networking at its finest!

A healthy family becomes a small community *within* a larger community. It becomes the building block of society. The reality is, without strong family units, we are weak and susceptible to many dangers – as individuals and as a nation.

During my college years I served as a counselor at Tall Timbers Youth Camp. The camp was founded in the late Sixties by retired baseball star, Ken Hamlin. Ken played for four teams in the major leagues but wanted to leave a legacy beyond sports. The camp is located in a small town called – don't snicker – Climax, Michigan. The boys, ages 10 to 16, would come to the forest and live in rustic cabins for two weeks of adventure and training. On the closing night of camp, Hamlin himself would build a huge bonfire. As the firewood crackled and popped, you could feel the heat on your face. The roaring blaze was bright enough to read by, and sparks shot upward like fireworks.

With all the kids sitting around the fire, Ken would begin talking about how the fire burns bright as long as all the sticks stay together. Then he would go up to the edge of the fire and kick one of the burning sticks out away from the rest. "Each of you is like one of those sticks," he said.

"You might think you can make it on your own, but you can't. I've tried it. It doesn't work."

As he talked, everyone watched the flame on the isolated stick slowly burn out. Ken explained, "If you stay connected with others, even though you will face tough times in your life, you will get through. You will have the help and encouragement you need to stick with it. You will be a bright light to the people around you." At that point he would kick the lone stick back into the pile. Everyone watched as the stick reignited and added to the flame's intensity.

Don't be a lone stick.

Find a "family" that's burning bright for a worthy cause and join up with them. You'll be amazed how bright your flame – and the flame of your family – will glow.

7F ACTION STEPS: FAMILY

- Take stock of your own gifts, talents and desires. (What are you good at? Carpentry? Cooking? Philanthropy?) Then look for organizations or groups with interests or goals that will allow you to express your gifts within that family.

- Go to *www.FoodforTalk.net* for 200 cards designed to initiate dinner conversation by helping parents and children establish a deeper, more meaningful connection. Soon, you'll be sharing feelings, values and experiences. Schedule other events that lead to bonding – like family activity nights (watching TV does not count!).

- Evaluate your family – any type of family – from a "cause" perspective. Is your family focused on protecting itself or on fulfilling a purpose worthy of dedicating your life to?

- Create a family values mission statement. Get the gang together and brainstorm about what's most important to you. Examples could be "always telling the truth," or "being kind to each other," or "sharing what we have with the less fortunate." Let everyone contribute what's personally meaningful to them, and when you've made the list, have everyone sign it as a sort of covenant.

- Conduct a family memories night. Bring out the scrapbooks and photo albums and some of that endless video footage you shot. Have each member share one vivid memory – from a vacation, a celebration or a milestone in their life.

- Consider becoming foster parents or adopting a child. If that seems out of reach, check out volunteering with Big Brothers or Big Sisters.

- Write a tribute to a significant person in your family. Tell them how they've made a positive impact on you and why they mean so much to you. I realize this may be tough in some cases. But if you try, you can always find something good to say. My own tributes to my father and mother follow this section.

o   o   o

Since I brought up this subject, can I be gut-level honest?

My parents weren't perfect. Neither were yours. And for some of you, thinking back to your childhood is a painful memory. But we can't wish away our past or re-choose our parents. Families – even broken ones – are forever, a permanent part of who we are. How we treat others for the rest of our lives is influenced by this seminal relationship that precedes and transcends all others. How we deal with our spouses, our kids, our bosses – everyone – is affected by our parent's influence. Even how we envision God is affected by whether our first authority figures were kind or cruel, caring or cold.

I hope your parents were warm, loving, and supportive. But even if they were far above average, it's likely they said and did certain things that disappointed you or maybe even scarred you emotionally. All families have some dysfunction, and all parent/child relationships have ups and downs. In *The Five People You Meet in Heaven*, Mitch Albom says, "All parents damage their children. It cannot be helped. Youth, like pristine glass, absorbs the prints of its handlers. Some parents smudge, others crack, a few shatter childhoods completely…"

As I said, no parents are perfect.

But to live an abundant life as an adult, you need to do two things:

First, you need to *forgive your parents.* Grant them grace for whatever major or minor mistakes they made. The best way to release the pain (or resentment or bitterness) you feel is to make a deliberate decision to forgive them for falling short – for who they were then, and who they are now if they're still living. They may or may not deserve it; they may or may not acknowledge it. But forgiveness is up to you, and the benefits accrue to you either way.

Secondly, you need to *thank your parents.* Don't thank them for being perfect people – I know they blew it – but thank them for all they've given you over the years, including your very existence. If that's the only good thing you can think of, start with the gift of life and work from there.

In his book *For One More Day*, Mitch Albom suggests we may owe mom and dad far more than we realize, "Parents, if they love you, will hold you up safely, above their swirling waters, and sometimes that means you'll never know what they endured…"

Bottom line? The power of saying "thank you" to our parents (or siblings or in-laws) can go miles toward healing a rotten attitude, rebuilding bridges, and maybe even reestablishing a better relationship with them now as adults. Don't just *feel* grateful; *express* it to them – either in conversation or in a written tribute. William Ward said, "Feeling gratitude and not expressing it is like wrapping a present and not giving it."

A TRIBUTE TO MY DAD

We haven't always seen eye to eye, but I am thankful to you for many things:

> *— For modeling a strong work ethic*

> *— For instilling in me the importance of being responsible*

> *— For teaching me there is a right way and a wrong way to do everything*

> *— For showing me what it's like to be a risk-taker*

> *— For providing materially for our family*

> *— For demonstrating the benefits of order and cleanliness*

> *— For emphasizing the importance of being courteous to others*

> *— For being a "straight shooter" and speaking the truth*

> *— For having fun with me outdoors hunting and fishing*

For these things and more, I will always be grateful to you. – Michael

A TRIBUTE TO MY MOM

A written list could never do you justice, but I will always be thankful to you:

> *— For believing in me and constantly encouraging me*

> *— For always being there when I needed you*

> *— For sacrificing your time and your own desires to help me accomplish mine*

> *— For loving me unconditionally*

> *— For your laughter and for seeing the humorous side of life*

> *— For not getting old mentally and being game to try new things*

> *— For the countless loads of laundry you washed*

> *— For all the delicious meals and desserts you prepared*

> *— For your faithful prayers*

For these things and more I will always be grateful to you. – Michael

C H A P T E R   6

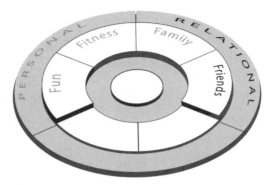

Friends

*A friend is someone who knows all about me, likes me for who I am and has
no plans for my personal improvement.*

Anonymous

At a Christie's auction in 1997, an anonymous buyer paid $114,614 for a
single bottle of wine. It was a 1945 Chateau Mouton-Rothschild, made
from what wine enthusiasts consider to be the finest vintage of the twentieth
century. With their complex subtleties, high-end reds are traditionally more
costly than other elite wines.

But really, ten grand a glass?

Compared to that, sipping my generic Bordeaux was a bargain. Sitting
with my wife at the bar of an upscale restaurant, I surveyed the drinks being
enjoyed by the patrons perched on tall stools flanking the bar.

On our left, a woman in her mid-forties was drinking a glass of red
wine. Judging by her couture outfit, Louis Vuitton handbag and perfect
coiffure, I guessed she was able to pop for the best house wine on the menu.

When she checked the time – it was approaching midnight – a diamond encrusted Cartier confirmed her net worth. Based on the ruby hue that half-filled her glass, I surmised her choice was the Chateau Lafite 1996. It's very dark with a bold flavor and silky texture.

A great choice for New Year's Eve.

On our right, a well-dressed man sat joylessly drinking a martini. His Armani suit and gold Rolex suggested high level executive. His silk tie had a hint of green that matched the apple schnapps coloring the Stoli in his final cocktail of the old year. I chuckled, recalling an observation by Oscar Wilde, "A well-tied tie is the first serious step in life."

What steps had led this sad-looking man to spend New Year's here?

As for us, we smiled between sips, hardly able to believe another year was just about in the books. It was December 31, and my wife and I were starting the evening at one of our favorite restaurants. The swank but friendly spot was always popular, and on this holiday night, it was especially jammed. When we arrived, there was an hour wait to be seated in the formal dining room. Rather than stand around, we decided to check out the crowded bar area where they also served dinner. We gladly grabbed the last two remaining seats.

The mahogany bar was a huge oval, shaped like a race track. We sat down near the far corner, a perfect vantage for people watching. The festive crowd was decked out for the occasion. Channeling the spirit of Joan Rivers, we critiqued each partygoer for fashion *faux pas*. The men looked dapper, sporting everything from cashmere coats to tuxedos on this special night. Not to be outdone, the women were at their most glamorous – jewelry, evening gowns, and plenty of politically incorrect furs were on display.

By outward appearances, everyone looked like they "had it goin' on."

As we scanned the menu, the woman with the red wine sighed and shifted uncomfortably on her stool next to me. She was alone, and stared down at her glass to avoid eye contact. Meanwhile, the well-groomed man with the Appletini swirled his drink without enthusiasm. In his mid-fifties, he was also alone. As Mary Ann and I talked, I couldn't help but notice how these two high-income individuals sat in silence, looking oddly stoic in a place bustling with people and ringing with laughter and music.

I thought to myself, *What decisions had these two made – or not made – that sent them out into the biggest party night of the year without a companion?*

Just then, a young couple elbowed their way through the people crowding around the bar to order drinks. The bartender asked to see their IDs. As soon as I heard his question, I knew I had an opening. It was so painful to see the woman next to me drinking by herself that I decided to take a chance. I asked, "Do you remember the last time you were carded?"

Her face lit up.

Someone was acknowledging her presence. Someone was engaging her in conversation. She was no longer left out.

She smiled, "It's been longer then I care to remember." Without any further prompting from me, she went on to talk (and talk and talk) about how the years had flown by, how she was glad to be out of her twenties and thirties and would not want to go back to that time in her life for anything.

It was like striking a geyser. She volunteered far more information than I cared to know. Based on the length of her response, it was clear she wanted to interact with someone, even if it was with a complete stranger. She had a desire to connect, even if it was just superficial talk with a person she would never see again.

As she chattered on, the man sitting by my wife also began to open up. Eager to start a conversation but wary of intruding, he asked how her dinner was. After a few minutes of tentative discourse, he warmed up and asked about our plans for the rest of the evening. He also desired to be acknowledged. His questions, lobbed in Mary Ann's direction, were like flags waving in the boisterous crowd saying, "I'm here too. I want to be part of the action. I want to be part of the fun."

With mixed emotions, we finished our meal and left the restaurant. Heading off to celebrate with friends, I wondered what those two solitary people would be doing when Dick Clark started his countdown. Would somebody toast them with champagne? Would somebody kiss them – or even notice them – when the ball dropped in Times Square?

From a school cafeteria to a greasy spoon to a five-star restaurant, one thing is universally true: Some diners will be surrounded by friends and some will eat alone. From childhood to old age, some people just seem to attract a large circle of friends while others have few, if any, companions. In this section, we'll look at why there's such a disparity.

The Four Foundations of Friendship

Why do some folks seem to have friends around every corner, while others struggle to find even one deep, lasting friendship? Issues like insecurity, immaturity, pride, low self-esteem and feelings of inadequacy are just some of the reasons certain people have difficulty "gelling" with others.

To offset those common inhibitors to friendships, we'll look at the foundations of every strong relationship. They are central to building and sustaining a solid friendship and require our ongoing attention. Hint: These four pillars are *not* fame, fortune, beauty, or sex appeal. They are respect, trust, love, and understanding:

1. RESPECT

The Queen of Soul said it best. Without a little R-E-S-P-E-C-T a friendship isn't going anywhere! Respect is simply having high regard or esteem for someone. It often starts on a surface level, based on the *performance* of the other person. That means you respect them for what they can do – their professional, athletic, musical or mechanical abilities, for example. But for a friendship to become meaningful, respect must advance based on the *character* of the individual, meaning "who they are and what they stand for" – their honesty, loyalty, generosity, etc.

Sports fans around the world agonized over the self-destructive tailspin of superstar golfer Tiger Woods. Countless admirers and colleagues alike lost respect for the golfer who many thought would be crowned the best player in history. Ironically, in the midst of Tiger's scandal, another professional golfer earned my respect by demonstrating "who he is and what he stands for" in a dramatic display of integrity during a PGA tournament in April 2010.

While tied for first place, golfer Brian Davis called a tournament official over to make him aware of a rule violation he may have committed. His error was so slight that it could have easily gone undetected. In fact, it was indiscernible except on slow motion replays. The fact that Davis was tied with fellow pro Jim Furyk – and in a sudden death playoff – heightened the drama.

It was ruled that Brian had indeed made an infraction and he was penalized two strokes. By turning himself in, he literally handed over the match to Furyk. Had he been silent, Brian Davis would still have been in contention. By speaking up and confessing his violation (he had merely brushed a loose reed during his backswing), he cost himself nearly $400,000 in earnings – the difference between first and second place.

If you were in that situation, would you have brought a small, unintentional violation to the attention of officials?

Davis did.

The next day, emails and phone calls streamed in from all over the country thanking him for doing the right thing, even though it cost him a bundle. Overnight, his reputation and level of respect soared. My guess is that those who personally knew Brian before this incident were not surprised. They already knew he was a man worthy of their respect.

Let's suppose that you or I were given the chance to meet and hang out with a guy like Brian. Would we be interested? Of course! After seeing how he handled this situation we'd be strongly compelled to connect with a man of his character. We admire that kind of behavior. We respect that kind of behavior. We are drawn to people like Brian – and this kind of person typically has a large flock of friends.

When you choose your friends, don't be short-changed by choosing personality over character.

W. Somerset Maugham, author

There are other, less dramatic, ways to win or lose respect. Rather than a single earth-shaking event, respect is usually enhanced or diminished over time by a thousand small actions: Do we tell the truth, show up on time, keep our promises?

This next principle is so basic and fundamental (or at least it should be) that it almost goes without saying. Respect is something we should extend to *every person* regardless of race, gender, age, income, belief, politics, opinions, or religion. Don't you wish that were practiced more today?

We should always take the feelings of others into account as we interact with them. Give respect, and you will (usually) be respected in return. Deny respect and you'll (usually) be disrespected – and friendless.

Here are the warning signs of **disrespectful** behavior:

- When we argue, we attack people on personal levels, disparaging them as a person instead of focusing on issues.
- When we're angry with our spouse or kids or co-workers, we humiliate them in front of others.
- We insist on inflicting our opinion on others without giving them a chance to express their viewpoints.
- We gossip or reveal sensitive information others have entrusted to us.
- We bully people, either physically or emotionally.
- We are rude, obnoxious, or self-absorbed in public places.

Think of the jerk on Bluetooth who's loud enough to entertain a shopping mall. Or the parents who let their crying baby spoil everybody's meal. The list goes on – from leaving a mess in the office kitchen to letting your dog bark all night to taking cuts in line. But all acts of disrespect have one thing in common: We are putting ourselves ahead of others. And we don't care how our selfishness may hurt, embarrass or disappoint anyone else in the process.

On the flipside, signs of **respectful** behavior are:

- We practice common courtesy at all times, even if it is not reciprocated.
- We actively listen to what others are saying, no matter how insignificant or incorrect we think their ideas are.
- We don't judge others – not on appearances, not on prejudices, not on third-party conversations.
- We're open-minded and sensitive to the feelings, fears, and problems of others.
- We accept people as they are; we don't push them to become something they're not.
- We refuse to be involved in name-calling or negative labeling of any kind.

When we were kids, all decent parents taught their children respect. It's sad that as we grow up we often forget the simple principles of civility. Everyone wants (and needs) to be respected, and if we dish it out liberally, we'll never have trouble attracting and keeping friends.

Remove respect from friendship, and you have taken away the most splendid ornament it possesses.

Cicero, Greek philosopher

2. TRUST

Shortly after the tragic events of September 11, 2001, former President Bill Clinton and Senator Bob Dole joined forces to raise $100 million in scholarship money for the stricken families.

The country was encouraged by this bipartisan act of charity. Grateful citizens congratulated the former adversaries. "But you know who *also* deserves a pat on the back?" Jay Leno mused. "Elizabeth Dole."

How so?

"Her husband Bob is a spokesman for Viagra and he's gone on the road with Bill Clinton," Leno explained. "That is one trusting woman!"

All kidding aside, the Doles had obviously built up enormous trust for each other during their decades of marriage. Their mutual respect led to mutual trust. The more respect you have for someone, the more trust you'll have in them. Here, the word *trust* means "the assured reliance on the character, ability, strength or truth of someone."

On the other hand, if Bob had a history of hitting on pretty young aides, his wife wouldn't trust him past the driveway. After all, you're not likely to give your full trust to someone who's abused it in the past. For example, the world trembled for decades as different Russian leaders broke one international treaty after another with their allies and enemies alike. During the Cold War, President Reagan was asked if he trusted the Soviets to keep up their end of the latest nuclear disarmament treaty.

His wise reply was, "Trust, but verify."

Trust is one of humanity's basic building blocks, not only of social discourse but of all civil interactions. Society breaks down when trust breaks down. Which explains why lawsuits and contract disputes and arbitrations are swirling around us today. It used to be that someone's word was their bond. If someone said they were going to do something, they did it. Famed billionaire Warren Buffet said he used to do multimillion-dollar business deals on a handshake.

Today, the need for binding contracts and mountains of red tape keep an army of lawyers busy – simply because we can't trust each other to fulfill our deals. There are 1.2 million active attorneys in America, with 45,000 more *juris doctors* graduating from U.S. law schools every year.

You can't trust a promise someone makes while they're drunk, in love, hungry, or running for office.

Joe Moore, educator

o   o   o

Trust is a fragile thing. And sometimes the oddest thing can shake it. The noted humorist Robert Benchley once applied for a bank loan. He was horrified when his request was promptly and unconditionally granted. He was so upset he closed the account. "I don't trust a bank," Benchley explained, "that would lend money to such a poor risk."

You can't buy trust.

You can't manufacture it.

We *earn* another person's trust when we make good on a promise. We build and strengthen trust each time we do what we say we're going to do. Trust is like a savings account that gradually builds, one deposit at a time. It can take years to build up but only seconds to empty. A reputation built on a lifetime of good judgment can be quickly tarnished by one misstep. Making one bad decision is like making a huge "withdrawal" from your trust account.

When that happens, the relationship is no longer on sure footing. Doubts creep in. Minds wander and wonder. Nietzsche said, "I'm not upset you lied to me. I'm upset that I can no longer believe you."

That's the consequence of shattered trust.

Once broken, a relationship may or may not be restored, depending on the nature of the offense and the individuals involved. Friendship is delicate, like glass. It can be fixed but there will always be cracks.

When there is a high level of trust, an equally high level of *freedom* can be extended. For example, in a healthy dating relationship, you don't worry when your "steady" goes to a party without you. In a healthy marriage, a husband isn't concerned when his wife goes away for the weekend with friends. Likewise, she doesn't mind when he goes off hunting with his buddies. In a healthy business relationship, when one partner is out on a business trip, he's not worried about what's being said about him by his partners back in the office. And likewise, they trust him to be doing exactly what he is responsible for on their behalf.

In my case, I would trust my business partners, Joe and John, with my life. In fact, I *do*. Literally. I would trust them with my personal checkbook, my house key, and my family. Why? Because they have demonstrated trustworthiness time and time again. I know they have my back and I have theirs. It's a great feeling to be in a friendship or relationship like that.

To be trusted is a greater compliment than to be loved.

George McDonald, poet & minister

○　　○　　○

One day a turtle was sitting by the edge of a pond getting ready to swim across. Just then, a scorpion came over and asked him for a ride. The turtle looked suspiciously at the scorpion, "Why should I give you a ride? You will certainly sting me and I will surely die."

The scorpion smiled, "Trust me. Why would I sting you when you're doing me the kindness of giving me a ride? Besides, I would also drown if I stung you."

The turtle thought about the scorpion's words and seeing the logic in them he allowed the insect to climb on his back. About halfway across the pond, the turtle felt a painful sting on his neck. He could feel the poison flowing through his body. Just before he lost consciousness he asked the scorpion, "Why did you bite me? Now we're both going to die."

The scorpion replied sadly, "It's just my nature."

If a person has a history of telling lies or stealing from work or cheating on a spouse, they will likely lie, steal and cheat again in the future;

it's just their nature. Don't expect a tiger to change its stripes. Be careful about placing your trust in any person with unproven character. Until you have some history with a person, you're wise to be cautious. If they have a reputation for being a compulsive liar or chronically unreliable, you're likely to get burned. Likewise, be careful around those with a quick temper. Avoid those who manipulate their friends or gossip behind their back. Know who you are dealing with. You cannot control the way other people are wired up.

You cannot "cure" them. They are who they are. Beware.

Be courteous to all, but intimate with few, and let those few be well tried before you give them your confidence.

George Washington, U.S. president

Speaking of caution, also beware of the "frenemy." A portmanteau of the words "friend" and "enemy," the word frenemy describes that two-faced guy or gal who sucks up to you all sweet and gushy, then stabs you in the back to advance their cause. You could call them a wolf in sheep's clothing or a snake in the grass, but by any name, those who pretend to be your friend and are actually your enemy are the most dangerous creeps of all. That doesn't mean your real friends have to be perfect, or that they won't annoy you sometimes, but they *do* have to be honest. Like Oscar Wilde said, "True friends stab you in the front."

Now, I'm going to step on some toes.

Do people consider *you* trustworthy?

Can they put their absolute confidence in you? Do you keep all of your commitments, big or small? Is your word your bond?

If so, you're likely to attract many friends. Good friends. The kind you can trust implicitly on a life journey that's surrounded by quicksand, potholes, speed bumps and booby traps. I know I would be lost without my faithful companions. Like former Beatle Ringo Starr, "I get by with a little help from my friends."

Good friendships are so valuable (and rare) that having just one trusted amigo close to home can be more helpful than importing a busload of family members with dubious character. A trusted friend will be there to comfort and console during times of sadness, provide perspective in times of confusion, and provide help in times of trouble.

Trustworthy friends can give us a pat on the back or a kick in the butt. They can dispense salty advice, give sweet hugs, or just simply be there for us when we need them most.

They're God's way of taking care of us.

Friendship doubles the joy and divides the grief in half.

Swedish proverb

○   ○   ○

Every August in Detroit, we have what's known as the Woodward Dream Cruise. Billed as the world's largest automotive event, it boasts 40,000 classic cars parading up and down Woodward Avenue. Over 1.3 million spectators line the road to watch an endless stream of muscle cars, exotics, and hot rods of every description. Every year the crowds get bigger. And every year I wish I still had my Camaro from college!

On one occasion, I got "sideways" with my dad over this gleaming white Chevy with red pinstripes. I don't remember what the issue was. All I recall is that he was going to take over possession of my car – a totally cool Camaro that we bought together 50/50. I was in the process of paying off his half when our disagreement occurred. The car was in his name. I was stuck. I needed transportation for work and school. Not to mention dating.

I went to my friend John and explained the situation. Without hesitating he wrote me a check for a little over $2,000 so I could pay off my dad. There was no contract, no collateral. He simply said, "I know you're good for it."

I soon got things worked out with my father. He wouldn't actually accept the money, so I was able to give John his loan back. But just knowing that my friend trusted me enough to cover me in a jam created a special place in my heart for him.

Somebody said, "A friend will help you move, but a true friend will help you move a dead body." I'm not advocating criminal behavior. And maybe hiding the evidence of a homicide is not a fair test of friendship, but you get my drift. You know who your *real* friends are. And I bet you can count them on the fingers of one hand. British writer, Thomas Fuller took it one step further, "If you have one true friend, you have more than your share."

How can you tell if a friendship is advancing towards this highest level? It's when your relationship becomes less about what you have in common and more about your lives feeling intertwined. Aristotle said a friend is a single soul in two bodies.

When you get to the point where it feels like you are living life together, you're on to something really good. When you know you can call a person at any time day or night – whether it's an emergency or just to talk – you've developed a valuable, trusting friendship.

It's the friends you can call up at 4:00 a.m. that matter.

Marlene Dietrich, actress

3. LOVE

In 1955, the lyrics that won the Oscar for Best Original Song proclaimed, "Love is a many splendored thing."

Or in the case of porcupines, a many splintered thing.

Sorry. What I mean is, the word "love" is almost impossible to define, and covers such a wide range of emotions and such broad levels of commitment, that we could never fully agree on its meaning – or what makes it happen.

High levels of respect and trust between friends may lead to feelings and expressions of non-romantic, non-sexual love toward one another. Have you ever had a friend look you in the eye and say, "I love you; you mean so much to me" in a sincere, heartfelt way?

If so, you're among a small percentage of people who've heard these powerful words voiced by a friend. Why so rare? Because very few people are willing to experience the depth of relationship it takes to get there. Most people have *proximity* to others but little or no *intimacy* with them. Most personal interactions have little depth because the conversation stays on superficial topics like work, sports, weather, the kids, traffic, etc.

Our interactions are a mile wide and an inch deep.

A 2012 article in *Atlantic* magazine titled "Is Facebook Making Us Lonely?" suggests that social networking might actually be fostering isolation instead of curing it: "Within this world of instant and absolute communication, unbounded by limits of time or space, we suffer from unprecedented alienation." The author, Jennie Rothenberg Gritz, concludes, "We have never been more detached from one another, or lonelier."

In her book *Alone Together*, Sherry Turkle says, "Insecure in our relationships and anxious about intimacy, we look to technology for ways to be in relationships and protect ourselves from them at the same time. The ties we form through the internet are not the ties that bind, but the ties that preoccupy."

So if the internet's stilted chat is interfering with real friendships, and Facebook's narcissism is insulating us from authenticity, how do we go deeper? How does an ordinary friendship turn into an extraordinary loving relationship?

Step one is pretty tough: Both people need high enough levels of respect and trust to go beyond superficial, day-to-day interaction.

Step two is even tougher: One person needs to be *vulnerable*. Someone in the relationship has to risk opening the door to their inner world to share a struggle or problem they have kept secret. When that courageous person opens up (and is not ridiculed or judged by their friend), then there's potential for something special to happen. When that courageous person is understood and accepted despite their flaws, a bond is created; a powerful connection is made.

This kind of non-romantic, non-sexual affection can occur man-to-man, woman-to-woman, or man-to-woman. It's the rarest form of friendship, and it's characterized by consistency and longevity that are not affected by geographic distance or time spent apart.

Against all odds, a loving relationship can develop as a result of two friends being transparent about significant personal challenges they face. But there's another way – it can also occur when someone in the relationship makes an unprecedented, selfless *sacrifice* for the other.

The world's bestselling book has a great example of this…

○   ○   ○

In biblical times, the friendship between David (the shepherd boy) and Jonathan (the son of King Saul) was well known. You may recall David's ticket to fame – he whacked the pesky giant Goliath with a slingshot. After that, he went on to slay thousands of annoying Philistines. But instead of being happy about the lad's success, King Saul became insanely jealous. Eventually, Saul's temper got the best of him. He couldn't take hearing one more pop song about how great David was. To ensure that his son Jonathan would inherit the throne, he sought ways to thwart the nation's newest hero.

But Jonathan stood up for his friend. Whenever Saul would curse David, Jonathan defended him, reminding the demented king of all the good things his friend had done. After each outburst, Saul would seem to relent, but his ravings grew more intense until it became obvious he was determined to kill his young rival.

Jonathan risked his life daily to keep David safe. He was even willing to sacrifice his right to succeed his father to the throne of Israel. Jonathan loved David "as much as he loved himself" and pledged on his honor to protect him. Upon discovering King Saul's plans to murder the innocent teen, he left the palace to warn him.

When David and Jonathan secretly met to say a final goodbye, they "kissed each other and cried together, but David cried the most" (1 Samuel 20:41). Jonathan said to David, "Go in peace. We have promised by the Lord that we will be friends."

Later, after David learned of Jonathan's death in battle he said, "I cry for you, my brother Jonathan. I enjoyed your friendship so much. Your love to me was wonderful, better than the love of women" (2 Samuel 1:26).

David referred to Jonathan as his *brother* even though they didn't share a bloodline. They demonstrated kindness, loyalty and self-sacrifice. They cherished their time together and would have willingly died for each other. Theirs is a beautiful picture of love in friendship.

That level of friendship is available to us, too.

4. UNDERSTANDING

Comedy director Mel Brooks said, "As long as the world is turning and spinning, we're gonna be dizzy and we're gonna make mistakes." No wonder we screw up so much – the earth is rotating at 1,040 miles per hour! Whether it's because we're dizzy, devious or just plain dumb, we all make mistakes.

We all disappoint ourselves and others.

No matter how hard we try to respect, trust, and even love our friends, the fact remains that we are still human and will eventually disappoint each other. We will let our friends down. We don't mean to or want to, but we will. That's when we need to demonstrate *understanding* – the fourth pillar in the foundation of any solid relationship.

They say ignorance is bliss. But it's the deadly enemy of a lasting friendship. There inevitably comes a point in any relationship when a person needs to become a "student" of their friend – to find out what makes them tick, to truly understand them.

But before we start analyzing our friends, we need to realize that all relationships cycle through four distinct stages. People living the 7F Life tend to work through all the stages; most other folks stop short for various reasons. The four phases in a friendship are:

A. Romance. When you first meet, it seems like your new friend can do no wrong. It's as if you're wearing rose-colored glasses and all you see are your friend's positive attributes. During this "honeymoon" stage, they seem to say all the right things, do all the right things, and care about all the right things.

B. Reality. Love is blind, but eventually – given enough time – reality will set in. At this stage, the honeymoon is over, the "halo" is gone and the "warts" start to show. You discover that your friend is not perfect. He or she has traits that start to bother and irritate you, even to the point of anger.

C. Rejection. I call this the rude awakening. For some reason, there's a breach in the friendship. Communication is strained or nonexistent. You think to yourself, *If I never see that person again, it's fine by me.* This is the critical point in any relationship. It's either going to be severed and tossed aside, or get mended and become stronger. No doubt about it, the easiest (and most popular) thing to do is to split up and look for someone else who's "more compatible." Just remember, if you do take that route, you'll soon find yourself right back in the same old situation with yet another "disappointing" person.

D. Redemption. Fortunately, life doesn't have to be a string of failed relationships. You don't have to be endlessly searching for a perfect companion. The fourth stage, redemption, can occur. You can forgive and forget and grow beyond the faults and flaws that we all possess. Novelist E.W. Howes said, "Probably no man ever had a friend that he did not dislike a little." How true! All it takes is a little understanding – and it must occur if you want to experience the benefits of a deep and satisfying friendship.

○   ○   ○

If you're married, I hope your spouse is your best friend.

If he or she is not, they can be. These four "pillars" of friendship are also the foundation of a solid, happy marriage relationship. I agree with Fawn Weaver, "A happy marriage doesn't mean you have a perfect spouse or a perfect marriage. It simply means you've chosen to look beyond the imperfections in both."

That means we can stop trying to change our spouses and work on enjoying them as they are. Isn't it more fun to celebrate our differences than to squabble over them? Isn't it more healthy (and fun) to be an encourager instead of a critic?

Maybe success in marriage doesn't come from *finding* the right partner, but by *being* the right partner. If you've fallen short, don't beat yourself up. We've all blown it at one time or another. Robert Anderson says, "In every marriage more than a week old, there are grounds for divorce. The trick is to find, and continue to find, grounds for marriage." That's liberating. You can't go back in time and change your past behavior, but you can start investing in a better future. Here's how: I suggest you turn *off* the TV some night and turn *on* the vulnerability. Be brave and ask your husband or wife to rate how well you're doing in each of these areas – respect, trust, love, and understanding.

Ask questions like, "Do you feel that I respect, trust, and love you? What could I do or say that would better communicate my respect for you? My trust? My love? Do you feel like I live with you in an understanding way?" Make up your mind in advance not to repudiate or retaliate.

Don't roll your eyes. Don't smirk. Don't make excuses. Just listen to your spouse's response and thank them for their honesty. This is not the time to debate or argue. This is the time to gather information that can save your marriage or give it a good tune-up. Speaking of tune-ups, you might discover some "leaks and rattles" that you had no idea needed fixing. But better to address them now than to have a breakdown later.

Remember, problems seldom if ever go away on their own. They only get worse. So even though the answers might sting a little, encourage your spouse to be totally honest. Your humility and willingness to improve can do more for a marriage than a mountain of candy and flowers.

I got gaps; you got gaps; we fill each other's gaps.

Rocky Balboa, from the movie *Rocky*

The Five Perks of Friendship

Did you enjoy the TV show *Insomnia Café*?

Never heard of it?

You probably knew it better by the name *Friends*. NBC changed the name prior to its launch in 1994. Good move. After 235 episodes, the series finale aired in 2004 to an audience of 51.1 million American viewers.

The sitcom – nominated for 63 Emmy Awards – was based on the idea that when all else fails, having good friends can get you through life's ups and downs. The ensemble of six wisecracking friends looked to each other for love, laughter and most of all, unconditional support.

Even the show's chart-topping theme song underscored the value of having a friend who knows you well and always has your back. Performed by The Rembrandts, it defined a true-blue friend as someone "who knows what it's like to be me." And as half the country sang along, they promised: "I'll be there for you, 'cause you're there for me, too."

And at least for 30 primetime minutes a week, Rachel, Monica, Phoebe, Joey, Chandler, and Ross *were* there for each other – even (as the *Friends* theme goes) "when the rain starts to pour."

But that's not reality. That's a well-written script. In real life, most companions turn out to be fair-weather friends at best.

Here's what I mean: As a kid growing up, I was fortunate to have an in-ground swimming pool in our backyard. And every summer, my number of friends magically doubled! I was the center of attention. As the cool kids tried to gain access to our pool, I felt pretty popular. But during Michigan's cold winter, these same "friends" wouldn't even acknowledge my presence in the hallways at school.

Being around a loyal, longtime friend is like slipping on a comfortable pair of your favorite blue jeans – it just feels good. No pretense, no formalities, no games. It's easy and relaxed to be around them. Rain or shine (or snow), they'll be there for you.

Litmus test? You can't imagine life without them.

What are some characteristics of these true-blue friends? What perks do they bring to the table? Here's a spotter's guide to the real deal...

1. GOOD FRIENDS WALK IN WHEN EVERYONE ELSE WALKS OUT

Remember when I was being sued, back in the Fitness chapter?

On the day I was served my court papers, the bad news reached its pinnacle. I was feeling attacked, stressed out and totally alone. Then the doorbell rang again. My heart sank – *more legal mayhem?* But instead of a courier, it was four close friends on my doorstep! They spent the better part of that day with me. They didn't offer any brilliant advice or come up with a magic escape hatch. In fact, it wasn't what they *said* that brought me comfort. It was their physical presence that bolstered me. Truth is, they hardly spoke because there wasn't much to say. None of what was happening made sense. I knew they couldn't stop the downward spiral, but I gathered enormous encouragement from their visit.

True friendship is sitting together in silence and feeling like it was the best conversation you've ever had.

Anonymous

There's an old expression, "Silence is golden." To which I would add, "and rare." That's one of the interesting things about good friends – they can be comfortable with silence if the situation calls for it. They don't feel the need to fill the air with the sound of their voices. The Catholic theologian, Henri Nouwen, said "The friend who can be silent with us in a moment of despair or confusion, who can stay with us in an hour of grief and bereavement... that is a friend who cares."

Great friends are sensitive to emotional conditions, and will be whatever their friend needs them to be at any given moment. American novelist, Edward Howe, put it this way, "When a friend is in trouble, don't annoy him by asking is there anything you can do. Think up something appropriate and do it."

○   ○   ○

Remember the story of the Prodigal Son?

A rich dad had two sons. One stayed home and worked hard, the other took off for a wild life in the big city. While the foolish lad was flush with cash from his father's inheritance, people flocked to his side, eating and drinking and sucking up to him. For months, these new friends partied hard on his tab. But when the money ran out, they left him alone and starving. The Bible says Mr. Popularity was reduced to eating garbage meant for the pigs he was tending.

Can you relate?

We can quickly determine the quality of our friendships when hard times hit. True friends plunge into the fray with you while others seek safer ground. Oprah Winfrey puts it this way, "Lots of people want to ride with you in the limo, but what you want is someone who will take the bus with you when the limo breaks down."

Sometimes during a crisis, it feels like you're being pulled in opposite directions. But with the right friends in your corner, you can make it through anything. Here's why – true friends are like a rope woven out of three separate strands. The harder it's pulled on from each end, the stronger and tighter the weave becomes. Likewise, the tougher the situation, the closer and tighter true friends become to each other.

Do not protect yourself by a fence, but rather by your friends.

Czech Proverb

2. GOOD FRIENDS TELL IT LIKE IT IS

What advice would *you* give if you knew you were going to die soon?

Speaking to an auditorium packed with students, Professor Randy Pausch said, "If I only had three words of advice, they would be, 'Tell the truth.' If I got to say three more words, I'd add, 'All the time.'"

Randy's advice was all the more powerful because he was terminally ill. Facing pancreatic cancer, the popular Carnegie Mellon professor summed up his entire life's wisdom in the now famous "last lecture" given at the university in September 2007. His remarks went on to become a best-selling book, *The Last Lecture*, and have been viewed on YouTube by millions. It's enormously inspiring and well worth your time if you haven't seen it.

Why is telling (and hearing) the truth so important?

Because we all have blind spots.

Have you ever been driving along and decided to switch lanes? First, you check your mirrors. Then you look in every direction to make sure it's safe. Then you check your mirrors again just to be sure. But when you crank the steering wheel you suddenly hear a car horn blaring right next to you! You swerve back to avoid a crash.

You didn't see them.

It looked clear.

But they were in your blind spot.

Even with today's accident avoidance technology and rear-view cameras, the only way to be absolutely sure it's safe to make a move is to have your passenger use *their* vantage point to check for hidden dangers. Same is true in life. The only way to become fully aware of what's going on and avoid relational collisions is to have a "passenger" in life with you.

Over the years, I've had a few teeth-clenching near misses with cars obscured by the rear quarters of my own vehicle. But there's another kind of blind spot that's equally dangerous. These psychological blind spots are unconscious patterns of thinking, behaving, and speaking that can hurt other people – unintentionally and without our awareness. Unknown to us, our actions or words can negatively influence our relationships at work, at home, anywhere. These blind spots often show up when we're stressed out – or ironically, when we're working at the top of our game, in the area of our greatest strengths.

That's why they catch us off guard.

Have you ever met a married person who is totally shocked when their spouse files for divorce? Or a boss who is stunned when a valued employee announces they're quitting? Both the spouse and the boss thought everything was going just fine, but the other party had the exact opposite feeling. That's a ginormous blind spot. They didn't know what hit 'em because their destructive words or behaviors – so obvious to everyone except them – were hidden in their blind spots.

We all have them. And if you think you don't, it's even more likely that you do!

If you're not living in authentic relationships with people who know you well, you'll fumble through life unaware of things about yourself that others know to be true.

And sometimes the truth hurts.

Okay, make that *most* of the time.

Typically these truths are not flattering, and we would just as soon ignore them. But believe me, we're far better off knowing our blind spots so we can address them and keep them from becoming stumbling blocks.

○   ○   ○

I have a friend who's the kind of guy who looks you straight in the eye and tells you (not in a condescending or demeaning way) when he sees something out of kilter. For example, he noticed I was shutting out a mutual friend because of some issues I was having with him. My observant friend said, "You may not think so, but your frustration is showing. You're not being as cordial to Kevin as you usually are. You're not taking time to really listen to him."

He was right. I hadn't noticed my rudeness. I went straight to Kevin and apologized. Our relationship was mended and actually grew stronger. Why? Because an insightful friend was courageous enough to challenge me. He was willing to risk being rejected if I disagreed with his assessment. After this potentially awkward incident, I respected him even more for his candor.

That's the difference between fake friends and faithful friends.

Sycophants will tell you what you *want* to hear ("Emperor, your new outfit is stunning!"), not necessarily what you *need* to hear (Emperor, you are buck naked!"). They'll say nice things to you that are actually meant to benefit them. Faithful friends, on the other hand, tell it like it is – even if it makes people uncomfortable. If there's a problem, they'll point it out, hopefully with the right attitude. Proverbs 28:23 says, "Those who correct others will later be liked more than those who gave false praise."

I've experienced this to be true, in my own life and as I look at history. During his presidency, Abraham Lincoln experienced both the most ferocious criticism and the greatest adulation of any U.S. leader. Yet he never caved in to his critics or gave special favor to his flatterers:

> I desire to so conduct the affairs of this administration that if, at the end, when I come to lay down the reins of power, I have lost every other friend on earth, I shall at least have one friend left, and that friend shall be down inside of me. I am not bound to win, but I am bound to be true. I am not bound to succeed, but I am bound to live up to the light that I have.

Speaking over 140 years later, the ailing Professor Pausch agreed with Lincoln, "Get a feedback loop and listen to it ... just one great man who tells you what you need to hear. The hard part is the listening to it."

Although few of us enjoy critique, Pausch reminds us we need to listen: "When you are doing something badly and no one's bothering to tell you anymore, that's a very bad place to be. Your critics are the ones still telling you they love you and care."

The best mirror is an old friend.

George Herbert, English poet

3. GOOD FRIENDS TAKE OFF THE MASKS

In television and movies, masks are used to hide secret identities, conceal disfigurements, or strike fear in people's hearts. Characters like Batman, Zorro, and the Lone Ranger never leave home without their iconic mask. From the Phantom of the Opera to Darth Vader, disguises are a central theme of great literature and films.

But what about real life?

Who's wearing a mask at the office? Or Starbucks? Or at the PTA meeting? The answer is "just about everyone." Most of us are hiding all or part of our true selves to avoid being rejected by our friends (or bosses or lovers or coaches or clergy or whomever). We think, *If they ever saw the real me, the ugly me, they wouldn't like me anymore and I can't let that happen.*

So we work 24/7 to keep up a false front.

But if a relationship is going to grow and flourish, the masks have to come off. There's a point when a person has to risk dropping their guard and say, "This is who I am, this is what I'm struggling with, this is what I fear."

Research professor, Dr. Brene Brown, understands fear: "In order for connection to happen we have to allow ourselves to be seen. Courage, when it came into the English language, was from the Latin word meaning 'heart.' The original definition of courage was to tell the story of who you are with your whole heart. People who connect well have the courage to be imperfect."

There has to come a time in a relationship when there is no more posing, no more hiding, no more positioning to achieve a desired outcome.

Someone in the relationship has to step forward and be genuine.

I remember thinking as a kid, *Why doesn't Lois Lane recognize that Clark Kent is Superman? His disguise is just a pair of glasses!* Even as a young boy I could tell they both wanted desperately to know each other better. Way better. But unless you're a crime-fighting superhero, why wait for the other person? Take the lead. If you want to experience a deeper, more meaningful relationship, be the first to drop the disguise.

Could you get burned by coming clean? Sure. Could you be embarrassed by dropping your guard? Yup. Could you be taken advantage of by risking it all? Absolutely. But there's no movement toward a better friendship until someone peels off the mask and takes the risk of transparency.

In *Spiderman*, Peter Parker could pull his mask off any time he chose. It was easy, like changing his socks. But how do you drop *your* mask? Start by taking a peek around it! Share a little something (please, don't reveal your entire dark side all at once) that the person you're talking with doesn't know about you and may be surprised to learn. See if this opening gesture is reciprocated – see if your acquaintance peeks from behind their mask, too.

From there, the two of you can peel the onion at your own pace.

○   ○   ○

I can almost hear you asking: "How do I know if my acquaintance is *wearing* a mask?" One way is by checking your relationship gauges. If months (or years) go by and your understanding and knowledge of this person doesn't progress, odds are good that a mask is firmly in place.

But it's not always easy to spot. Masks can be tricky.

They're not ugly like Hannibal Lecter's in *Silence of the Lambs*, or scary like Jason's in *Friday the 13th*. Just the opposite. They're beautiful. They're captivating. The masks we put on are usually positive attributes like self-confidence (even if we're scared), humility (even if we're jealous), or happiness (even if we're angry). We can also hide behind activities that seem exemplary, like physical fitness, business success, or even doing good deeds.

Remember, a mask can be anything we think will make people like us or love us or accept us.

As kids we quickly learn to hide behind anything – false bravado, stiff upper lip, extreme niceness – that gets us the results we want. As adults we carry on the tradition. We need to shed whatever false pretenses – fashion, athleticism, obsession with appearance – that we are consumed with and stop portraying ourselves as something we're not.

Masks may attract positive attention temporarily, but they make it impossible to develop a long-term, authentic relationship. If we're faking it, the person who becomes our friend is attracted by someone we're really *not*, and it takes all of our energy to maintain the false persona they think is us!

It's wiser to be real with people from the onset and skip the make-believe. The energy it takes to conceal our identities keeps us from enjoying the 7F Life. As my pastor friend, Steve Norman, says, "How exhausting it is to stay a step ahead of our secrets."

What's the solution? Be honest, open and authentic.

Shakespeare said, "To thine own self be true." That means, be yourself. Don't be what you think others want you to be just to earn their love or fit in with the crowd. Stop pretending to be richer, smarter, or younger than you are. No false pretense – not even one that appears wholesome – can be a legitimate long-term source of your acceptance.

Without masks, you can experience deeper, more meaningful relationships. You can cultivate a more intimate bond. And best of all, you can relax. A relationship where "I can be me and you can be you" is priceless. When the masks come off in a friendship, each person feels the freedom to be who they are and explore directions they've dreamed about taking, without fear of rejection or judgment.

So take off your mask and let the chips fly. Let people see the real you. The ones that like what they see are the ones worth investing your time in.

Your friend is the man who knows all about you and still likes you.

Elbert Hubbard, American publisher

4. GOOD FRIENDS MAKE YOU A BETTER PERSON

My buddy Jeff traveled to India with a friend who has multiple sclerosis. His friend was still able to get around to some degree, but at a much slower pace than what's considered "normal." This was a challenge for Jeff because he's a high-energy guy who loves to be on the go – continually exploring, moving, negotiating, and so on. Obviously, on this trip he couldn't walk or work as fast as usual because he had to match his friend's protracted pace.

Jeff said at first this was frustrating, but after his internal RPMs slowed to match his external RPMs, something wonderful happened. His senses were sharpened and he started noticing things around him in a new way: Details in a temple doorway. Patterns in a silk robe. Shades of color in a market stall. He heard laughter and music and peacocks. He smelled incense and baking bread and exotic spices. By slowing down, he enjoyed the rare beauty of their surroundings and the incredible tableaux of faces streaming by. To this day, the sights and sounds are etched into his memory. But he would have missed it all if it hadn't been for his friend.

When we connect with friends and actively engage with them, they help us see our world – and ourselves – differently.

One of the greatest benefits of going away to college or overseas for work is the "melting pot" we're dropped into. When you rub shoulders with students or co-workers from different backgrounds, you grow by leaps and bounds. Making friends with people raised in other states, countries, or totally dissimilar cultures helps us see the world through an entirely new lens.

When we allow people with differing perspectives and politics to get close to us, we're often surprised at how one-dimensionally we may be viewing the world. And this awakening can be a two-way street. By making friends from outside our circle, we can expand each other's viewpoint, making us both aware of how skewed or narrow our thinking may be.

Every person is a new door to a different world.

From the movie *Six Degrees of Separation*

5. GOOD FRIENDS AGE WELL

If you went to high school any time after 1983 (or have a child who has), chances are you've heard the song, "Friends" by Michael W. Smith. He's sold over 15 million albums, but it's his signature song that's played at every grad party, prom and homecoming ceremony in the Western world. The nostalgic lyrics include zingers like, "A lifetime's not too long to live as friends" and the heart-tugging chorus, "Friends are friends forever."

Friends forever. It sounds good. It feels good. And it makes the angst of graduation bearable for young adults saying farewell to classmates. But is it really possible? Yes and no. Unlike the song, friendships in the real world have different reasons and seasons...

SOME FRIENDSHIPS ARE FLEETING.

Sometimes a person crosses our path and makes a significant impact in a very short time. We met Mitch and Ruth when we moved to Fort Lauderdale. They arrived there from Minnesota about the same time we moved down. My wife and Ruth worked together at a women's apparel store. Mitch was a first-year teacher like me. We were both athletic and liked to work out. We quickly became pals. The four of us got together whenever possible. We took trips to Disney World and other attractions. We always had a great time together.

It seemed like we'd always be friends.

But today, I have no idea where they are or what they're doing.

We never had a fight or a problem. We simply changed locations. We left Florida after one year to take a teaching position closer to home. Maybe the subconscious reason we became friends was to get through a turbulent year of great change – newly married, cross-country move, new job. Or maybe it was to learn and grow from their positive influence. But whatever the reason, it was mutually beneficial. We haven't talked since, but that doesn't minimize the importance of our brief friendship.

SOME FRIENDSHIPS ARE SEASONAL.

Bill was a friend I made during graduate school in Texas. We were both enrolled in a rigorous Master's program and met during the first semester in a language class. We hit it off and started meeting to wrestle through the complexities of Greek and Hebrew. We studied together and relaxed together. Bill's passion was carving ducks. His finished sculptures were amazing, detailed, precision works of art. He even helped me carve a fairly recognizable duck. I'm sure we both did better in class because of our time together; the intensity of our program seemed far less daunting thanks to our friendship.

After graduation he went back to Alabama and I stayed in Dallas. We haven't had a reason to talk since. But embracing that season of friendship during four years of laborious study was a great benefit for both of us.

SOME FRIENDSHIPS ARE FOREVER.

Someone said it takes a long time to grow an old friend. But sometimes you intuitively sense a friendship will be special right from the start. Something just clicks when you meet this special person. For some mysterious (non-romantic) reason, you grasp almost immediately that this is someone you'll want to know and grow with for the rest of your life. Eleanor Roosevelt once said, "Many people will walk in and out of your life, but only true friends will leave footprints in your heart." That's the kind of timeless friendship I'm talking about here. The kind that gets better with age, like a fine wine or a priceless violin. In fact it's probably the best thing about getting up in years. Writer Robert Brault jokes, "Say what you want about aging, it's still the only way to have old friends."

In his book *The Girls from Ames: The Story of Women and a 40-Year Friendship*, Jeffrey Zaslow chronicles the lives of eleven girls who grew up together in Ames, Iowa. Linked by 40 years of experiences and memories, these women demonstrated the power and lifelong benefits of friendship. When one of the "girls" was asked what she still had in common with the others she responded, "We root each other to the core of who we are, rather than what defines us as adults – by careers or spouses or kids. There's a young girl in each of us who is still full of life. When we're together, I try to remember that."

A similar project at Flinders University in Australia tracked 1,500 women as they aged. The study found that close friendships – even more so than close family ties – helped prolong women's lives. Those with the most friends lived 22 percent longer than those with the fewest friends.

Researcher Zaslow concurs with this discovery, "As we age, friendships can be crucial to our health and even our sanity. In fact, a host of scientific studies show that having a close group of friends helps people sleep better, improves their immune systems, and staves off dementia."

○   ○   ○

Here's a bombshell: *Men and women are different.*

Which is why us macho dudes have a much harder time sharing our emotions and being transparent with others than women do.

Women can seemingly open up to strangers at the drop of a hat – at the mall, at the salon, at the kid's soccer practice, wherever, whenever. But men typically build their friendships around *activities* (fishing, hunting, coaching a team, etc.) or connect while doing a *project* (restoring a classic car, rehabbing a house, raising funds, etc.). If you're a man looking for connection, find a group with interests similar to yours and enjoy building friendships as you pursue those activities. Guys especially enjoy doing and discussing things that require special skills (like golf or playing guitar) or knowledge (like fantasy football or picking stocks) and can most easily form a bond around careers, sports or hobbies.

With or without common interests, women seem to have an easier time building both casual and lifelong friendships. By the time women are in middle age, most have built the friendships that will last a lifetime. But even as they age, they never shut the door to making new friends like men tend to do. Women are more open to making fresh acquaintances and then allowing them to grow into deeper relationships – friends they can know and trust, friends who can become socially and emotionally significant.

Strangers are just friends waiting to happen.

Rod McKuen, poet

SOME FRIENDLY ADVICE

Despite gender differences, we are all designed to connect with others in meaningful friendships. This section contains some tips to move that essential but mysterious process along.

First of all, friendships should start with both parties on equal footing. Nobody should seem desperate. If one party is needy or clingy, the friendship will be short-lived. And kind of creepy. If you absolutely "need" a certain person to be your friend, it's not likely to last. It's better for a friendship to grow from an *invitation* than from a *need*.

When you have a mutual interest in each other, when you voluntarily welcome each other into your lives, there's a far better chance the relationship will grow.

Disclaimer: This advice will work for most people. But there are a few unlucky folks who have a gift for offending others. Like Mr. Magoo, they're oblivious to the havoc they leave behind them. They've perfected the art of disrupting potential friendships and then wonder why they're short on friends.

If you'd like to join their lonely ranks, here are a few (tongue in cheek) ways to hinder any budding friendship…

- When borrowing something, return it broken. Better yet, don't return it at all.
- Dominate all conversations. Talk only about yourself and how good you are at everything you do.

- When you promise to do something, don't do it. Say you forgot.
- Ask for things frequently and give nothing in return. Make it all about you.
- Don't ever share anything personal about yourself. Stick to superficial topics.
- If you're asked to keep something confidential, share it with others. Online if possible.
- Cut people off in the middle of their sentences and blurt out what you want to say.
- Act like you know absolutely everything. Exaggerate or fabricate when necessary.
- Demand that your friends be perfect. Bring up their mistakes – remind them over and over again of their blunders.

Some cause happiness wherever they go; others whenever they go.

Oscar Wilde, writer

Obviously I hope you'll try hard to do just the opposite and honor your friends. After all, having true friends is a privilege. The moment we start thinking we're *entitled* to someone's friendship – whether it's a work relationship, marriage partner, family member, or school buddy – we risk damaging it.

The harm comes when we start taking the other person for granted and making bad assumptions. For example, we might assume that we can perpetually take more than we give back, or that someone is obligated to like us simply because we have some circumstantial connection.

Too often we offer friends our "leftover" time, creativity, and energy – allowing them to be an afterthought rather than an integral part of our life. Willful or unintended neglect can strain any friendship to the breaking point. No wonder the poet Khalil Gibran warned, "Friendship is a sweet responsibility, not an opportunity."

Here are some ideas for building true and lasting friendships...

- Ask someone to tell their story, then really listen. Asking questions to expand or clarify will demonstrate your level of interest.
- Ensure that what's important to your friend becomes important to you.
- Give your friends the freedom to be who they are. Don't try to reshape them in your image. One of you is enough.
- Look for ways to do ordinary, daily activities with a potential friend. Ask them to join you on a shopping trip or fun errand.
- Have a teachable spirit. We're not always right about everything.
- Find common points of interest and enjoy them together.
- Do what you say you're going to do – on time, in full.
- Stay in touch. Long periods with no contact can cause a relationship to grow cold or dormant. When someone crosses your mind, contact them.
- Be vulnerable and appropriately transparent. Be willing to share something personal that reveals a side of you not currently known.
- Always keep in confidence what you have been asked to.
- Laugh together. Cry together. Travel together. Serve together.
- Don't brag about your accomplishments, let others praise you.
- Do recognize the accomplishments of others, either verbally or in writing.

Building meaningful and lasting friendships is not for the faint of heart. It involves risks. It requires patience. It may necessitate sacrifice. And it will take diligent effort to go below the surface. You don't just stumble into friendships. There's no friendship lottery to win. But the rewards are worth every ounce of energy it takes.

You don't make friends, you earn them.

Anonymous

The Five Steps to Building Friendships

Obviously, making friends is not a scientific formula with precise steps and ingredients that can be duplicated in a laboratory. However, while studying this subject, I did discover certain basic principles or "best practices" for building friendships. As you read them, think of people you know who do a good (or poor) job at each principle:

1. LISTEN

One of our most basic needs is to be *heard and understood*. When we listen to someone, we acknowledge their presence (no one likes to feel invisible or left out) and elevate their value. The human body gives us a clue about how much listening we should do compared with speaking – we have two ears but only one mouth. Follow this two-to-one ratio and do twice as much listening as talking. How else can we really understand the person we're trying to connect with?

If we flip that ratio (and do twice as much talking as listening), most people will tune us out. Even though it *looks* like they're listening, they're not. They're daydreaming or making a shopping list or planning an escape. Caution: Make sure you're not just listening with the intent of topping the other guy's story. If your friend says he's on a Jell-O diet after his tonsillectomy, avoid saying, "I was eating beef jerky and jalapenos two hours after my surgery." If we take that tack, we make our friends feel inferior, weak and defensive.

Not good ground for lasting friendships.

2. BE AWARE

Awareness is a high-level friendship building skill requiring tact and sensitivity. Sooner or later, we all have *unspoken* or *unrecognized* needs in our lives. Maybe we don't feel comfortable sharing them, or maybe we have a blind spot in that area. Keep an eye and an ear out to pick up on these.

Watch for nonverbal communication, body language and emotional signs of distress.

Example: Suppose a friend frequently voices frustration and anxiety about his work. Maybe you should suggest that your friend's skill set and passion are not in line with his work. Maybe you should suggest he consider a new career.

Or suppose a friend finds himself in a financial squeeze but is too embarrassed to talk about it. If you're "aware" and meet that need – anonymously or otherwise – you've honored your friendship and optimized the benefits of your relationship. When we're tuned in and responsive, we're able to support and surprise our friends.

3. FACILITATE

Figure out where your friend is heading and help them get there. Learn what they're trying to achieve and help clear the path. What resources can you share that would move your friend closer to their goal? What connections could you offer? What cause is your friend interested in that you could support? What need could you fill? Hint: It's likely we'll already know these things if we're doing a good job of listening and staying aware.

One day my friend Tom overheard my wife talking about diamond rings in a particular setting called "Forever." A few days later, he walked into my office with four stunning examples. I said, "Wow, these are gorgeous! Who are they for and what are they doing here?" He replied, "I heard Mary Ann talking to my wife about getting a new ring someday with this arrangement of stones. A buddy of mine owns a jewelry store. If you think Mary Ann would like one of these, I can get you a significant discount."

It just so happened that our twentieth wedding anniversary was coming up. I bought one and she wears it to this day.

Tom made me look like a hero because he was listening and because he shared a resource. Do you know someone who's running for office that you could assist? Could you open a door of opportunity for a friend selling a product? Can you recommend a mechanic to a co-worker who needs transmission work? When we enrich someone's life – even in small ways – we endear ourselves to them. The fabric of relationship is strengthened.

4. CULTIVATE AND COMMUNICATE

Cultivate a diverse group of friends. Having friends that all look alike, sound alike, and think alike isn't beneficial. It's the bland leading the bland.

Years ago I served on a board made up of diverse members. I got along with everyone there except a woman named Sheri. She and I just didn't click. We got off to a bad start. To be honest, I found her a bit abrasive. Her communication style was more direct and sharp-edged than I was comfortable with. We saw things differently. With time, though, I came to value and appreciate her approach and perspective. I realized that more often than not she saw things I didn't because of my biases. Our friendship grew and my respect for her kept increasing.

As a result, I became a more valuable board member.

It was a rocky road, but Sheri and I eventually grew closer because we kept the lines of communication open. Friendships cannot happen without constructive communication. In your conversations with others, keep these three criteria in mind. Before you say something, ask yourself:

Is it true?

Is it kind?

Is it necessary?

Let's say we're at a party, and a young lady I know walks in. I turn to you and say, "She demonstrates the stereotypical characteristics of a ditzy blond." That may be true but it certainly isn't kind. Or I could say, "Her father served time in prison." That may be true, but it isn't necessary. Or I could say, "She's the world's greatest financial expert." That's very kind but it surely isn't true.

Find something to say that hits *all three buttons* and you're on the way to making – and keeping – friends.

5. Be the Kind of Friend You Want to Have

Imagine having a friend who is loyal, protective, loving, helpful, and undemanding. Okay, that's a golden retriever. But wouldn't you love to have a *human* friend like that? We all would. Guess what? If you want to enjoy that kind of friendship, be that kind of friend to others first. Be proactive without being manipulative or obvious, and you'll both reap the benefits of having another quality friend in your lives.

The old adage says "opposites attract." But that's not true – or desirable. In his book, *The 21 Irrefutable Laws of Leadership*, John Maxwell says, "Who you attract is not determined by what you want. It's determined by who you are."

Work on becoming more like the kind of friend you wish to attract. Follow these five tips, get out there in the world, and you will never be short of friends.

The only way to have a friend is to be one.

Ralph Waldo Emerson, poet

Super Glue for the Soul

I once saw a sign outside a welder's shop: "We fix everything but a broken heart." That's funny, but how *do* you patch up a broken friendship?

Maybe you need to swallow your pride and go apologize. Whether or not it was your fault, be the one to start the healing. Especially if you're hitched. Ruth Bell Graham said, "A happy marriage is the union of two forgivers."

Maybe you need to take the initiative and go break the ice. Don't wait for a friend to come to you and admit they screwed up. Keeping anger or resentment bottled up will ruin your chance for a balanced 7F Life.

Perhaps you need to step up and "speak the truth in love" to someone who's on a bad trajectory. Sharing wisdom is like a splash of antiseptic. It hurts for a while, but you're stopping an infection that can only get worse.

Or it could be that silence is called for instead of offering advice.

Whatever the case, when a relationship is struggling, we need to ask ourselves some hard questions: "Should I devote more time and attention to this person? Do I have something my friend needs? Am I understanding enough? Patient enough? How can I be more supportive and encouraging?"

Warning: Someone in the relationship is going to have to sacrifice.

Bigger warning: It will most likely be you.

You may have to sacrifice your pride or your plans. You may have to sacrifice your position on an issue. You may have to give up your time or share your finances. You won't know what particular sacrifice is needed until you reach out and invite your friend into an open conversation.

And that can be scary.

Remember the TV show *Fear Factor*? That's kid's stuff compared to this. Most people would rather lie in a box of tarantulas than get real with another human being. Entering the darkness of a busted relationship to bring issues out into the light is daunting. That's why most of us let old friends just slip away.

Earlier we looked at the four stages of a relationship – romance, reality, rejection, and redemption. If you're courageous enough to have a hard conversation, you'll at least give your faltering friendship a chance to get back to that first stage, "romance."

From there, you just might restore the relationship. It may take considerable time and work, but you can usually mend it.

Be humble. Be brave. Be the one to take the initiative to work through problems. Step into the "tunnel of chaos." You'll benefit from it regardless of outcome. You'll become wiser and more mature. You'll grow in your understanding of yourself and your friend. While the redemption process may not be pleasant, there's much to gain.

After all, there was something in your previously-likeable friend that drew you to them in the first place.

Rediscover that something.

Whoever said friendship is easy has obviously never had a true friend.

Bronwyn Polson, Australian author

7F ACTION STEPS: FRIENDS

Women, are you feeling challenged by trying to meet that special friend? Try some of these ideas:

- Invite the moms that come to your child's birthday party over to your place for a wine and cheese tasting night.
- Form a group with a purpose, like a book club, cooking co-op, scrapbooking posse, investment club, board game night, etc. This will help prioritize your time for friendship building.
- Write a blog about your life. Others may leave comments about your posts. By responding, you may discover common interests and concerns that could lead to a face-to-face at the coffee shop.

Men, remember that building true friendships takes effort. Make a point of intentionally getting together with other men:

- Invite a few friends to join you on a hunting or fishing trip. The chance to walk and talk together in a laid-back atmosphere is sure to strengthen relationships.
- Plan a road trip with friends to watch your favorite team play an away game. Hang out for the weekend. Take in the sights, sounds and action. Eat wings, nachos and grinders. Enjoy the conversation, laugh out loud and mix with the locals.
- Join a group that's centered on your favorite hobby or activity. Even if you're terminally shy, jumping into a special interest group is the easiest (and most painless) way to make new friends.

A good friend is a connection to life – a tie to the past, a road to the future, the key to sanity in a totally insane world.

Lois Wyse, ad executive

7F FAMILY AND FRIENDS

As you've seen on the 7F diagram, Family and Friends have a ***Relational*** focus. People who develop healthy relationships have tremendous support in pursuing their personal and vocational goals. This network lifts us up when we're down, affirms us when we're on the right track, and corrects us when we're not. Family and Friends are an integral part of an abundant life. You limit yourself without them, and life is *certainly not as much fun!*

Next, we'll move on to the ***Vocational*** aspects of the 7F Life.

The Firm

When I worked at my job I made a living. When I worked on myself I made a fortune.

Jim Rohn, business philosopher

How dangerous is your job?

For those of us in the white-collar world, our list of occupational hazards is pretty brief. Paper cuts. Blackberry thumb. Maybe an occasional headache. Clearing a jammed copier or loading a stapler is about as high-risk as we get. And even if you work outside the office, you probably don't face death on a daily basis.

Unfortunately, that's not true for all wage earners.

Danger is a way of life for the Alaskan fishermen who risk life and limb in the job made famous on Discovery's *Deadliest Catch*. The show follows a few of the 100 or so crab boats that fish Alaska's treacherous Bering Sea. Because they work between October and January, winter storms and 90 mph winds are common. The resulting sea spray coats everything from crab traps to fishermen with ice. Beyond the obvious misery, there's a greater danger – the icy veneer adds tons of weight that can capsize the boats.

At my office, about the heaviest thing I lift is my laptop. But these guys hoist 800-pound steel cages overboard. That's some serious man code, my brother males. Did I mention the traps are smeared with herring meat? Rancid, putrid herring? Several hundred of these fragrant cages are lowered overboard while the skipper fights to keep the boat upright on waves topping 30 to 40 feet. When enough crabs crawl inside to get the chum, the traps are reeled up and the writhing catch of pincers and claws is unloaded and sorted by hand.

Tired of the 9 to 5? Average shifts on a crab boat last 18 hours, and in the Alaskan winter, that means a scant three hours of daylight. So add darkness and fatigue to the stress of operating hydraulic winches on an ice-covered deck that thinks it's a Tilt-A-Whirl. But a mangled arm is a minor inconvenience compared to being swept overboard by a rogue wave or caught up in coil lines and dragged to the bottom.

Do your co-workers complain about the weather? On the Bering Sea, temps can dip to seven below, and being wet makes it worse. Way worse. Cold water removes heat from the body 25 times faster than cold air. The salty sea is just above freezing, so if a fisherman falls in, he'll likely inhale while under water (the involuntary gasping reflex) and drown without coming back to the surface. If he's lucky enough to stay afloat, he'll be dead in two minutes anyway. That's how long it takes for hypothermia to chill his body's core to the fatal 80° threshold.

Pretty daunting. In fact, the fatality rate for crab fishermen is 90 times higher than the average U.S. worker. So why sign up for such a dangerous job?

Here's a hint: the answer starts with a big fat "M."

As in *money*.

Deck hands can cash out with as much as $50,000 to $60,000 each for a few weeks' work. The captain pulls in six figures for his share. And if the harvest is good, the ship's owner nets in the neighborhood of $450,000.

CHAPTER 7: THE FIRM

People might claim they work for any number of noble reasons, but 99 percent of the time it's strictly for the green stuff (how many Lotto winners continue working?). Since the very first shopkeeper traded a stone ax for a fur hat, people have relied on some form of monetary exchange to get by.

And that unbridled, primeval capitalism was my sole motivation for scanning the help wanted ads in 1978...

WELCOME TO THE MACHINE

It was the summer before my sophomore year of college, and I desperately needed to find a job. I was almost broke, and I needed to pay for food, tuition, and gas (a whopping 63 cents per gallon). Not to mention buying gifts for my lovely new girlfriend, Mary Ann. Now there's a motivator. One day over coffee, I saw an ad in the local newspaper: "Landscape Laborer Wanted, $9.00 per hour, full-time employment."

Nine bucks an hour? My pulse quickened. *Wow, I could stash some big cash in a hurry at that rate.* Back in the late Seventies, that was unheard of money for unskilled labor. I was a fit young lad; I worked out with weights, played sports and felt like I could handle anything this landscape company could throw at me. Besides, how difficult could it be pushing a lawn mower or raking leaves?

I applied immediately and to my delight I got the job.

My joy quickly turned to pain.

My first day on the job, I walked into the company yard with my new boss, Vince. A gruff man in his fifties, he looked like a prizefighter and had the personality of a prison guard. Without any chit-chat to break the ice, Vince led me to an intimidating tower of noisy, clanking machinery. The menacing rig had a huge conveyer belt that transported material about three stories up. From there it fell into what looked like a giant meat grinder. The rotating head had six-inch steel teeth, each spike about two inches in diameter. The jagged teeth were staggered in rows and spun around, pulverizing whatever came into contact with them. I had never seen or heard anything like this before, and the awful machine looked like something the Mafia would invent to get rid of guys with big gambling debts.

Vince motioned for me to climb up to a tiny platform situated above the moving conveyor belt.

At the low end of the device was a huge metal funnel. Dump trucks would back up to this receptacle and unload soil mixed with boulders, metal, glass, missing labor leaders, etc. This mixture would land on the conveyor belt and ride up to where I was standing, about 35 feet above the ground. My platform had a sturdy metal floor and a great view of the northern hemisphere but no guard rails. My job was to bend over, reach down, and grab unwanted debris off the belt so only dirt and clay were left to fall into the giant Mixmaster that would pulverize them into fine top soil.

If my arm got snagged or caught on something, I could lose my fingers or even a hand. But there was a worse scenario. If I lost my balance for even a second, I could fall in and be ground into hamburger.

As the machine sprung to life, I quickly realized why they were willing to pay such a high wage for grunt work – this was DANGEROUS. The conveyor belt moved rapidly below me, carrying a rough mix of soil and debris at a blurring speed. If I didn't yank out the nasty stuff in time it would fall into the grinder and jam the machine to a halt. The screeching result of a concrete chunk getting past me didn't make my ill-tempered boss happy. It meant "down time" for his employees, and the sight of workers standing around while the machine was being repaired enraged him. I was the cause of his lost revenue, and he used some colorful language to let me know it.

As a 21-year-old student athlete I didn't fear much. But this was back-breaking, life-threatening work. After three days I concluded, *I don't care how badly I need the money, this is crazy. I'm out of here.*

My job from hell reminds me of the classic *I Love Lucy* episode where Lucy and Ethel get jobs at a chocolate factory. The inept gals screw up one task after another until they're transferred to the wrapping department.

They're instructed that every piece of candy must be wrapped before it gets into the packing area or they will be fired. At first, the chocolates come down the conveyor belt at a reasonable clip and the duo does fine. But when their supervisor speeds up the belt, they start to panic. The girls struggle to keep up, but some candy slips by. To avoid getting fired, Lucy and Ethel start stuffing chocolates into their mouths, down their blouses, under their hats – anywhere they can find to keep candy from leaving the room unwrapped.

If it's been a while since you've watched this scene, you owe it to yourself to Google "I Love Lucy – Candy Factory." It's hilarious. But unlike this comedy sketch, there was nothing humorous about my stint on the conveyor belt.

I always wanted to be somebody, but now I see I should have been more specific.

Lily Tomlin, comedian

Still in need of income, I answered another landscaping ad. This help-wanted posting indicated more traditional outdoor activity and the pay was attractive. I applied and got the job. From day one I sensed a totally different work environment. It was a respected, family-owned business, with two generations running the company. When I arrived, owners and employees alike showed an interest in getting to know me and asked about my future aspirations.

Once again, the labor was strenuous – unloading truckloads of sod in the rain, for example – but this time I found the work to be interesting and even fun. Many days we'd load a truck with supplies and head out to the beautiful neighborhoods along Lakeshore Drive in Michigan's wealthy Grosse Pointe area. We would drive past Edsel & Eleanor Ford's historic estate en route to work at fabulous homes with manicured lawns and sculpted gardens. There I learned how to install brick pavers and prune ornamental trees. I learned which plants require acidic soil, which need direct sunlight, and which require shade. My bosses took time to teach me insider secrets like which groundcovers are best for color, which curtail weed growth, and much more.

As I reflected back on my two landscaping jobs, I thought, *what a contrast*. Both were in the same industry, but they couldn't have been more different. The second job involved people I enjoyed being around and work I found interesting. That summer, I discovered how much I enjoyed helping things grow and creating beautiful environments.

Obviously, I liked the second job more than the first. But the opposite might have been true for someone else. To a certain type of individual – the crab fisherman type – working on the conveyor belt might have been a thrill! Either landscape job could have provided a gratifying experience for somebody because *we're all wired differently*.

○ ○ ○

How about you? Is your work cutting it?

Do you view your job as a jail sentence or a joyride? Does it feel like the gates of hell or a stairway to heaven? Be honest: Do you find what you do energizing, satisfying, interesting and rewarding? Are you eager to get to work? Or does your spouse need a cattle prod to get you out the door?

I have a friend who sets his coffee pot timer to turn on fifteen minutes before his alarm clock goes off. That way, there's a tempting aroma of coffee in the air to motivate him to climb out of bed. Only his love for java can overpower his disdain for his job.

If that's you, it could be time for a career change.

It's estimated we will spend approximately 93,000 hours of our life at work. Doesn't it make sense to spend that time doing something we love? Somehow we *must* find work that is fulfilling and rewarding – for us and for others. To live an abundant 7F Life, we need a job where we gladly expend all that we are and all that we have on things that matter.

Take this Job and Shove it. (Or Love it.)

Has this ever happened to you?

You walk into a store with a question. The employee mumbles something and continues doing what he's doing (texting, homework, sports betting, whatever) without looking up. You persist until finally, with a sigh of annoyance, he begrudgingly turns around and points in the general direction of the product. Instead of buying what you came for, you leave the store, vowing to return when Hades freezes over.

This is a classic example of bad customer service, and it's repeated endlessly in modern America. Cable and utility companies are known offenders. A promise of "We'll be there sometime between nine and noon," is installer code for "We probably won't show up." And if they do come, they'll botch your order. When you call customer service (I use the term loosely), you'll talk to someone in Bangladesh, then ask for a supervisor who speaks English, then spend most of your adult life on hold. Crummy service is so common that many businesses have lost credibility with the public.

So are long waits, crabby clerks and broken promises all we can look forward to?

Nope. From Nordstrom to Costco, certain businesses – including Apple, Lexus, Hilton, Southwest, and Disney – have reputations for exceptional customer service, with employees who actually seem happy to cater to a customer's every need. Staff morale is high and turnover is low.

That such extreme disparity exists raises the question: "What spells the difference between, 'We have your money, now get lost' and 'Thanks for choosing us, please come back' out there in the trenches?"

Answer: Workers fall into one of three categories. Which one you bump into determines the quality of your interaction…

1. THE "HAVE-TO" WORKER

Some people take a particular job simply because they *have to*. Perhaps jobs in their field of expertise aren't hiring. Or maybe house payments or student loans or medical bills are piling up. So they take whatever job they can find just to get by.

Sometimes circumstances require this – plenty of college grads are delivering pizzas to make ends meet. But a "have-to" worker is seldom happy, and it shows. If they remain there long, they run the risk of becoming sour, easily agitated and no fun to be around.

When you're in a store and you feel like an employee is doing you a huge favor by assisting you, that's a "have-to" worker.

When you're in a restaurant and the waiter treats you like an unwelcome interruption, that's a "have-to" worker.

One group of diners recently experienced this at a national chain restaurant (nameless, so you won't boycott them). Midway through their meal, they saw a mouse dart out between two booths. They called their server over and described the furry patron. He nonchalantly replied, "That's cool" and walked away. When they complained to the manager, he scolded them, "All restaurants have mice whether you see them or not. There's nothing I can do about it."

(Dining tip: If someone says rodents are normal, hygiene may not be high on the establishment's list of priorities.)

From store cashiers to car rental clerks, beware of the "have-to" worker – they can be snippy, lippy or comatose.

2. THE "CAN-DO" WORKER

This group works at jobs they *can do* – but secretly hate doing. These "can-do" workers possess the intellectual capacity, physical strength and talent to do their jobs, but the work really doesn't interest, challenge or excite them.

Why do they sign up for a gig that's not their passion? The work may have offered good pay, robust benefits, convenient location, growth opportunities or job security, so they took it. It met their basic needs; it may have even offered a certain status in the community. But if these people are honest, they will admit their work doesn't really stir positive emotions within them – like my stockbroker friend who'd rather be a meteorologist.

Living in limbo, these people have little or no enthusiasm for their work. They exert no more energy than necessary. They tend to do only what's required and nothing more. The "can-do" worker can fly under the radar for quite some time, even years, without showing any outward signs of discontent. But it's in there, smoldering under the surface.

Money and security are big reasons people stay in jobs they're not excited about. But there's another reason. Many felt pressured by their parents or spouses to go into a certain field because of the prestige, power or perks it offered. There are lots of outwardly successful people who studied hard and became well-paid lawyers, doctors or accountants. But if you asked them privately, off the record, what they'd *really* like to be doing, they'd admit their real passion was to be a pilot or a musician or a chef, whatever.

Of course, there's nothing wrong with the legal, medical or financial professions, and there are folks in those jobs who deeply love their work. I'm just saying don't sit at a computer screen if your dream is to be a forest ranger. Don't crunch numbers in a six-by-six cube if your dream is to captain a charter boat. Don't drill teeth if you'd rather be drilling for oil!

If you're doing your job to please someone else, you are in the "can-do" camp and should consider making a change.

Warning: It takes an exceptional spouse to encourage their mate to take a risk and pursue a dream (especially if it pays less money).

Warning: It takes visionary parents to see their child's strengths and urge them to follow their star (especially if they don't fully understand their kid's choices).

Warning: It takes a courageous person to leave a guaranteed salary with pension and benefits and lots of vacation days and a designated parking spot to take a complete shot in the dark (especially if you're getting up in years). But regardless of your age or current level of success, I say *go for it*.

Gutsy folks who took the plunge include...

- Sylvester Stallone worked at a deli counter. Nobody would hire him as an actor so he wrote, directed and starred in his own movie. Written in just three days, *Rocky* became a franchise with five sequels. Yo, Adrian!

- Martha Stewart was a stockbroker until the recession of 1973. Then she started a food catering business. In ten years it was worth $1 million. Today she's a media mogul and a household name.

- Jerry Springer was mayor of Cincinnati until switching from politics to TV talk show fame. Okay, bad example.

- Colonel Sanders was a steamboat pilot, insurance salesman, farmer, and railroad fireman. He didn't start cooking chicken till he was 40, and didn't start franchising the secret recipe until he was 65.

- John Grisham exchanged the routine of practicing law for the freedom of writing novels. His second book, "The Firm," became a best seller and a hit movie. Also the title of this chapter. Nuff said?

3. THE "GET-TO" WORKER

I call the third group the *get-to* gang. When Sunday evening rolls around, they start thinking, *Yippee! I get to go to work tomorrow.* Monday is not blue for them. Wednesday is not hump day for them. In fact, for this lucky group, work doesn't feel like work. Somebody said, "Do what you love and you'll never work a day in your life." Even putting in overtime doesn't feel like a chore.

The "get-to" workers love what they do and the people they're doing it with. Their work is something they would do for free if they didn't have bills to pay. I have a friend who has never looked at his paycheck. He doesn't know what he's made in a year until he gets his earnings statement and does his taxes. He's the rare person who is not in it for the money but for the love of a job well done.

These "get-to" workers are surprised when they look at the company clock because they can't believe how fast the hours fly by.

I know. In what universe does *that* happen? But if it all sounds like a fairy tale, let me quickly add that "get-to" workers also experience frustration and disappointment at work. They have good days and bad days like the rest of us. But these zealots see challenges and failures as lessons learned and opportunities to get better at what they love doing.

Instead of living for the weekend, they bring contagious energy and creative ideas to improve their company's product or service. Instead of grumbling, they're grateful. Instead of shirking work, they look for ways to make a positive difference for co-workers and customers.

I can almost hear you saying, *I'd feel that way too if I was so-and-so working at such-and-such.* (Insert your dream occupation here.) My own personal fantasy is hosting *Jeopardy*. I mean how hard is that? He already knows the answers! And he makes millions! Seriously, it's not that the "get-to" workers got lucky and found the most exciting, rewarding, desirable jobs ever. It's more about the "good fit" they've found between their work environment and their individual strengths, personality and passions.

Maybe you doubt this level of job satisfaction is even possible. If so, it's likely you haven't yet found a place where the real you can be fully utilized and appreciated.

Let's close with a tough question: Does your job give you the opportunity to do what you love and excel at every day?

If not, don't give up hoping and don't let the status quo rule you. Keep growing, keep learning, and keep working toward your ideal job.

After all, Alex Trebek can't live forever.

Never get so busy making a living that you forget to make a life.

Anonymous

Your Blueprint for Success

Just as a contractor needs a set of detailed plans before beginning a project, we need to develop a personal blueprint before we launch into building a career. Your blueprint is unique to you – just like your fingerprints – and following it will help you find fulfilling and rewarding work. There are four components to your personal blueprint:

1. YOUR HEART'S DESIRE

Cinderella said a dream is a wish your heart makes.

Sit back and allow yourself to dream for a minute. If you could wave a magic wand and make it happen, what kind of job would you wish for? Go ahead, imagine it. If money wasn't an issue, if location wasn't an issue, if family wasn't an issue, what would you do and where would you do it?

What kind of work setting would make you pinch yourself to be sure you're not dreaming? What kind of job would make you wake up in the morning and think, *I can't believe I actually get paid to do this*?

Whatever that image is – butcher, baker, environmentally-friendly candlestick maker – it's probably your true heart's desire.

> *What we really want to do is what we are really meant to do. When we do what we are meant to do, money comes to us, doors open for us, we feel useful, and the work we do feels like play to us.*
>
> Julie Cameron, writer & artist

When I talk about your heart, I'm not describing your blood pump. I'm talking about the core of your being – your mind, will, and emotions – that makes you aspire to certain things and behave in certain ways.

I'm talking about the internal compass of our lives.

Here's how it works: When you see, hear, or experience certain things that touch your heart – things uniquely meaningful to you – your pulse quickens and your attention is riveted. Perhaps you're listening to a certain speaker when suddenly you find yourself sitting up, leaning in, focusing intently on every word. Your heart beats faster. Your spontaneous, reflex reaction inspires you to take action. The ideas you're hearing strike a chord within you, and suddenly you're dreaming up ways to get involved.

That's your heart's desire talking.

But who takes the time to listen?

Henry David Thoreau said, "Most men lead lives of quiet desperation and go to the grave with the song still in them."

Nothing is sadder than that. Yet so many of us walk around like disembodied spirits, not quite dead, but certainly not fully alive either. We've settled for lukewarm because we're not on fire about anything. The sameness of life and the drudgery of work have made us comfortably numb.

Is that you? Have you forgotten what fire in the gut feels like? Can you remember the last thing you were passionate about? Do you secretly doubt if *anything* on earth can stir you up anymore?

Here are three exercises to help you identify your heart's desire:

First, locate your hot buttons: Grab your favorite newspaper. As you read, begin circling the issues or causes you feel strongly about. Your blood pressure will rise when you read something you're passionate about. When you're sucked into a story, you're getting close to your heart's desire.

Ask yourself, "What topics get me fired up? What gets my motor running? What keeps me talking until the wee hours of the morning?"

Next, try this assessment: Imagine you're filming a documentary on yourself. Look back over the years. What issue or cause would you be most proud of for having made a difference in?

At the end of your life, what would make you feel really good about the way you used your time, talent and resources?

Finally, ask yourself this dangerous question: "What would I attempt if I knew I couldn't fail? What activity would I try? What cause would I be part of?"

Finding your heart's desire is the first component of your personal blueprint.

You can only become truly accomplished at something you love. Don't make money your goal. Instead, pursue the things you love doing, and then do them so well that people can't take their eyes off you.

Maya Angelou, American poet

---

2. YOUR UNIQUE ABILITIES

Is it really true that no two snowflakes are exactly alike?

Better yet, grasshopper, if two identical flakes *did* fall some winter's day, how would we know? Pardon my Zen, but since we can't possibly check them all, who can say for sure?

I can.

I'm going to stick my neck out and say that every snow crystal in the history of our planet has been unique.

Skeptical?

Consider this question: How many ways can you arrange 15 soup cans on a kitchen shelf? There are 15 choices for the first can, 14 for the second, 13 for the third, and so on. Multiply it out and there are over a trillion ways to arrange them! Now, let's say a snowflake has 100 molecular components (they actually have many more). The number of different ways those 100 separate features can occur is a 1 followed by 158 zeroes. That's more options than there are atoms in the entire universe.

So the chance of identical-twin snowflakes is pretty slim.

And because a human being is far more complex than a snowflake, I can guarantee that you are unique! There is *no one* on this planet exactly like you. No one possesses the unique blend of qualities that make up you. Which means no one has been given just an "average" ability. We each possess talents and gifts that are unique – talents that can be developed as a powerful force for good.

We're all born with certain innate talents and abilities. If you have siblings, you know that despite being from the same parents, your skills and interests are different than your brother's or sister's. Each of the 7 billion unique human beings alive today was born with a built-in knack or aptitude for certain activities.

And *not* for others.

For example, I'm not mechanically inclined. Okay, that's an understatement. When a warning light appears on my dashboard I don't reach for my toolbox, I reach for my wallet. I may humor myself by lifting the hood to stare at the engine for a few seconds, but I have absolutely no idea what I'm looking at. I might as well be peering at the insides of a spaceship – I have no clue what to do and no desire to do it.

In contrast, there are people who love getting under the hood of a car and fine-tuning it. My father-in-law pulled the engine out of his Mercury Marquis and dismantled it down to the last bolt. He rebuilt the worn parts and put it all back together. It ran like new and he enjoyed every minute of it. I guarantee that if I tried to rebuild an engine (even a lawn mower engine) I'd have a bushel basket of parts left over and a worthless hunk of metal.

Likewise, there are people who can turn five yards of fabric into a beautiful garment and those who can't sew on a button... people who can remodel a house and those who can't drive a nail... people who can cook a perfect soufflé and those who can't defrost a frozen – excuse me, my microwave's beeping.

People rarely succeed at anything unless they have fun doing it.

Dale Carnegie, writer & speaker

o   o   o

How do you *know* if you have a gift?

Sometimes it's obvious. Mozart started composing at age 4 and wrote his first opera at 11. By the time he turned 18, he'd written 33 symphonies. If you're a child prodigy or an American League MVP, the whole world pretty much knows you're special. But usually it's not quite so easy to identify a gift.

Fortunately, there are clues. A gifted pianist can sit down and elicit sublime beauty from a piano. Using the exact same instrument, I can only approximate a bad rendition of "Chopsticks." Same piano, different levels of talent. Whether it's music, athletics, academics or some other area, you probably have a gift when you are able to do something dramatically better than most people, and it just "comes naturally" to you.

Like Robert Redford hitting home runs in *The Natural*, operating in your area of giftedness is second nature to you – like breathing.

In fact, maybe you're not even aware you *have* a gift, because high achievements in a certain field have always come easily to you. Because you excel at something with little or no effort, you assume it must be easy for everyone. Believe me, it's not. In fact, that's another clue that you may be exceptionally gifted: You find people of normal, average skill to be incompetent or lazy. You unconsciously project onto them the expectation that their achievements be at the same level as your own gifted ability in this field. That is unrealistic.

Some of the abilities you possess may have been identified while you were growing up, like the young Mozart. Others may have surfaced and been honed later on in the classroom or on the playing field. Some gifts don't become obvious until even later, in college or in the corporate world. Even as a mature adult, you still may not be aware of all the skills you possess. Published studies suggest that the average person possesses 500 to 700 skills.

Here are three steps that could help you identify your abilities. I picked up these tips from Rick Warren of Saddleback Church in California:

Write your autobiography. What were your most satisfying and rewarding achievements in life? What excited you as a child or young adult? What significant challenges did you overcome?

Take inventory. What do you consider your natural talents to be? What skills have you acquired? What do you enjoy doing most and why? Reflect on how you'd like to spend your time if you didn't have pressure or obligations. What do you get the greatest satisfaction from doing? What kinds of problems do you enjoy solving? How have you spent your happiest moments?

Gather feedback. We tend to discount skills that come easiest to us, so unless someone points it out, we may not recognize it. For example, you may have a talent for active listening. So you automatically think that everyone else does, too. You may not realize you could use your gift as a counselor or therapist. A friend's perceptions of your strengths and abilities may be quite different from yours. What special abilities have they seen you exhibit? What do they think is holding you back?

Some skills are more marketable than others. Throwing a perfect pass like an NFL quarterback will earn you considerably more than carving a perfect duck like my friend from grad school. But that's not the point. The bottom line is this – pursue the gift that means the most to *you*, the one that gives *you* the most pleasure, the one *you* are able to do almost effortlessly.

Focus on the gift that feels as natural as breathing. Then work hard at refining and developing that ability to a high level. If you do, chances are that others will recognize your talent and value it (because they can't perform it at the same level) and will reward you monetarily for your services.

○   ○   ○

Highly successful people *discover* their unique abilities and then *delegate* everything else so they can focus on using their talents.

Why would Alan Mulally, president and CEO of Ford Motor Company, spend his time installing bumpers on Fusions? Why would he leave the boardroom to be on the assembly line? Manufacturing is important work, but it's not what Alan is uniquely qualified to do. He was hired to exercise his world-class leadership ability – and delegate everything else to competent, trusted people with different gifts.

Related to this is the question of studies. If you're trying to figure out what to major or minor in at college or grad school, follow this principle: Always play to your strengths. Don't pursue an area just to "round yourself out" even though you find that topic boring. I'm not a counselor, but my advice is *fuhgeddaboudit,* as they say in Brooklyn. You may be able to struggle through it, but it won't serve you well in the long run. You're better off putting time and energy into areas where you have a natural affinity and aptitude. Develop your skills in those areas and you'll likely be in high demand upon graduation.

Finding your unique God-given ability is the second component of your personal blueprint.

3. YOUR PERSONALITY

There are certain people I can't wait to see again. And there are others I would do anything within the law to avoid being around. (You know who you are.)

But seriously, why do some folks rub us the wrong way while others make us feel like hugging them every time they show up? The invisible, intangible force that repels us or attracts us is their *personality* – the sum total of all the behavioral and mental characteristics that are peculiar to a certain person.

What about you? Maybe your personality is so appealing that others are drawn to you like a magnet. Or maybe you fit Henny Youngman's description of a guy he knew, "You have a nice personality, but not for a human being."

Chances are you're somewhere between the two.

Man's main task in life is to give birth to himself, to become what he potentially is. The most important product of his effort is his own personality.

Erich Fromm, psychologist & philosopher

Personality is an area that I misunderstood for years – particularly as it relates to the workplace. What I discovered is that discontent and friction on the job are not always caused by differences in business philosophy or aptitude, but by a failure to understand the differing personality types.

Whether or not I'm able to get along with others and be successful at work largely depends on being aware of strengths, weaknesses and biases – my own and those of my co-workers. We're all different and that's a good thing. We need to value each other's uniqueness. But we can't value what we don't understand.

Fortunately, there are great resources to help us understand our own personalities and those of others. Three I use and recommend are:

A. The Meyers-Briggs Type Indicator. This has been an extremely valuable tool in my business as well as in my family. It's helped us gain deeper insight into how human beings are wired up – personal preferences, communication styles, and the type of environment a person is most comfortable in. It helps us understand if we have a preference for introversion or extroversion, sensing or intuition, thinking or feeling, judging or perceiving.

Because it identifies strengths and weaknesses, the Meyers-Briggs assessment can provide important career guidance, like what types of tasks we're most suited to perform and where we are naturally happiest. It can also assist in managing employees by helping us understand a person's natural capabilities and in what areas they'll most likely find success and satisfaction. It can provide valuable insight into managing interpersonal relationships by helping us recognize personality types and how to best communicate within each type.

B. The Kolbe A Index. This looks at human behavior from a different angle. It's another important tool that we've used extensively at work and home, and it identifies our instinctive strengths and natural talents. It has nothing to do with whether you're an introvert or extrovert or math whiz. It deals with a part of the mind that's different from your personality or intelligence. It deals with the "conative" part of the mind – our willful determination to act on natural impulses and instinct.

Let me explain. While the *cognitive* part of the mind has to do with thinking, and the *affective* part of the mind has to do with feeling, the *conative* part of the mind has to do with "doing."

Kolbe identifies four primary action modes, each involving a different approach to doing things. We all have natural strengths in each action mode that help us make better decisions. Knowing which type of doer we are is incredibly helpful, because it lets us know how *much* info and which *kind* of info we need in order to be comfortable in making a decision.

Knowing our "Kolbe type" tells us our best way of dealing with risk and uncertainty. It tells us what activities or situations to seek out (because they energize us) and which to avoid (because they produce stress and drain us). It lets us know how to get more done in less time when we focus on our primary mode of operation or instinct. It gives insight on how to maximize each workday in light of our instinctive preferences.

C. StrengthsFinder. Does hearing the words "report card" still make you nervous? In most homes, a student's grades are a source of tension. Doing poorly can lead to loss of privileges, cutback in allowance, etc. But maybe we have it all backwards. Suppose your child gets an "A" in art and a "D" in algebra. Which subject will get the most time and attention? At our house, my folks would have lectured me on my weakest subject, taken my car keys, and signed me up for a math tutor. And that kind of thinking carries into adult life. We spend far more time trying to fix our shortcomings than developing our strengths.

A useful assessment tool that can reverse that tendency is based on the bestselling book, *StrengthsFinder*. This Gallup publication uses an online assessment to reveal your top five talents. Why is this critical? According to author Tom Rath, "People have several times more potential for growth when they invest energy in developing their strengths than correcting their deficiencies." By finding where you have the greatest potential for success, you can concentrate on developing and applying your natural talents in that area. *StrengthsFinder 2.0* provides you with a personalized Strengths Insight Report, an Action-Planning Guide and a web-based Strengths Community.

See the Action Steps at the end of this chapter for access info on all three of these resources.

You cannot be anything you want to be – but you can be a lot more of who you already are.

Tom Rath, leading business thinker

HOW THE ANGELS KEEP THEIR WINGS

Using these various assessment tools is like taking an X-ray, allowing us to see inside ourselves and better understand what makes us tick. Another way to hone our skills – and one we should practice daily – is asking for feedback from our friends and colleagues.

Ken Blanchard is the management expert who coined the adage, "Feedback is the breakfast of champions." Sorry, Wheaties, but Ken is totally right. Leading without constructive feedback is like trying to shave without a mirror. Business author Jonathon Simpson agrees, "Self-confidence without self-awareness leads to self-destruction." Ouch.

It takes a little humility to ask others for critique, but it pays huge dividends. No matter how successful you may be, don't assume you're doing something right just because it's the way it's always been done.

Feedback is necessary whether you're just starting out in business or you're the "top gun" at what you do. Literally. The U.S. Navy Blue Angel pilots put on 70 airshows a year. Speeds hit 700 mph, and maneuvers range from collision course passes to inverted aerobatics. They are rightly considered the best pilots in the world. And who could argue? Applicants need a minimum of 1,250 tactical jet hours and must be carrier qualified. That means taking off via steam catapult (0-to-165 mph in 2 seconds) and landing a 45,000-pound fighter by snagging a cable on a pitching deck. In total darkness. Carrying explosives. And a $21 million price tag.

These elite flyers exemplify guts and skill, with lots of well-earned bragging rights. Surely *they* don't need feedback.

Or do they?

Since 1946, the Blue Angels have been seen by over 260 million spectators. Pilots and maneuvers have changed over the years, but one thing remains constant: After every single performance, the pilots hold a debriefing – a gloves-off meeting that lasts roughly twice as long as the actual flying time! Behind closed doors, they critique *everything* – from the way they marched to the planes to the smallest nuance of each loop, spin and formation. They readily admit their mistakes and set a plan in motion to make improvements before the next exhibition. And it's not only pilots who share their input, but Blue Angel staff members who sit in the crowd watching the show. The Blues are wide open to constructive feedback because they know it's the only way to improve.

Contrary to popular opinion, practice does *not* make perfect.

Practice only makes permanent whatever you do over and over again, good or bad. A gymnast can perform a somersault countless times, but if she's not listening to her coach and watching videos and talking to teammates, she'll never get any better at it. Unless she hears feedback from others, she'll never perfect the move.

From pilots to gymnasts to business leaders, it's the same formula for all of us: *Practice plus feedback equals progress.*

Each of us is hard-wired to have a primary mode of operation. We need to know what that is. We all have preferences that affect our flow of energy, how we take in information, how we prefer to make decisions and the basic lifestyle we prefer. Make every effort to discover what makes you thrive and act accordingly.

For all of us, the key is to pay close attention to which activities make us feel most alive and in love with life – and then try to spend as much time as possible engaged in those activities.

Nathaniel Branden, psychotherapist & writer

Learning your personality type is the third of four components in your personal blueprint.

4. YOUR EXPERIENCES

Einstein said the only source of knowledge is experience.

But we all know experience can be a tough teacher. By the time we reach adulthood, we've all experienced heartbreak, conflict, illness, loss and disappointment. Mexican singer Luis Miguel once said, "We all wish we could erase some dark times in our lives. But all of life's experiences, bad and good, make you who you are. Erasing any of life's experiences would be a great mistake."

I agree. The sum total of what we've seen and done makes up our experience, and it shapes us dramatically.

Nobody wants to endure pain or inconvenience. Nobody looks forward to setbacks or frustration.

We'd all prefer to live a life of uninterrupted bliss.

But sooner or later, it rains on everybody's parade. Fortunately, there is an upside. A lifetime of experiences can toughen us up and teach us valuable lessons. Think back on the hard knocks you've endured. Buried in most of them is a kernel of wisdom; things to do, things not to do. While painful at the moment, bad times can be most useful in helping us pick a vocation

– pointing us towards certain pursuits and away from others. They provide clues to the kind of work we would find most fulfilling and most miserable.

During my tweens and teens, I observed my father spending an inappropriate amount of time at work. I saw firsthand how overemphasis on acquiring money and things strained and severed relationships between parents, children and relatives. Even the neighbors suffered collateral damage. These experiences instilled a desire in me to help others avoid such costly and painful mistakes. They fueled me to prepare myself to work as a wealth coach.

Partly because of my experiences at home, my firm takes a broader, more comprehensive view of wealth management than most. When people hear the word "wealth" they usually think of the dollars and cents they have in their bank or brokerage accounts. While finances certainly comprise a significant part of your wealth, they're only one slice of the pie. We believe your overall status includes your wealth of relationships, wealth of knowledge, wealth of experiences, and so on.

What we strive to do is help our clients understand and capture their true and complete wealth, then leverage it toward the things that matter most to them. In fact, helping people experience abundant living (however they define it) is the mission of our firm. What I do as a wealth coach today is a good fit based on what I've experienced personally in the past.

How about you?

Have you examined your past experiences and considered how they might have prepared you for your work today? If not, take out a piece of paper. Think for a few minutes about those experiences that are most memorable – the biggies. Include positive and negative events, uplifting and discouraging circumstances.

To get started, jot down things like hirings and firings, awards and demerits, breakthroughs and setbacks. Include health complications, personal challenges, changes of location, parental involvement and home life. Stretch yourself. Try to write down 25 or more experiences.

Now look over your list and ask yourself these questions:

- What life lessons and insights did I learn from each experience?
- Is there a job out there where I can utilize my key learnings?
- Which of my experiences point to areas where I would like to make a difference if I had the opportunity?
- What would I want to help others avoid?
- Who can benefit most from what I've learned?

Life experience is the fourth and final component of your personal blueprint, along with heart's desire, unique abilities and personality type.

Putting Your Plan into Action

Now that we have the four "ingredients" for a maximized career, how do we utilize them to create (and sustain) enough motivation to reach our goals? We've learned about how we're wired up and we now have the right tools in place, but turning any plan into reality requires *action steps*. Without them you run out of willpower and your motivation motor stalls.

This next section reveals six positive, proactive steps to find or create your ideal job based on your own unique blueprint. Lots of self-help materials teach you to talk yourself into being happy; but that's backwards. I say, talk yourself into action and happiness will follow...

1. IMAGINE YOUR PLACE IN THIS WORLD

Disneyland opened in 1955. Since then, over 600 million people have visited the original park located on 160 acres outside of Los Angeles. Millions more have visited Disneyworld in Orlando. Disney Paris, Tokyo and Hong Kong are huge global attractions. From theme parks to motion pictures to cruise ships, the Disney brand is virtually a guarantee of success. Annual revenues for the Walt Disney Corporation are estimated at $35 billion.

But it wasn't always that way.

Despite his success as a groundbreaking cartoonist and animator, Walt Disney faced huge obstacles to developing his theme park. Despite winning Academy Awards (he eventually won 26 Oscars), he was denied loans over and over again by banks refusing to back his dream of building the world's best amusement park. For years, he relentlessly shared his imaginative ideas with potential backers until he finally obtained the $17 million he needed. Countless people have benefited because Disney doggedly pursued his dream to change the face of entertainment forever.

Of course, not every dream is achievable.

Your dream should line up with your personal blueprint – your heart's desire, your unique abilities, your personality, and your experiences. If it does, let yourself go. In the words of Disney himself, "If you can dream it, you can do it. Always remember that this whole thing was started with a dream and a mouse."

So give yourself permission. Don't resist it, don't resent it. Pursue it. There are no guarantees of success, but without the dream, the reality is not possible.

Imagination is more important than knowledge.

Albert Einstein, physicist & philosopher

2. FIND YOUR PLACE

What's your idea of the perfect job?

You know, the one you fantasize about when your mind drifts off at your current employment?

If you have a mental picture of that fantasy career, let me ask you an obvious question – *why aren't you doing it?*

Maybe you're afraid of failure, or feel trapped by circumstances. Perhaps in the past you heard someone say, "Only in your dreams, pal!" And that little put-down caused you to back off from your true feelings.

Don't let it.

There's an old saying: "Opportunity favors the prepared mind." By taking a personal inventory of how you are wired, you're much more likely to end up in an environment you'll love. Armed with a better understanding of who you are, you can confidently seek employment that suits you – or create employment for yourself.

Anthony Mullen was a highly motivated man who did just that.

Because of family circumstances, Mullen's dream of going to college and becoming a teacher was deferred. To make ends meet, he worked on an assembly line and later spent 20 years as a New York City police officer. While walking the beat, Mullen learned about life on the streets for troubled youth. As a cop, he worked with disadvantaged kids – generations growing up without the benefits of education and positive adult role models. In such a tough environment, these kids were destined for prison unless someone stepped in to intervene. Mullen vowed to be that role model and eventually completed his Master's degree in elementary education and special education.

When Mullen retired from the police force, he began to mentor and teach teens with severe behavioral and emotional problems. The former cop said, "I knew my biography and work experience would provide me the empathy and skills necessary to help such young people."

In 2009 he was named National Teacher of the Year. When he accepted the award, he said, "A teacher can receive no greater reward than the knowledge that he or she helped recover a lost student." Mullen says the keys to his drive as an educator are "passion, professionalism, and perseverance."

Anthony Mullen found his place in this world by taking into account his work experience, his heart's desire, his temperament, and his unique abilities. You can do the same. Whether your place in this world is serving in the public sector, a corporate environment, the entertainment industry or a nonprofit arena, seek the place that gives you the best opportunity to express what you're most passionate about, most prepared for, and most compelled to do.

You'll make an impact there *and* experience greater fulfillment.

3. EARN YOUR PLACE

How far a person goes in their career depends on many factors, but few are more important than character. A person's character is critical to the type of work opportunities they'll be given. Business trainer Zig Ziglar said, "If people like you they'll listen to you, but if they trust you, they'll do business with you."

A person who can be trusted is usually the one who is given additional responsibilities, positions of influence, and increased compensation.

But as desirable as trust is, it's a rare commodity. In our efforts to get wealth and power, compromises are made. Rules are bent. Promises are broken. And the result is a society that distrusts big business, organized religion – even our own government. A recent poll showed public trust in Congress was at an all-time low, with only 34 percent of Americans showing any measurable confidence in the legislative branch in Washington. The executive and judicial branches fared slightly better, but ranked their lowest since the 1970s.

Psychologist Alfred Adler, observed, "Men of genius are admired, men of wealth are envied, men of power are feared, but only men of character are trusted."

Sometimes it seems like we live in a world where crooks, liars and schemers profit while people who play by the rules get steamrolled. Do it anyway. Humorist Mark Twain said, "Always do right. This will gratify some and astonish the rest." So do something astonishing. Stand up for what's right even if you feel like you're the only one in your arena who is acting with integrity.

Warren Buffett, CEO of Berkshire Hathaway and one of the wealthiest men in the world, stated, "I look for three things when hiring people. The first is personal integrity. The second is intelligence, and the third is a high energy level. But if you don't have the first, the other two will kill you."

He's right on. Without the development of our character, intelligence and energy can lead us astray. And we'll drag others down with us! A person with mature character boosts their own job security because the employer knows that person can be trusted when no one is looking and will endure when the going gets tough.

Our character is what we do when we think nobody else is looking.

H. Jackson Brown, author

4. MAKE YOUR PLACE

Odds of winning a Powerball lottery are 1 in 176 million.

Sorry.

If you're going to have anything of real value in life, you're going to have to work for it. No one is going to hand it to you. The tooth fairy stopped putting money under your pillow a long time ago. And despite borrowing billions from China, the government fairy can't pay your allowance.

If you or someone you love confuses Uncle Sam with Uncle Santa, here's my two-step rehab program:

Step one – Rid yourself of any sense of entitlement. No one owes you any freebies. Not your parents, not your employer, not your government.

Step two – Rid yourself of any tendency to play the victim. You'll be at odds with most of society, but if you want to break free, you need to take personal responsibility for your own actions.

Author and Jesuit priest, Brennan Manning, observes, "If we continue to blame others for our weaknesses and failures, we refuse accountability for the present direction of our life."

Blaming is easy (and profitable).

Finger pointing is rampant (and profitable).

Victimhood has replaced self-respect and pulling yourself up by your bootstraps. Which is why we're drifting toward a society of cradle-to-grave social programs. Already, over 60 percent of our federal government spending is on entitlements. Gerald R. Ford had it correct when he warned, "A government big enough to give you everything you want is a government big enough to take from you everything you have."

Across Europe, governments are in deep recession. Some have crossed into depression. Why? They are collapsing under the exponentially increasing weight of state-run healthcare, pensions and benefits. Yet any attempt to curb spending on entitlements results in national strikes, violence and riots. The European Union's debt crisis should be an object lesson for the U.S. The bailouts of Greece, Spain and Portugal should be proof that socialism – or progressivism as it's called in America – doesn't work. But the shrill voices that call for us to curtail capitalism and copy this failed statist model grow louder each year.

Perhaps you've heard it asked, "Is it fair that some people in the U.S. are better off than others?"

That's a complex question, of course. But forget politics and labels for a minute and let me address it with an empowering statement by Ronald Reagan: "America isn't a land of equal *outcomes*, but a land of equal *opportunities*."

Granted, some have to overcome more difficult obstacles and barriers than others. Some are born into wealth, some into poverty. Some are born with healthy bodies, some with physical and mental challenges. Some will get better schools, better parents, better environments, better language skills, and so on. But negative circumstances *can* be overcome.

Because they refused to be victims of circumstance, groundbreakers like Pablo Picasso, Winston Churchill, Thomas Edison, Leonardo da Vinci and William Shakespeare all overcame obstacles and disabilities to shape and influence world history in incredible ways. So can you.

Every day, millions of Americans refuse to let their limitations define who they are and what they can achieve. So can you.

When you have a clear vision of what you want your life to be about and possess the persistent drive and passion each day to take a step in that direction, you will run, walk or drag yourself toward your goal.

Opportunity is missed by most people because it is dressed in overalls and looks like work.

Thomas A. Edison, inventor

Be inspired. Read stories about people who beat the odds. Emulate people like Ben Carson – an inner city kid from a broken home in Detroit who became a neurosurgeon at Johns Hopkins Hospital (and is world famous for separating conjoined twins). Be inspired by people like Stephen Hawking – a severely disabled victim of Lou Gehrig's disease who became the world's foremost theoretical physicist and cosmologist. Look up to people like Brenda Holmes – a penniless, homeless crack addict who became a highly respected educator.

When the "experts" say you can't make it, remember that the experts told a young German boy named Albert that he would "never amount to anything." Officials actually told Einstein's parents that their son's persistent questions destroyed class discipline, and that he would be better off to quit school altogether.

Fortunately for us, the daydreamer's parents didn't listen.

o   o   o

Looking for work? As an employer, I've interviewed plenty of job applicants over the years. First off, finding the right environment to showcase your talents is absolutely critical. Secondly, before you go in for an interview, do your homework. Know yourself (as described in this chapter), but also get to *know the field* you're interested in. Talk to people working in that industry; beg them for the pros and cons, the inside story. Ask them for any info that can set you apart from the herd of less-prepared applicants.

If possible, do an internship. It's a great way to dip your toe in the water to see if you like that type of work. Or wade in by taking a part-time position.

When you're ready to start applying for a permanent position, find out all you can about your potential employer. Go to their website. Study their mission and core values. Examine your own core values and work philosophy. Compare the two. Would you be a good fit? When you finally go in for an interview, share how you could help the organization accomplish its purpose through the use of your talents and strengths.

5. MAKE A PLACE FOR OTHERS

Some people just naturally love to lead.

To be a follower is against their grain. They have strong ideas about what should be done, who should do it, and how it should get done. They tend to be visionaries – always seeing opportunities where others see obstacles, always thinking about ways to improve and advance their services. These folks love to take educated risks. They don't lose any sleep about putting all their resources on the line to pursue their vision. In fact, they find it exhilarating. If they're pursuing their dream and they find that things aren't working, they don't throw in the towel and give up. They just reevaluate their situation.

That's exactly what the founder of FedEx did.

Just three weeks after launching his company, Fredrick W. Smith knew he didn't have the right business model in place. He shut everything down, made adjustments and reopened. The rest, as they say, is history. People with this sort of internal wiring understand and accept delayed gratification. They are willing to give up immediate payment for a bigger reward later. They understand that the greater the risk they take, the greater the potential reward.

I've had great fun turning quite a lot of different industries on their head and making sure those industries will never be the same again, because Virgin went in and took them on.

Richard Branson, entrepreneur

These people are typically referred to as entrepreneurs. Webster's dictionary defines entrepreneur as "one who organizes, manages, and assumes the risks of a business enterprise." They're the jet fuel that powers the private sector and they're responsible for creating jobs and opportunities wherever they go.

Often attributed to Revolutionary War hero Thomas Paine, the "Entrepreneur's Creed" is their call to action:

It is my right to be uncommon. I seek opportunity, not security. I prefer the challenges of life to the guaranteed existence, the thrill of fulfillment to the stale calm of utopia… I will not trade freedom for beneficence nor my dignity for a handout… It is my heritage to stand erect, proud and unafraid; to think and act for myself, to enjoy the benefits of my creations."

Entrepreneurs make their own paths.

Their mindset is "Let's give it a go and find out." Things don't need to be spelled out for them in advance. They are comfortable figuring it out along the way – learning what works and what doesn't as they go. Entrepreneurs prefer blank white boards to write on. They love the challenge of creating something from scratch, of designing structures from the ground up. The fact that something's never been done before does not dissuade them – on the contrary, it inspires them.

They learn from the work done by others in their field, but they innately believe their leadership and ideas can make a drastic improvement over the status quo – and they want to be the one to make it happen.

Even when the odds are overwhelmingly against them…

○　　○　　○

When Andra Rush was 23 years old she started a trucking company. All she had was a beat-up van, a pair of pickup trucks, and the conviction that she could make a difference. While pursuing her MBA, she interned at an airfreight company, where the speed of package pickups and deliveries drove profits.

After watching the process, Rush concluded, "I thought I could do it better." She borrowed some money from her parents and accepted every delivery job she could find. Within six months she had ten employees and clients like Ford and GM. Soon, Ford offered her the business of trucking parts between plants and suppliers. 26 years later, Andra was running a $400 million trucking business, Rush Trucking.

But there's more to the story.

Rush is a member of the Mohawk First Nation of Ontario, Canada, and employs many of her 1,000 workers from reservations near her operations. When she was a teenager, she visited an Ontario Native reserve and was struck by the poverty and hopelessness. Instead of pointing fingers or wringing her hands, she decided to take action.

Recalling her motivation – "I really wanted to make a difference" – she tells of joining forces with a Canadian parts maker to design and assemble automotive components. She then built plants near Indian reservations, creating life-changing opportunities where jobs had been nonexistent.

To some people, being an entrepreneur sounds exciting and impressive. But this path is *not* for everyone. I've seen people go down this road and discover it wasn't a good fit with their personal blueprint. Because of that, their choice ended up causing a lot of stress and heartache. If you think you might be an entrepreneur, but aren't sure, ask yourself these questions:

- As a youngster, did you organize kids in your neighborhood to form a club or start a team?
- When you were in college, did you lead any student organizations?
- Have you ever run for school board, town council or other public office and won?

- Have you started a new ministry or program at your church or synagogue?
- Have you devised new marketing initiatives for your company?
- Have you ever raised money to support a significant cause in your community?
- John Maxwell said "Everything rises or falls on leadership." Does the thought of being the point person – having everything rise or fall on your actions – excite you?

If you answered "yes" to most of these questions, you may have the internal wiring to start your own business or nonprofit organization.

How to begin? In short, *find a need and fill it.*

Taking into account your personal blueprint, identify a need that people have in an area that you're passionate about and matches your abilities. Then figure out a unique or better way to meet that need.

That's what a take-charge guy named Truett Cathy did.

Back in 1961, Truett was running a small diner in Atlanta, called the Dwarf Grill. One day, a local supplier asked him if he might want to buy pieces of chicken that were too small for other uses. Seeing the opportunity to acquire chicken at a good price, he hatched (sorry) a new idea – why not develop a chicken breast sandwich?

Truett Cathy remembered an old cooking technique his mother used for keeping chicken juicy, and found that by using newly-developed pressure cookers, he could cook the meat in just four minutes. He spent two more years experimenting with different spices and doing consumer testing until he found just the right blend.

In 1967, Truett opened his first Chick-fil-A restaurant. He turned his idea for a chicken breast sandwich into a chain of 1,500 stores that annually cook up $3 billion in sales. Hungry for profits like that? You can read about it in *How Did You Do It, Truett?*

○   ○   ○

The old business adage, "Find a need and fill it" is still valid. But there's a twist on it that can ring cash registers even faster – "Find a want and fill it."

Here's what I mean: A minivan fills a *need* – a sports car fills a *want*. Deodorant fills a *need* – perfume fills a *want*. Tap water fills a *need* – bottled water fills a *want*.

Okay, you get the point. But here's why it matters – folks will pay way more for wants than needs. Don't believe it? Bling H20 water sells for $40 a bottle, complete with hand-applied Swarovski crystals, frosted glass and a cork!

Whether you fill needs or wants, be true to who you are.

Trying to be somebody you're not in a career you hate will inevitably lead to frustration and fatigue. Then you'll be annoying to everyone. So do the world a favor – celebrate your unique qualities by putting them to good use in work you find meaningful, fulfilling and fitting.

The best way to predict the future is to invent it.

Alan Kay, computer scientist

6. MAKE IT MATTER FOR A LIFETIME

Do you dream of spending your golden years playing bingo?

Do you dream of senior discounts and 4:00 p.m. dinner specials?

I hope not! As you might guess, I'm not a big proponent of "shutting all systems down" during the latter years of life. Think about it. By the time you've reached 62 or 65 (or whatever you deem an appropriate age to transition out of your present work), you will have accumulated a wealth of experience, knowledge, connections, and maybe even finances. My point is this – you've never been more valuable. What you can provide for your family (adult children, grandchildren, etc.) and what you can offer to your city, state, or country is too valuable to be wasted by sitting around some retirement community.

Should you reduce your work load? Perhaps.

Should you decrease the number of hours you work? Maybe.

Should you reduce your stress and responsibilities? Probably.

But if you are doing something you love to do, why quit doing it altogether? Why stop contributing to a society that needs your skills and your maturity? I've talked with many retirees who flipped the switch from working a full schedule to doing absolutely nothing and they were beside themselves with boredom in a very short time.

One well-off client told me, "I've played every golf course from here to Timbuktu. There's only so much golf you can play. I have to find something meaningful to do with my time, energy and resources."

You've heard the saying "use it or lose it." That's true physically; it's also true mentally, so find a way to keep your mind active. Perhaps a consulting role (where you can control the amount of time you work and who you work with) would be a good fit for you. Or offer your skills to a nonprofit organization you care about. They would love to have you share your wisdom with their staff and the people they serve. Or get creative. Start that new venture you've always dreamed about doing "someday."

When an old man dies, it is a whole library which burns.

African proverb

If you're up in years, you now have the time and resources to do something significant. So make it happen. Instead of re-tire, you can re-fire.

Even if you're 90.

Richard McNeilly of Detroit was 90 years old and working full time at the Better Business Bureau when a newspaper reporter interviewed him. Asked what keeps him going, Richard replied that he loved "doing something that makes the city or the country a little better, rather than just having a job where you go to work and you get paid and that's it."

Richard had learned the importance of linking what he does with what's important. He was motivated, even at 90, to make a positive difference in the lives of others. He wanted his work to be connected to a mission, something more important than just paying the bills.

○　　○　　○

Connecting your work with your personal mission is powerful. As Donald Clifton and Paula Nelson write in *Soar with Your Strengths*, "Mission is at the heart of why you do what you do. Goals, on the other hand, are often steps to its achievement. Mission is altruistic. A goal does not necessarily have to better the world. Mission has an eternal quality – the benefits often extend far beyond a lifetime."

A mission motivates us, gives us conviction, and gives our work significance. That result is possible in any field. One good example of a heartfelt mission is found in this statement of purpose from Ringling Brothers Circus, written in 1899:

> Our mission is to create smiles, to loosen the chains that hold man captive to his duties and return him better fitted for his obligations… To give flight to the caged soul, to soften the wrinkles of sorrow, and make smiles of frowns. This is the mission of the circus, with its joy and power to make all men and women children again for at least one day.

Can you imagine how that made circus workers feel about their job? From the ringmaster in the spotlight to the guy who followed the elephants, it brought meaning and purpose to every task.

Joe Colavito of Wells University conducted a lengthy study of centenarians. One of the men he interviewed was particularly active. At age 95, this elderly man opened a general store inside the assisted living center where he resided. For more than a decade, he rose early to make popcorn and coffee – complementary for his customers. At age 106, he still worked six hours a day "because people need me."

Forget human growth hormone or fanciful diets. For this man, and for all the other centenarians Mr. Colavito interviewed, doing meaningful work was the fountain of youth.

Work and live to serve others, to leave the world a little better than you found it and garner for yourself as much peace of mind as you can. This is happiness.

David Sarnoff, radio & television pioneer

THE CABBIE'S SECRET WEAPON

Columnist and speaker Harvey Mackay tells a story about a cab driver he met with unusual passion and purpose for his work – and the unusual results it produced. The story's been told and retold in lots of variations, but the lesson is crystal clear…

Harvey was waiting in line for a cab at the airport. When one pulled up, the first thing he noticed was that the taxi was polished to a shine. Smartly dressed in a white shirt, black tie and pressed black slacks, the driver jumped out. His name was Wally, and he quickly opened the door for his passenger.

While loading his bags, Wally handed Harvey a small card with the driver's mission statement: "To get my customers to their destination in the quickest, safest and cheapest way possible in a friendly environment."

This blew Harvey away. Sitting down, he noticed the inside of the cab was also spotlessly clean. As Wally slid behind the wheel, he asked Harvey if he'd like a cup of coffee – he actually had regular and decaf onboard. Harvey said jokingly that he'd prefer a soft drink. Wally replied that he had a cooler filled with soda, water and juice. Wally offered Harvey a selection of reading material, and as they pulled away, he handed him another card, this one listing radio stations he could listen to. Wally asked if the temperature in the cab was comfortable. He then advised Harvey of the best route to his destination for that time of day. He also let him know that he'd be happy to tell Harvey about some of the sights or to leave him quietly to his thoughts.

That cab driver is a perfect example of the "get-to" type of worker we looked at earlier in this chapter. Harvey asked Wally if he had always served his customers this way. Wally replied, no, it had only been during the past two years. For five years before that, he had been like all the other griping, discontented cabbies. One day he decided to stop complaining and start differentiating himself from his competition by the quality of his service. "All the cabs were dirty, the drivers were unfriendly and the customers were unhappy. I decided to make some changes."

Harvey asked if people responded. Wally replied, "The first year, I doubled my income. This year, I'll probably quadruple it."

It doesn't matter what line of work you choose, as long as it's in sync with your heart's desire, unique abilities, personality and experience. If you work smart and hard and deliver extraordinary service, you will stand out like a beacon in the night and you will be handsomely rewarded – and have a great time doing it.

○   ○   ○

I've heard it said that the richest places on this planet are not the diamond mines of Africa or the oil fields of the Middle East. The richest places on earth are the cemeteries scattered across the globe. Why there? Because it's in those graves that men and women took with them all the songs that were never sung, books that were never written, ideas that were never acted upon, inventions that were never produced, and organizations that were never formed – but should have been.

Please don't smother your talents; don't put things off, don't wait for someone else to step up, we need you to express your gifts while you're above ground.

If you were to die today, what ideas and aspirations would die with you? Remember, no one else can sing your song, paint your self-portrait or write your life story.

From the moment you woke up this morning to the moment you fall asleep tonight, everything in between *was* and *is* your choice.

Make bold choices.

7F ACTION STEPS: THE FIRM

The four components of your personal blueprint are: Heart's Desire, Unique Ability, Personality Type, and Life Experiences. For each of these four areas, write a summary sentence that best describes you. You should see a picture emerge of what makes you tick. This will identify the type of work you will likely experience success and satisfaction in.

- Go to *www.personalitypage.com* to take the Meyers-Briggs Personality Assessment.
- Go to *www.warewithal.com* to take the Kolbe A Index Assessment.
- Go to *www.strengthsfinder.com* to take the StrengthsFinder Assessment.
- Read *Soar with Your Strengths* by Donald O. Clifton and Paula Nelson.
- If you're an entrepreneur or in charge of an organization, read *Traction: Get a Grip on Your Business* by Gino Wickman.

Our imagination is the only limit to what we can hope to have in the future.

Charles Kettering, engineer & inventor

CHAPTER 8

Finances

Money isn't the most important thing in life, but it's reasonably close to oxygen on the "gotta have it" scale.

Zig Ziglar, author & speaker

Today's real estate market is choked with bargain hunters hoping to cash in on short sales and foreclosures. But the urge to get a sweet deal isn't new. In the 1986 comedy *Money Pit*, actors Tom Hanks and Shelley Long play a couple who decide to buy a suburban New York mansion for next to nothing.

The seller admits the house needs a few repairs, but at just $200,000, it's a distress sale they can't pass up. Unfortunately, the moment Walter and Anna move into their dream home, it begins to fall apart. Literally. The staircase collapses, the wiring catches fire, the bathtub crashes through the floor, the chimney crumbles. Worst of all, a promised two-week renovation drags on for four excruciating months. Frustrated by delays and rising costs, the exasperated Walter dubs his disintegrating fixer-upper the "money pit."

Like Hollywood's Walter and Anna, real-life home buyer Amanda

Reece was shelling out some serious bucks to renovate her own 90-year-old money pit. But unlike the fictional characters, Reece wound up in the black, not the red.

How? By finding a fortune in cash stuffed inside the walls!

In May 2006, Reece hired contractor Bob Kitts to do some remodeling. While tearing out a section of plaster, Kitts made a weird discovery. Knee-deep in debris, he called Reece to say he'd found a hidden treasure in her master bath. Reece told reporters, "I opened up one of the envelopes, tore open the corner and there's a $50 bill. I thought I was going to pass out." The total stash was $182,000 in cash, most of it in rare bills dating from 1929, worth an estimated half-million dollars today. The money was apparently socked away by a wealthy business owner who built the home near Cleveland and died without a will or heirs. The mystery man carefully concealed a pair of metal lockboxes behind his medicine chest and never retrieved them.

The loot was hidden away during the Depression – a grim time of bank collapses and joblessness. People were nervous about the economy and distrusted Wall Street. Sound familiar? In today's uncertain economy, people have once again taken to hiding big piles of cash under their mattress.

Which, according to police, is the first place every burglar looks. Duh.

Okay, I can hear you asking, *So if my Posturepedic is too obvious, what's a safer spot to park a few Benjamins away from prying eyes?*

First off, I do think it's a good idea to keep a little cash in your home for emergencies – at least enough to buy a week's groceries and a night or two in a hotel. But because this money will not be earning interest (and is subject to being burned up, chewed up, forgotten or stolen), I would limit the amount.

Here's what experts call the best hiding places for that wad of dough:

In the freezer. Assets frozen? Put 'em in a Ziploc, stick the bag between two steaks and wrap it in aluminum foil. Or how about stashing your bling in a box of Pizza Rolls? (Federal agents found $90,000 in Louisiana congressman William Jefferson's freezer.)

Behind a picture frame. Smart thieves pull pictures away from the wall to see if money is taped to the back. But they won't take the time to look between the cardboard backing and the picture itself. Just don't sell that Thomas Kincade in a garage sale by mistake.

In the hollowed-out pages of a book. This feels positively Victorian. Using a hobby knife or box cutter, carve out a few dozen pages of your least favorite novel. Hide your cash inside the book and return it to the shelf. Don't try this with a Kindle.

Inside a kid's toy. Kid's rooms are notoriously messy, and toddlers aren't known for keeping large sums of money. Take Mr. Potato Head apart and hide your cash inside. Return the toy to the bottom of the pile in a closet or toy chest, and it should be safe.

Fake drain, fake heater vent. Build a false drain in the basement floor and you can hide a pipe full of money forever. We've all seen the vent cover ruse on way too many TV shows, but it actually works pretty well – remember, burglars are in a hurry.

Digging holes. Ask Captain Jack Sparrow – burying treasure is an age-old trick. The key is remembering where you put it and keeping it safe from the elements. Pirates recommend PVC piping. It keeps dirt and moisture away, and prevents critters from eating it.

Tampon box. I'm not joking here. Leave a little "product" in the box for realism, tape a wad of cash to the inside, and you can be sure a robber won't think to check it for your bankroll. Also thwarts that nosy husband or broke boyfriend.

Now that we know the best spots, what are the worst? The cops talk about a guy who hid money in the battery compartments of his electronic toys. Sounds smart. But during a break-in, thieves stole the devices – and got the cash as a bonus. Other silly hiding spots are dresser drawers, cookie jars and in the pockets of old clothing.

Some more really bad ideas:

Toilet tank. Except for the Tidy Bowl man, who thinks this will fool a burglar? Crooks hide guns in there, dealers hide dope in there, and mobsters keep their gambling vig in there. The only thing you should hide in your toilet tank is a brick to save water.

Prescription medicine bottles. Most thieves are looking for drugs in the first place. Double duh. The junkie's two big destinations are your bedside table and master bathroom. They'll empty your entire medicine cabinet into your favorite pillow case and sort it out later.

Diversion safes. These are common household products that look real, but have hidden compartments. Best-selling fakes include Ajax, Dr. Pepper, and Desenex Foot Spray. Downside? Thirty seconds on Google can alert crooks which products are faux faves.

Of course, if you're really worried, you can always fall back on bad housekeeping. Just make sure your house looks semi-robbed all the time. By the time thieves figure out which pile is concealing your treasure, they'll be too old to spend it anyway.

Above all, tell someone. Really. If you should die or lose your memory or be abducted by aliens, would anyone know where you hid your cash? Be smart. Write it in your will. Tell a close relative. Inform a true-blue trusted friend about your secret location.

Or just tell *me* where it is.

That's what my mother did.

Let me explain. My family was what you'd call upper middle class. I grew up in an affluent suburb, and there always seemed to be plenty of money around.

Unfortunately, there was an equal amount of tension and strife to go with it...

COLD HARD CASH

My father put himself under tremendous stress.

Especially at his business.

I know this firsthand because I worked for him from age 13 until I left for college. Dad worked long hours and was a great provider for our family. We enjoyed two beautiful homes and had most of the toys people equate with happiness – new cars in the drive, swimming pool in the backyard, powerboat, snowmobiles, ski equipment and all the trimmings. His work ethic afforded us many advantages, including private school education and world travel.

But it strained my parent's relationship.

Dad usually came home from work tired and edgy. Who wouldn't be after a 12-hour workday? With his workaholic zeal setting the stage, my parents would get into heated arguments over what seemed like the most trivial things – a crumb discovered on the carpet, a refrigerator door that wasn't closed quickly enough, a light left burning in an empty room. These arguments weren't the typical two-way sparring between couples, but one-sided rants, with my dad totally going off about the things that irritated him.

When mom couldn't take any more of the verbal warfare, she'd leave home for varying lengths of time. One of her escapes happened during the summer before I left for my first year of college in 1977. After being gone for two weeks, she returned home unannounced and asked me to do her "a favor."

I remember that day perfectly. It was a sunny afternoon and my dad was at work. I walked in the door and was pleasantly surprised to see my mother standing there. After catching up on family news, she made a startling request: "When I left, I took some money from a canister your father keeps in the freezer in the basement. Here, take this and replace the money I took so your dad doesn't find out. He keeps the cash in bundles of $1,000. Find out which bundle doesn't add up to $1,000, and replace whatever is needed. I don't want him to know about this – it would likely cause another argument."

I remember thinking, *That is a major understatement.*

Glancing out the window, she continued, "I'll stay upstairs to keep a watch out in case he comes home unexpectedly."

I was dumbfounded. "Sure."

I went downstairs to our finished basement and into the laundry room. Inside the freezer, I found a gray, cylindrical canister. It was a little larger than the canisters used at a bank drive-through, and covered in frost. I took the container and sat down on one of the barstools in our kitchen area. Slowly, I unscrewed the lid and emptied the contents onto the counter. I had never seen that much cash in my life. The bills made my fingers numb. I chuckled to myself, *So this is what they mean by "cold hard cash."*

I started counting out bundles of $1,000. Five, ten, fifteen, twenty, twenty-five – I quickly found myself staring at $30,000 dollars. I carefully counted each roll, trying to find the one that was short. At one point I remember sitting back in my chair, staring at all that cash, thinking, *This is ridiculous. They have all this money, all these wonderful things – and yet my parent's marriage keeps hemorrhaging.*

As I repacked the rolls of bills, I thought about my older sister. She had left home at 17 and never came back. She couldn't stomach the ranting and raving. We enjoyed a high standard of living, but was it really so "high" if it ripped our family apart? I thought, *Is it worth having $30,000 or $50,000 or even $100,000 in the freezer if your home cannot be a place of peace, joy and refuge?*

Sitting in that beautifully furnished basement, surrounded by the trappings of success, I would have preferred a harmonious family to any amount of cash.

○   ○   ○

I learned early on that money cannot ensure happiness. It can't produce solid relationships or sustain a romance. And it cannot guarantee that a person will lead a life of positive impact.

In 1963, a very young John Lennon sang, "Money can't buy everything is true. But what it can't buy, I can't use." How wrong he was. It's exactly what it *can't* buy that we need *most*. Money can buy the toys and trinkets that dazzle the eyes, like the expensive stuff my parents accumulated. But it can't buy the invisible things – the priceless things – like unconditional love, inner peace and lasting joy.

In 1968, an older and wiser Lennon penned this lyric: "I'd give you everything I got for a little peace of mind." Found in the Beatles' song "I'm So Tired," this insight puts fame and fortune in a whole different perspective.

I'm not down on money. There's nothing wrong with having a bundle of it. Even a super-sized bundle. I'm just saying keep it in perspective. What matters most is not what you have, but what has you.

Money is a tool. It will take you wherever you wish, but it will not replace you as the driver.

Ayn Rand, novelist

We've all heard the adage, "Money is the root of all evil." But that's actually a misquote. The Bible verse actually reads, "The love of money is a root of all kinds of evil." It's not the money itself that's evil; it's the *love of money* – and what people do to get it – that can be evil. It's why robbers rob and killers kill and swindlers swindle.

But the money itself is not to blame.

Money by itself is neither good nor evil. It's simply a tool, like a hammer or a violin or even a pistol. In the hands of a policeman, a gun protects our safety. In the hands of an outlaw, the same pistol wreaks havoc on society. Whether it's used for good or evil depends entirely on who is holding the gun – or the money.

Money can build up or tear down. You can send a kid to college with it or you can waste it on cocaine. You can invest it wisely or blow it on the ponies. Either way, money does not define "you" at the deepest level. But unless you determine its proper place, it may influence the way you think about yourself and others.

Now, may I ask a question that will step on some toes? It's one I have to ask myself on a regular basis: *Is your self-esteem closely connected to your net worth?*

If so, you're standing on shaky ground. During 2008, the Standard & Poor's 500 Index saw a 38 percent decline in value – that's a huge drop. When it happened, did you feel 38 percent worse about yourself? Did your self-image and self-worth decrease 38 percent? I hope not. Your value as a human being has nothing to do with your financial portfolio or your productive output.

> *The real measure of your wealth is how much you'd be worth if you lost all your money.*
>
> Scottish proverb

Back to money – what *is* it good for? It's the electricity that sparks innovation. It's the energy that puts people and products in motion. It's the key that opens doors to opportunities. Money can improve quality of life. It can provide for our personal needs and be shared with those less fortunate. It can even benefit future generations long after we are gone. Irish immigrant, Nelson Henderson, wrote, "The true meaning of life is to plant trees, under whose shade you do not expect to sit." Or in today's terms, "to invest money you don't expect to ever spend on yourself."

Money is our society's medium of exchange, and as such, requires management responsibility on our part. In wise and prudent hands it is a *blessing* – Bill Gates has donated $28 billion to charity. In reckless and foolish hands it is a *curse* – seven out of ten lottery winners go bankrupt.

The Four Pillars of Financial Success

Let's look at four areas we need to master if we're going to avoid the most common mistakes people make with finances. For some this will be remedial, for others it will be new information. I've boiled down a library of advice into a brief synopsis of time-tested principles for managing your money – making it, growing it, keeping it, and distributing it.

PILLAR NUMBER 1: MAKING IT

Legendary investor Warren Buffet is the third-richest man in the world, with a net worth of $44.4 billion. So he's not hurting for cash. But what about the rest of us? Fortunately, you don't have to be a professional money manager to have ample financial resources. Nor do you need a high IQ or connections with the movers and shakers of Wall Street. You don't even need good timing or good luck. And contrary to popular opinion, your financial strength is not dependent on a generous government program or robust economic times. You do, however, need to believe in (and act upon) certain axioms if you want to build your bank account and portfolio.

Here are three "non-financial" principals that affect your income:

A. THE GREATER THE RESPONSIBILITY, THE GREATER THE COMPENSATION.

A person leading a business or organization will be paid more than someone working at an ice cream parlor or dog kennel. Not that the person scooping butter pecan or grooming poodles is any less valuable as a human being, but as the level of our responsibility increases so does our compensation.

Take for instance a teacher who has responsibility over a classroom of 30 children versus a principal who is ultimately responsible for all 650 students, teachers, administrative staff, and maintenance crew at their school. Who's going to be paid more? The principal. You can argue whether that's right or not, but it's true nonetheless.

That hard truth brings up two questions: How much responsibility are you *willing* to take on? How much are you *able* to take on? We all have different capacities, different workloads that we are capable of. How you answer those questions will determine, to a certain degree, the amount of revenue you receive.

Some people prefer a job with Dolly Parton hours – you know, 9 to 5. When their shift is over, they "punch out" both physically and mentally. They don't think about their work when they're not on the job. When they leave, it's Miller Time. The ups and downs of the company that pays them is somebody else's concern. You have the freedom to choose a career like that. But realize that you've just constructed a financial ceiling over your head and capped your earning potential. In contrast, if you are willing to take on more responsibility than most, you open the door to the potential of greater financial reward. The choice is yours and mine. Again, how you decide does not affect your worth as a human being.

It does however affect your paycheck.

Money is better than poverty, if only for financial reasons.

Woody Allen, filmmaker

B. THE MORE PEOPLE YOU SERVE WELL, THE MORE YOU RECEIVE.

The more people you help get what they want or need in life, the more likely it is your finances will improve. The more focused you are on understanding what your customers or clients are looking for – and providing it – the more successful you will be. If you focus on serving *yourself*, you shrink. If you focus on serving *others*, you expand. Henry Ford put it this way, "A business absolutely devoted to service will have only one worry about profits – they will be embarrassingly large."

Integral to this principle is *access*. Is your product or service accessible only to people who live near your business? Or is it available worldwide? My wife and I visited a sleepy little town in northern Michigan called Hale, population 4,292. We walked into a modest looking house that had been converted into a business selling unique home decor. I asked the owner how business was going. Her response just about floored me: "Well, our international business is booming, particularly Europe and Japan."

I would have never guessed this housewife-turned-entrepreneur could run such a bustling business in a one-stoplight town. She explained how she travels to New York and Chicago to buy her pieces, then posts them on her website. Wow, did I underestimate this dynamo. It was a lesson worth learning – it doesn't matter where you're located, what business you're in, or what the local economy is doing, there are people somewhere on this planet interested in your services. We just need to make ourselves accessible to them. It's the law of high numbers. The more people who know about what you do, the more likely it is you will find buyers.

Also integral to this principal is *appeal.* Does the product or service you provide appeal to a narrow audience or a wide one? Take art for instance. Not everyone appreciates fine art. But let's assume you enjoy seeing how a Michelangelo or a Rembrandt used color, texture and chiaroscuro to create mystery and emotion in their paintings. Not many can appreciate it, and even fewer can afford it. On a percentage basis, the number of people who can spring for museum caliber art is infinitesimally small. On the other hand, bazillions of people crave pictures of sad-eyed clowns and kittens – and they're as affordable as a blue-light special.

The best modern day example of *access and appeal* is the personal computer. Virtually everybody wants the benefits of owning a device that can calculate, automate, organize, educate, and entertain. Way back in 2004, there were already 600 million users of Microsoft products. By 2011, Apple's world market share of personal computers was approximately 330 million users. And with the access and appeal of the iPhone and iPad, Apple zoomed even higher.

How much higher? In the first quarter of 2012, Apple's stock market value topped the $500 billion mark, another record high for what was already the world's most valuable company. Only five other companies in history have ever topped the half-trillion dollar valuation – Microsoft, ExxonMobil, Cisco, General Electric, and Intel. Apple's valuation is now higher than the gross domestic product of Poland, Belgium, Sweden, Saudi Arabia, or Taiwan.

This is not to say that mass-market technology is more important than limited edition fine art. In fact, many would make a case for the opposite. It's simply to point out that products and services have different audiences. Generally speaking, the greater the access and appeal, the greater the potential revenue stream.

Which is why velvet paintings of Elvis outsell Picassos.

C. THE MORE UNCOMMON YOUR KNOWLEDGE, THE GREATER YOUR COMPENSATION.

How can you acquire this "uncommon knowledge?"

Basically, you have two choices. You can acquire it with the help of others – by choosing a formal education (high school, college, grad school). Or you can acquire it on your own – by choosing a non-formal path (apprenticing, mentoring, trial and error). Whether you choose a fancy college or the school of hard knocks, *learners are leaders* and will more likely experience financial reward.

The more we know and understand, the more potential earning power we have as entrepreneurs, employers, employees or public servants.

Countless people have been wildly successful after completing a *formal* education. Their ranks include college grads like Ann Richards, governor of Texas (Baylor); Colin Powell, Chairman of the Joint Chiefs of Staff (NYC University); Andrea Jung, Chairman of Avon (Princeton); Donald Trump, billionaire (Wharton); Clarence Thomas, Supreme Court Justice (Yale); and Wes Craven, film director (Wheaton College).

On the other hand, equally successful leaders have taken a *non-formal* educational path to success. Movers and shakers who never sat in a college classroom (or dropped out) include Michael Dell, founder of Dell Computers; Andrew Carnegie, industrialist; Mary Kay Ash, founder of Mary Kay Cosmetics; Winston Churchill, British Prime Minister; Grover Cleveland, U.S. President; Richard DeVos, co-founder of Amway; Walt Disney, developer of Disneyland; and Thomas Edison, inventor extraordinaire.

Dropouts often make incredible contributions to society. Dropouts from Harvard *alone* include Mark Zuckerberg, founder of Facebook; Bill Gates, founder of Microsoft; Matt Damon, Oscar-winning actor; and

William Randolph Hearst, media mogul.

Those who took an unconventional path to the top of their field had an insatiable desire to explore and learn – just like those who took a more traditional path. However, their "classroom" was the garage they worked in while inventing their product, or the basement they toiled in while launching their business. They learned from their successes and – more often than not – their failures along the way. They learned from others in similar fields. They learned from every person who worked alongside them and increased their understanding each step of the way.

Clearly, success depends on possessing uncommon knowledge. And there are lots of ways to getting it. But essential to whatever road you take is the commitment to learn from all available sources and to never stop. There are exciting, financially rewarding opportunities awaiting those who keep their mind sharp, curious, and eager to explore.

Michigan's Oakland University has a unique motto: *Seguir virtute e canoscenza.* If your Italian's a little rusty, it means, "Seek virtue and knowledge." Found in Dante's *Inferno*, they are the final words of Ulysses' speech to his men, urging them to sail on in pursuit of knowledge and to experience the world at large.

To get context, ponder the three-line stanza the motto is taken from: "Consider your birth… you were not made to live like brutes… but to follow courage and knowledge (virtue, wisdom, and learning)."

Developing these lofty attributes will serve you well, regardless of your career path.

PILLAR NUMBER 2: GROWING IT

As I write this, there are 1,210 billionaires in the world. At the same time, there are 1.4 billion people who live on less than $1.25 per day. I'm guessing you're somewhere between the two extremes. There's a widening disparity between the richest and the poorest, but the one thing that most people have in common is the universal desire to *make more money*.

Let me state at the outset that money can be powerfully seductive. The more of it we have, the more of it we want. You may recall that when multimillionaire John D. Rockefeller was asked, "How much is enough?" he replied, "Just a little more."

In an upcoming section I'll share what I believe is the key to balancing money's downside (its alluring, enticing nature) with its upside (countless beneficial and humanitarian purposes).

Until then, let's follow the advice of English rockers Pink Floyd to "grab that cash with both hands and make a stash."

How?

When you boil it all down, there are really only two ways to produce income: By having *people* at work or having *money* at work.

Most of us are already working hard at our job. We give it our best. We give it our all. We work smart in the area of our passion. (At least, I'm assuming you are. If not, please re-read Chapter 7, "The Firm.")

Because you are working hard, it's imperative that your money *also* be working hard!

By "working hard" I don't mean taking on unreasonable amounts of risk. I mean having your money invested in instruments that are appropriate in light of the purposes you have for it. That means fixed income instruments such as bonds, Certificates of Deposit and Treasuries for *short-term* income needs, and equities, commodities and real estate for *long-term* growth and inflation protection.

Stuffing money in a coffee can and keeping it nearby may be comforting in the short run, but it's physically dangerous (it's exposed to fire and theft, for example) and financially risky (it won't keep up with cost of living increases and it deadens a potential growth resource).

At some point in life, your *work* will no longer be able to provide the lion's share of your income needs. Your *money* is going to have to take over and work for you.

To have something to invest, you need to follow two basic principles:

A. ACCUMULATING LITTLE BY LITTLE OVER TIME AMOUNTS TO MUCH

Avoid get-rich-quick schemes. If something sounds too good to be true, it probably is. Let me give examples from two decades...

In 1985, something crazy happened in the exotic car market. Republicans were in office, and investors were bullish. Speculators were buying spots on waiting lists for Ferraris that hadn't been built yet. They were willing to pay double the sticker price in hopes of finding someone who'd pay *triple* the sticker. Credit was loose, and people were buying and selling 12-cylinder Testarossas without ever seeing an actual car. Eventually, the world ran out of dummies, and the bubble burst. There were no "greater fools" left to repurchase the obscenely overpriced vehicles.

Something similar happened in 2004 during the Florida real estate boom. At its height, people were buying homes and condos that hadn't even been built yet and "flipping" them to other investors in hopes of making a quick profit. Some did realize sizable gains. But others, hearing about the easy money to be made, bought at the height of the market only to see prices decline, leaving them unable to find a buyer.

When the music stopped a lot of people were standing without chairs.

As prices plummeted, both sets of unwise investors ended up with a boatload of financial burdens. Some had to carry additional mortgages or backbreaking property taxes. Others were stuck with huge car loans they were upside down in. Some had to liquidate other assets at an inopportune time to cover their payments.

But don't get me wrong. It's not that it's impossible to make quick money. Sometimes it can be done. It's just much more difficult than people think and it happens less frequently than most imagine.

I tell my friends who visit Las Vegas, "Never bet more than you can afford to lose. Set a limit on your losses and go have fun." The smart ones quit before it starts to hurt, and walk away from the tables with a shrug. No harm done. Same for investors. If you're going to take a chance on a quick profit, only do so with true risk capital. By risk capital I mean expendable money – money you can afford to lose without jumping off a bridge. That way, if the investment goes belly up and all you're left with is a piece of paper, it's not going to wreck your world.

It's odd that I have to give this warning to grown-ups, but folks, there are far more scams and gimmicks out there than there are genuine good deals.

Did you get that?

It takes a lot of investigating, analysis, and intelligence to pull off a score. If you're going to pursue a "quick hit," stick to a field that you are very familiar with, one where you know the players and the history of the industry. Make sure it's one where you know *all* the potential risks and rewards.

Money will come when you are doing the right thing.

Michael Phillips, banker & author

○　　○　　○

If legit windfalls only come once in a blue moon, how *should* you accumulate assets? One method is to rob a bank. Not recommended. Another is to marry a millionaire. If it's too late for that, try this: Invest a fixed amount each month into diversified investments. Because of the normal fluctuations of the financial markets, this approach buys more shares when assets are lower priced and fewer when shares are at higher prices. This method is referred to as dollar cost averaging. The net result is that investors lower their overall price per share or unit.

A great vehicle to use in this regard is your organization's 401(k), 403(b) or 457 plan. If your employer offers a matching (typically up to six percent) contribution, please, *please* participate with at least the same six percent of your pay. If you don't, it's like turning your back on free money. If you do, it's like giving yourself a six percent raise!

Another method is to time the purchase of your investments. When employing this method, be a contrarian. When everyone else is buying, think about selling. When everyone else is selling, consider buying.

When the financial crisis hit the United States full force in late 2008, most investors headed for the hills and parked their money in stable, low-yielding instruments. That seemed like a prudent thing to do. But the savvy, experienced investors did their homework and identified investments selling at deep discounts. These contrarians bought when almost everyone else was shivering on the sidelines, waiting and hoping for a recovery before they got back into the markets. John Q. Public sat out until it felt safe to re-enter – and after prices had increased.

For example, an investment in emerging markets in February 2009 (when financial markets in the U.S. were still in steady decline) could have returned over 54 percent by the end of that year. Often I will ask my son Drew, "When's the best time to buy a snow blower?" He now knows to say, "In the middle of summer, Dad, when they're on sale."

You get the idea.

If you don't have the time, interest or expertise to do your own investing, hire a competent financial advisor and work together to accomplish your goals.

And please don't make the mistake of thinking you need to have a huge portfolio or a super high-paying job to make your money work for you. Years ago, there was a program on PBS called *The Wealthy Barber*. It was based on Dave Chilton's bestseller of the same name, first published in 1989. (Since then, Chilton's book has sold three million copies and led to a sequel in 2011.) It was based on a local barber sharing his financial wisdom with three average customers with very modest incomes. By following his advice, the three working stiffs went on to accumulate significant wealth.

My point? If someone can become wealthy on a barber's salary, the rest of us can, too!

In the book, Chilton's fictional barber shares nuggets with his young customers that we can all learn from. Consider his advice on investing…

- *"Wealth beyond your wildest dreams is possible if you follow the golden rule: Invest ten percent of all you make for long-term growth. If you follow that one simple guideline, someday you'll be a very rich man."*

- *"If your financial plan hinges on predicting the future, you're in trouble. Instead, stick to a balanced, diversified portfolio and focus on long term."*

- *"The only thing worse than a bad investment is a bad investment made with borrowed money."*

B. MULTIPLE REVENUE STREAMS ARE BETTER THAN ONE

Three things that are gone forever: cheap gas, polyester pants, and job security.

In today's unpredictable world, you can be well paid and highly regarded by your company one minute and unemployed the next. With jobs vaporizing all around us, it is prudent to have a number of revenue streams flowing into your bank and brokerage accounts. You never know when any one of those streams is going to dry up or start gushing.

Gone are the days when a person worked 30 years for the same company and could count on a healthy pension and benefits package to carry them during retirement. Today it's estimated that the average worker will experience four to six major career changes. More and more, our future financial position is determined by what *we* do for ourselves rather than expecting our *employers* to take care of our retirement needs.

Case in point: I have a client who worked for a company with $3 billion in annual revenues. Employed there for almost 30 years, he literally rose from the mailroom to the boardroom. As an officer of the corporation, he travelled the world from Melbourne to Shanghai on their behalf. Then without warning, he was called in for a meeting and fired. Terminated. Not a performance issue, just "restructuring."

The meeting lasted *less than ten minutes.*

So don't count on loyalty or honor or decorum to rule the day. Count on having multiple revenue streams to fall back on in case you get an unplanned phone call from your HR department.

When I refer to multiple revenue streams, I simply mean having money coming in to you from a variety of diversified sources, ideally not from within the same industry.

My friends, Tom and Bob, are good examples of this diversity. In one pursuit, they've developed raw land by putting in roads, drainage, and power in preparation for its sale. In another pursuit, they've purchased or built assisted living centers in strategic locations (anticipating increased demand as Baby Boomers age). In other fields, they've invented numerous automotive and technology products. They also own interests in businesses ranging from rock quarries to medical sanitation. If one of these income streams dries up, others will still be flowing.

This principle works on a smaller scale as well. Many of the unique abilities and talents we personally possess can be expressed in a variety of ways in a variety of settings. For example, let's say you teach writing at a community college. With the same skills, you could also submit articles to magazines in a field you're passionate about or write a book and get it published. If you create made-to-order curtains for a living, you could also offer tailoring services or design custom dresses and suits. It doesn't matter what your gifts or talents are, you can express them in numerous ways and have potential for generating different income streams.

Money never starts an idea. It is always the idea that starts the money.

Owen Laughlin, U.S. Senator

Big or small, multiple income streams are an important part of your money-making toolbox. But they aren't created without a plan or in a vacuum. Again, my friends Tom and Bob are a good example. They formed a group called G5. This "success team" consists of a small group of friends who possess a broad set of skills in a variety of industries including electronics, mechanics, software, and marketing. The G5 group meets weekly to discuss and explore new inventions, market trends, demographic shifts, product enhancements and more. As a result of their teamwork, they hold patents on numerous products and others are patent pending.

So go for it. Have some fun with the skills you possess!

PILLAR NUMBER 3: KEEPING IT

I'm not bragging, but in my line of work, I get to know lots of wealthy people. Many are self-made business owners, many are entrepreneurs. Many have clawed their way up by working multiple jobs. Others have taken financial risks to get there. Others just plain got lucky. But being around rich folks for most of my life has taught me one thing: It's easier to *make* money than to *keep* it. Whether their success came from rags-to-riches toil or from a windfall inheritance, a good chunk of my clients and friends tell me the same story – when it comes to money, it's easy-come, easy-go. A surprising percentage of big earners say it's like having holes in their pockets or purses. The big fat paychecks just can't keep up with the big fat bills.

And they have no idea how to fix the leak in their piggybanks.

To help you hang onto your hard-earned assets, here are six principles:

A. SPEND LESS THAN YOU MAKE

This first principle for keeping your money is almost insultingly obvious, but it's surprising how many struggle with this concept. It doesn't matter if you have a five, six, or seven-figure income – *you have to have more coming in than going out.*

I've seen people with high incomes have very little discretionary income to invest. And I've seen people with relatively small incomes devote a high percentage of their income to investing. The size of the income isn't the issue. The daily decisions on how you spend it are the key. Even though you *can* buy something doesn't mean you *should*. Having the means to purchase an item doesn't necessarily make it right.

This principle of not buying just because you can is often challenged by human emotions. Too often we get our *needs* confused with our *wants*. Do I really need those new clothes or new tools? Or do I simply want them? There's nothing wrong with wanting something as long as you can afford it and it doesn't sidetrack your overall investment strategy.

According to the International Council of Shopping Centers, there are 1,122,703 retail stores in America, and every one of them wants your money. Retailers are experts at playing on our emotions through the use of sales, discounts and promotions. Just remember, signs shouting "On Sale" or "Buy-One-Get-One-Free" don't necessarily translate to "good deal" or "appropriate purchase."

Have you heard about the "zone of seduction?" That's what author Martin Lindstrom calls areas in supermarkets scientifically designed to trigger subliminal buying responses. In his book, *Brandwashed: Tricks Companies Use to Manipulate Our Minds*, Lindstrom warns, "Next time you go grocery shopping, take a look at the signs, the floor and even the carts. Every element has been designed with an eye toward getting you to grab three cans of something that wasn't even on your list."

The odds of going to the store for a loaf of bread and coming out with only bread are three billion to one.

Erma Bombeck, columnist

I recall being at my in-laws when my wife and her mother returned from a shopping spree. My mother-in-law excitedly told my father-in-law, "Herman, you won't believe how much money we saved you!" To which he replied with a smile, "Right, you've saved me so much I now have to work overtime to pay for those savings!"

Too many of us operate on actress Bo Derek's dubious philosophy, "Whoever said money can't buy happiness simply didn't know where to go shopping."

SHOPAHOLICS ANONYMOUS

Earlier, we discussed Dave Chilton's success at helping ordinary folks get rich over time by judicious saving. In his new book, *The Wealthy Barber Returns*, Chilton's emphasis shifts from increasing our saving to cutting our spending: "It's not that we're bad savers, it's that we're fantastic spenders. Until we get spending under control, saving never takes place."

He's a big proponent of living with less. But does he walk the talk? A reporter asked if the wealthy author practices what he preaches. Chilton replied, "I live in a 1,300 square-foot house – including the basement. I don't even know what granite countertops look like."

Obviously, he knows what money can and cannot do. He's famous for saying that those who spend less than they make are happier: "This drive toward consumption and possessing as much as we possibly can is not translating into better happiness levels. In fact, it may be doing the opposite by creating tremendous stress."

Chilton says North Americans need to rediscover the virtues of spending less. He chides parents and young marrieds, "The most important personal finance advice is getting young kids to save, whether they're in their 20s or 30s, and to live within their means. Living within their means is what financial planning is all about; it's what we struggle most with."

That struggle was well portrayed in *Confessions of a Shopaholic*. In this romantic comedy, the film's charming heroine, Rebecca Bloomwood (Isla Fisher), is unable to live without the exhilaration that shopping brings. Her addiction progresses until her credit cards are declined by merchants and she is harassed by bill collectors. But despite the embarrassment, her compulsion to shop trumps all logical thinking. Grappling with her debilitating obsession, Rebecca even attends Shopaholics Anonymous meetings.

Seeing her apartment stuffed with piles and piles of unopened purchases may seem like a Hollywood exaggeration. But in real life, her story is repeated thousands of times over. Psychologists say about ten percent of Americans are full-fledged compulsive buyers. Some experts put the addiction on a par with alcoholism, eating disorders or even substance abuse – about one in three shopaholics say the act of buying gives them a "high" like a drug.

Compulsive spending can be triggered by a need to feel special or to combat loneliness or to compensate for low self-esteem. But shopping can't satisfy any of these needs long term, so the shopper's behavior escalates like a drug user who craves ever-increasing doses. And like other addicts, spenders experience emotional peaks and valleys – vacillating between endorphin-fueled highs and guilt-ridden lows.

When the buying binge is over, the shopper is regretful, depressed and guilty. In order to cope with these yucky feelings, the addicted person will often self-medicate with another purchase. The psychological term for this unhealthy cycle is *oniomania*, meaning "the compulsive desire to shop till you drop" (or at least till your credit score drops).

Kidding aside, the real-life consequences of oniomania can be anxiety, bankruptcy, ruined marriages, even suicide. Compulsive spenders are prone to shop in secret as their condition worsens. Debt builds, and shoppers start hiding their habit from family and friends.

I would bet that we've all experienced at least a twinge of this disorder and probably know somebody who is certifiable. And no wonder. The pressure to spend is at an all-time high. In his book, *The Good Life*, Jay McInerney says, "When people from Tennessee to Alaska are getting the same message from the culture, 'Live to spend, dress to kill, shop your way to happiness,' there will always be some who are without protection against being swallowed whole."

And I would add, it's the same message in Mexico or India or China, too. Global media, social networking and online shopping drive the spending mantra across borders. Called the first "postmodern addiction," consumerism is spreading to every land where there's even a whiff of a free market.

And we, dear shoppers, live in the epicenter…

KEEPING UP WITH THE JONESES

According to industry data, America has over 7 billion square feet of shopping center space – or about 23 square feet for every man, woman and child!

Simon Crompton, author of *All About Me,* warns this incessant drumbeat to "spend, spend, spend" is loudest in "capitalist societies dependent on consumption, where ubiquitous marketing and advertising promotes a culture where high material aspirations drive consumer booms by encouraging the creation of artificial needs."

Did you catch that – "artificial" needs?

The whole job of Madison Avenue advertisers can be summed up in five words: *Make consumers feel perpetually unsatisfied.*

Billions are spent to keep us discontented – to make us nervous about falling behind the coolness curve, worried that our apparel is dated, fretting that our smart phone is obsolete. Instead of enjoying things that are perfectly serviceable, we're concerned that our trusty vehicle (or running shoes or vacation spot or gas grill or whatever) no longer impresses the imaginary Joneses we've been trying to keep up with our whole lives.

Every week, we are bombarded by thousands of ads that link our deepest emotions and insecurities to products: *I'm not pretty enough. I'm not thin enough. I don't fit in. Nobody loves me. Nobody respects me.*

Every emotional impulse is exploited to make us buy something: *Fear of loneliness, fear of failure, hunger for relationships, craving for sex.* Marketing skillfully links our basic human needs with products – by promising us that "things" will deliver what they never can. Advertisers convince us to not only buy certain brands, but to seek our identity (and our fulfillment) through what we buy.

A million times a year, advertisers persuade us that the pathway to happiness and love and self-respect is the consumption of material things.

Why are we so susceptible?

Because we're copycats by nature.

The most basic learning method of any living being is *imitation*. That's how we learned to walk and talk and hold a pencil. It's how we learned to use a spoon and comb our hair. Same for adults. Only now we imitate what we see in movies and magazines and reality shows.

Which is why everyone is Gapped, Starbucked and Appled.

And why kids in Kenosha, Kazakhstan and Kenya all want Nike.

But here's the difference: In most of the world if you can't afford something you see on TV, you go without it. In America, if you can't afford something you see on TV, you simply *charge* it.

And that option is our biggest enemy…

○   ○   ○

It would be bad enough if Americans went to the local mall and spent 100 percent of their paycheck on boots and perfume and blenders. That would be awful. But in reality, many Americans are actually spending *more* than they earn.

We're in negative savings territory, taken captive by the twin monsters of easy credit and the I-deserve-it-now attitude of entitlement. Actor Will Smith puts it this way, "Too many people spend money they haven't earned to buy stuff they don't need to impress people they don't know."

Plunking down the plastic is literally ruining their lives.

Credit cards enable easy, unplanned spending way beyond our means. It's how a hotel maid can wear Versace. How a lawn boy can dress himself at Barney's. The result? American consumers owe $849.8 billion in credit card debt (Federal Reserve's 2012 Consumer Credit Report). On average, U.S. households owe $23,346 in consumer debt (not including mortgages), or about $2.78 trillion.

Someone stole all my credit cards, but I won't be reporting it. The thief spends less than my wife did.

Henny Youngman, comedian

Easy credit and impulse buying can rob us of a solvent future.

But there's another pitfall that robs our investment resources. It's called "retaliatory spending." It occurs when you don't need or even particularly want something, but by gosh, you're as angry as hell and you'll buy what you want! New York psychologist Bonnie Eaker Weil calls it "P.O.P." spending – "pissed-off purchases." Before publishing her book *Financial Infidelity,* Dr. Weil did a survey and estimated that "revenge spending" accounts for over $400 billion in purchases each year.

Such retaliatory purchases can result from a fight with your boss, spouse or best friend, according to Weil. One of her clients dropped $500 at Saks because her husband gave one of her beat-up old jackets to charity without asking her first.

Here are a couple of ways to avoid getting sidetracked from building your financial nest egg:

Pay yourself first. Before spending money on things you may not need, have a predetermined amount of money each month deposited directly into your various bank and brokerage accounts for *saving* (emergency and short-term needs) and *investing* (long-term growth).

Guard your eyes. What we see is what we get. Avoid tantalizing places you know will tempt you to spend money that could be used for more important purposes. Wandering through the mall (or marina or shoe store or Craig's List) is dangerous to your wealth.

By systemizing the use of your funds (i.e., using direct deposits) and censoring what you see, you can avoid the pitfalls of letting your emotions rule. Here are a couple more tips – a little closer to "meddling" than purely financial advice:

Count your blessings. Be thankful for what you have. Cultivating an attitude of gratitude is the antidote to being envious of others. When we stop comparing and competing, we step out of the rat race that drives us to out-spend, out-drive, out-dress and out-do.

Visualize a junkyard. Realize that everything you ever buy will end up in a landfill. Sooner or later, every car, boat, hot tub, and plasma TV goes in the junkyard. The crockpots and computers and couture we shop for so carefully will eventually be sold for pennies on the dollar at Salvation Army. So why accumulate?

o   o   o

Where is your money going? Where can you plug the leak?

Take a good hard look at your monthly expenses. Some of them are fixed (mortgage, car payment, insurance bills, etc.) and some are variable (food, entertainment, cell phone bill, clothing, etc.).

Variable expenses are usually where you can make immediate adjustments that could free up additional cash for investment. Cutting out $6 lattes, $60 manicures, and $600 club dues can free up cash overnight.

Fixed expenses are tougher to trim. You may be locked in for a while. It may take a little time to pay down, pay off, or refinance before you can improve your cash flow.

If you haven't done it for a while, keep track of all your expenditures for a month (see the Action Steps at the end of this chapter, and the 7F Life Cash Flow Tracker in the Appendix). The simple act of measuring something almost always leads to improvement. You cannot control something if you don't measure it. This expense analysis may be painful, fun, or somewhere in between. But like avoiding the dentist, putting it off will only create bigger, costlier problems down the road.

Budget: a mathematical confirmation of your suspicions.

A.A. Latimer, writer

B. Saying "Yes" to One Thing Means Saying "No" to Another

There's a beautiful hunting lodge not far from my home. I enjoy taking friends, clients and family members up there to hunt pheasant, partridge and quail. In addition to the great camaraderie, the wild game dinners following the outings are fabulous. But what I like best about this premier resort is the high priority they place on safety. Before heading out into the woods, the hunting guide gives every guest a lesson that ends with one very important instruction: "Remember, once you pull the trigger, it's forever."

In other words, once you release the bullet from the chamber, it's not coming back. Ever. So make sure you actually want to fire the weapon – and that you're fully prepared to live with the results.

The same is true with our spending decisions.

Once we say "Yes" to purchasing something, we instantaneously release the money in that direction. Assuming you don't return the item for a refund, that currency is gone forever, never again available for other uses. When we say "Yes" to buying (or renting) one thing, we automatically say "No" to many, many other things.

When we spend any amount of money, we say no to saving it. We say no to investing it. And we say no to sharing it. To avoid buyer's remorse now and a skimpy retirement later, give some serious thought *before* you pull the money trigger.

The art is not in making money, but in keeping it.

Anonymous

C. Minimize Your Taxes

Arthur Godfrey was immensely successful. No personality on early television enjoyed more acclaim or a higher salary. A man of the people, Godfrey once quipped, "I'm proud to pay taxes in the United States; the only thing is, I could be just as proud for half the money."

Ain't it the truth!

Federal income taxes as we know them today were created in 1913 with the adoption of the 16th Amendment to the U.S. Constitution. For American citizens, four words in that amendment have been especially costly. They gave Congress the power to tax incomes *"from whatever source derived."*

These sources now include earnings on investments as well as income from salaries and wages, lottery winnings, unemployment payments – even jury duty per diems! In a little less than a century, these four words have translated into $19 trillion flowing from individual U.S. taxpayers to the government coffers.

Have you gotten your money's worth?

If your answer is "No," fight back by reducing your taxes to the minimum legal amount. In the case of Gregory vs. Helvering, U.S. Court of Appeals Judge Learned Hand said:

> Anyone may arrange his affairs so that his taxes shall be as low as possible; he is not bound to choose that pattern which best pays the treasury. There is not even a patriotic duty to increase one's taxes. Over and over again the Courts have said that there is nothing sinister in so arranging affairs as to keep taxes as low as possible. Everyone does it, rich and poor alike and all do right, for nobody owes any public duty to pay more than the law demands.

Is that not beautiful music to your ears?

The good judge reminds us that it is our *right* to take full advantage of tax reduction regulations that are within the scope of the law.

If April is the only time you think about taxes, you're probably leaving money on the table. Those who plan ahead avoid paying unnecessary taxes. The only way to be confident that you're not overpaying is to review your tax situation throughout the year. Here are just a few of the areas to consider for tax planning:

Reduce your taxable income. Take advantage of employer-sponsored (and other) retirement plans that allow you to accumulate assets on a tax-favored basis. You contribute to these types of plans with pre-tax income, which lowers the amount of your income exposed to ordinary income tax each pay period.

Take advantage of lower capital gains tax rates. When it makes sense to do so, consider holding appreciated stock 12 months from its purchase date before selling to receive more favorable capital gains tax rates, as opposed to paying higher ordinary income tax rates (as is the case at the time of this writing). Be careful, though – I've seen people get so focused on the tax savings that they held on to an investment longer than was prudent. The result was losing significantly more on the devaluation of their investment than they gained from their tax savings.

Maximize credits and deductions. Credits are more valuable tax reduction tools than deductions because with tax credits the taxpayer is usually able to negate each taxable dollar with each eligible tax credit. Tax credits include the Hope and Lifetime Learning Credits, the adoption credit, the dependent care credit, etc. Check to see whether you are eligible for any of them. Significant tax deductions may include job-related moving expenses, medical insurance for the self-employed, student loan interest, self-employment taxes and alimony – whether you itemize your deductions or not.

Make charitable contributions. Making charitable donations, whether in the form of cash or merchandise (giving a seldom-used car to charity, for example) can reduce your tax liability. In addition, giving highly appreciated stock can be a great way to maximize both your gift to a charity and your deduction.

Refinance mortgage points. If you have refinanced your home within the past 12 months and paid points, you may be able to take the deduction for points paid.

The list of opportunities – and pitfalls – goes on and on. In 2006, the U.S. tax code was a whopping 6,845 page document. By 2010, it was a staggering 71,684 pages long.

Think you can understand all that?

Tax laws and regulations change regularly. The Internal Revenue Code is a voluminous and complex moving target. Hiring a competent Certified Public Accountant can be well worth the fees to ensure you're not paying more than you should.

By the way, a CPA's fee to prepare your tax return is deductible as well.

It ain't enough to get the breaks. You gotta know how to use 'em.

Huey P. Long, U.S. Senator

D. DON'T FALL IN LOVE WITH YOUR INVESTMENTS

It's okay to fall in love with a person.

It's not okay to fall in love with an investment.

People who have allowed a particular stock to dominate their portfolio are on hazardous ground. Just ask the stockholders of Enron (2001), Global Crossing (2002), WorldCom (2002), Delta Airlines (2005), Lehman Brothers Holdings (2008), Borders Group (2011), or Hostess Brands (2012). These were some of the largest, most respected companies in America, if not the world. Yet they went under like the Titanic and took their stockholders down with them.

Concentrated stock positions may occur as the result of an inheritance. Or they may build up over time because you purchased discount shares of the company you work at. Sometimes the accumulation occurs because you know an insider who tips you to "hang on a while longer; they're turning this sinking ship around." Or maybe you helped launch a business and have an emotional attachment to it.

Whatever the case, if you have an individual security that comprises more than ten percent of your portfolio, you should consider diversifying that asset or, at the very least, hedging it.

E. Use Hedging Strategies

When you make an investment, it is prudent to take measures to minimize the potential downside of that investment. That's where hedging strategies come in. Think of a hedging strategy as a safety rope connecting one mountain climber (investment A) to another climber (investment B), limiting the potential fall of each climber. Hedging strategies come in many forms. The goal is to reduce the risk of an existing investment.

The strategic use of cash in a portfolio is a hedging strategy. Cash is a position just as stocks, bonds, real estate and commodities are positions. Cash, such as money market funds, treasuries bills and short-term CDs, reduces the overall volatility in a portfolio.

Options can also be an effective hedging strategy. When you make an investment, one way to reduce adverse price movement in a security is to take an offsetting position in a related security, such as an option. Options are a right – but not an obligation – to buy (a "call" option) or sell (a "put" option) a specific amount of a given stock, commodity, currency, index or debt at a specific price during a specific period. As protection, options can guard against price fluctuations in the near term because they provide the right to acquire the underlying security at a fixed price for a limited time. Examples of hedging strategies include selling covered calls on stocks, buying puts on an index or on specific stocks, shorting the index, and selling naked calls (that sounds a lot sexier than it is). Entering stop-loss orders on existing positions is another hedge against downward price movement.

If your eyes just glazed over, I totally understand. I suggest you ask your investment advisor to walk through these strategies with you.

I'm not as concerned about the return on my money as I am with the return of my money.

Will Rogers, cowboy & entertainer

○   ○   ○

Question: What's the ugliest word in the dictionary?

If you answered "inflation," you win.

Basically, inflation is the rising cost of goods and services. It's usually caused by having more demand than supply in a market. Let's say there's a big ice storm where you live. Lines are down and power is out. If 20,000 shoppers are suddenly competing for 50 generators, a shrewd retailer will "inflate" the price of those units. What used to cost a week's wages now might cost a month's wages.

As inflation progresses, every dollar in your wallet is worth less.

Even small fluctuations in inflation can make a dent in your finances. But big fluctuations can destroy an entire economy. The classic example of "hyperinflation" occurred in Germany following World War I. In 1923, one U.S. dollar purchased *four trillion* Deutschmarks! Postage stamps cost *50 billion* DMs, and it literally took a full wheelbarrow's worth of currency to buy a single loaf of bread.

An inflation hedge is an asset that loses little value in periods of rising prices. A variety of instruments can be used as hedges, or protection, against inflation. For example, Treasury Inflation Protection Securities (TIPS), high-quality stocks, land, silver, wine, managed futures and other instruments can be used as hedges against inflation.

A nickel ain't worth a dime anymore.

Yogi Berra, New York Yankees manager

○   ○   ○

Another important way of protecting against financial loss is to use various insurance products. Unless you are independently wealthy, you may want to use disability income continuation policies to protect your most important asset – your ability to work and earn an income. Most of your life's plans are likely based on having an uninterrupted flow of income to fund your goals. A disability policy can provide replacement income (a percentage of current income) during periods of illness or injury. Financial instruments such as annuities may also be used as a helpful hedging tool, depending on how they are structured. Some can be obtained with guaranteed minimum income benefits, guaranteed withdrawal benefits, etc.

Please keep in mind that anytime you increase the certainty of a desired outcome and decrease risk, a cost is involved. If you are going to transfer the bulk of your investment risk to an insurance company, for example, you're going to pay for that protection. Understand up front what you are doing, what you are getting, and what you are going to pay for that safety.

For example, I talked to one person who recently purchased an index annuity. When I asked what it had cost him, he replied "There were no costs." There may not have been any traditional fees or sales charge, but the issuing company was getting paid somehow – how many companies do you know that are in business to provide free service? Sometimes it's as simple as limiting the amount of upside participation you have in the contract (they keep the difference). My point? Know what you are investing in, how it works, and why it makes sense in your particular situation.

Advice on hedging can be about as confusing as Yogi Berra's classic suggestion, "When you come to a fork in the road take it." Which is why it's best to consult a financial expert. Yogi could have been describing Wall Street when he uttered this famous malapropism: "You've got to be very careful if you don't know where you're going, because you might not get there."

F. DEATH AND TAXES

The IRS doesn't forget about us after we die.

In fact, they would love a "parting gift" from us.

Depending on the size of your estate – everything you own minus everything you owe – your heirs may have to pay an estate tax. When you die, and all the assets you've worked a lifetime to build (and have already paid tax on!) transfer to your loved ones, the IRS may assess one more tax – and it's a whopper.

If your estate is large enough and a tax payment is due (go to *www.irs.gov* for current estate tax tables), your heirs have a maximum of nine months to pay the tax after you pass away.

The estate tax can be one of the largest tax payments you (through your estate) ever make. One way your heirs can avoid having to liquidate cherished assets at an inappropriate time, and keep the assets that took you decades to accumulate in the family, is to purchase second-to-die or survivorship life insurance. This type of policy insures two lives (typically husband and wife) and pays out on the death of the second spouse. The policy provides tax-free money to the beneficiaries, typically the children of the deceased, to pay estate taxes.

Survivorship policies are a cost-effective way – typically costing pennies on the dollar – to pay your estate taxes.

G. CREDIT CARDS ARE A SUCKER DEAL

Ever have a dripping faucet keep you up at night?

Then you know how annoying a small, but persistent leak can be.

During the interrogation technique known as "Chinese water torture," a victim is restrained while cold water is slowly dripped onto their forehead. In itself, each drop is harmless, but the incessant drip-drip-drip eventually drives the victim insane.

At first, the unfortunate soul is confident: *I can handle this, no problem.* But after about two hours, each little drip starts to feel like a sledge hammer. Soon after that, the prisoner will start screaming for mercy.

That's how carrying credit card debt can feel. At first the debt is almost unnoticed. But if you don't make large enough payments to pay down the principal (over and above the required minimum payments), the debt forms a steadily increasing "drip" of interest payments that will begin to feel like torture. Those innocent-looking interest charges start out like a tiny drop but grow into a fire hose aimed right at your forehead.

Eliminate that drain on your income as soon as possible. Develop a game plan: Write "Cash is king" on your forehead with a marker. Then start by paying off the card with the highest interest rate. Make payments over and above the required minimum payments even if it hurts (it will). Whoop it up big time when you pay a card off. Then move on to the next card and do the same.

Don't allow credit card debt to undermine your ability to create wealth. If you are carrying credit card balances on a regular basis, *you are overspending*. Pure and simple. But at least you have company. Lots of company. According to the editors of industry site *CreditCards.com*, the average balance due per U.S. household with credit card debt is $15,956! And it's not just private consumers in trouble – credit cards are now the most common source of financing for America's small business owners.

Which means it's time to break out the scissors and cut up some cards. (It's going to take a lot of snipping – there are 610 million credit cards held by U.S. consumers.)

But there's another compelling reason to grab the shears.

We've all heard the old Dun & Bradstreet study (it's often quoted by gurus like Dave Ramsey) that claimed people spend about 15% more when using credit cards versus using cash. That statistic has come under fire recently for lack of documentation. But new studies at Carnegie Mellon, Stanford and MIT now back up D&B's premise.

George Loewenstein, professor of Economics and Psychology at Carnegie Mellon University, says "Credit cards effectively anesthetize the pain of paying. You swipe the card and it doesn't feel like you're giving anything up to make the purchase, unlike paying with cash where you have to hand over the bills."

Makes sense to me. Plastic doesn't feel like real money so it's easy to grab whatever strikes my fancy. With plastic I don't worry about the consequences until the VISA bill comes in the mail. Then I go into atrial fibrillation. So I agree with Loewnestein. When we're handing over a hard-earned $50 bill, our brain feels a pain-like reaction. Plastic numbs that experience. If you don't believe it consider this: McDonalds reportedly did a study that shows their average sale goes up from $4.50 to $7.00 when customers use plastic!

That's like saying "super-size me" to our personal debt.

The best way to avoid the credit card crunch is to eliminate your need to rely on credit. If you haven't already done so, build a discretionary "rainy day" account of liquid assets – consider an amount totaling three to six months living expenses. Whether it's a savings account or money market fund, have a slush fund you can draw on for unexpected expenses (car repairs, home repairs, etc.), travel opportunities and so forth. By having a discretionary account, in essence, you become your own bank, drawing funds interest free.

That's a good way to keep more of what you've worked hard for.

Some debts are fun when you are acquiring them, but none are fun when you set about retiring them.

Ogden Nash, poet

PILLAR NUMBER 4: DISTRIBUTING IT

Remember the old Office Depot theme song?

I still hum "Takin' Care of Business" when I'm on a roll at the office.

This working class anthem by Bachman Turner Overdrive was all about chasing the almighty dollar. Pop diva Donna Summer also described the pursuit of wealth in "She Works Hard for the Money." Notorious B.I.G. gangster-rapped his way to gold with "Mo Money." And the biggest hit from Pink Floyd's *Dark Side of the Moon* was, you guessed it, "Money."

Why all the fascination with cash?

Because it's what most of us think about most of the time.

Okay, that's a slight exaggeration. Sex is way up there, too. But consider how much time and effort we devote each day to making, saving, investing, and protecting money. It's enormous! It comprises the bulk of our non-sleeping hours. It controls most of our thoughts and activities. We're so busy scheming and dreaming about how we're going to get more, save more, borrow more and shelter more that we almost become a *slave* to it.

That's a strong term, but I don't use it lightly. For many people, there's a ball-and-chain relationship between them and their money, and there's only one surefire way to break the bondage – by giving it away.

Giving puts you back in control of your money.

By giving some of it away – even small amounts – we are in essence telling our money: "You don't control *me,* I control *you.* There's a new sheriff in town."

Why the tough talk?

Because if you don't master your possessions, they can end up mastering you.

Here's an example. Former First Lady of the Philippines, Imelda Marcos, reportedly owned 3,000 pair of designer shoes. The wife of dictator Ferdinand Marcos will forever be remembered for the mountains of pumps, flats, and high heels discovered in the presidential palace after a people's revolt overthrew her husband in 1986. While her constituents toiled in extreme poverty, she collected rooms of intricately beaded and gold-trimmed shoes (size 8½ if you're wondering) from Charles Jourdan, Gucci and Ferragamo. She also left behind 15 mink coats, 508 gowns, and over a thousand luxurious handbags.

Who owned who in *that* closet?

THE JOY OF GIVING. REALLY.

Giving a portion of our assets to a worthy cause can be liberating (it reminds us who's in charge) and inspiring (we see the positive effects we set in motion). It feels great to know that our lives are valuable – not just for what we're able to accumulate or produce, but for what we're able to distribute to people and causes we love.

In his book, *The Treasure Principle*, Randy Alcorn writes, "Giving infuses life with joy. It interjects an eternal dimension into even the most ordinary day. You couldn't pay me enough not to give."

Giving allows us to see the value of money apart from what it can do to meet our personal needs and wants. It moves us to see a hurting world that exists just outside our daily routine – a world of opportunities waiting for us to make an impact.

By using money exclusively for our own personal benefit, we release only a fraction of its power and potential. Unleashing it to help others generates a universe of possibilities. People can receive hope. Families can be restored. Communities can be transformed. Money is ready and waiting to do good.

It simply needs direction from us...

For years, people in Kansas City heard rumors about a "Secret Santa" who walked up to random strangers and handed them a $100 bill. This nameless benefactor approached hundreds of people in need, wished them a "Merry Christmas" and slipped away. Appearing each holiday season, he eventually handed out over a million bucks in cash to the poor and elderly.

The anonymous giver turned out to be Larry Stewart, a self-made success who earned a fortune in cable TV and phone service. Born into a welfare family, he was penniless and hungry when one night the owner of a diner gave him a $20 bill to buy a meal. He never forgot that act of kindness and vowed to do likewise. His identity as Secret Santa only became known when he became ill with cancer in 2006. Before dying, he wanted to share what he had learned about the immense joy and satisfaction that giving to others produced. He explained to curious media that the key to a happy life is to give away what we value. Stewart's legacy included building a YMCA, supporting the Salvation Army, and funding scholarships for the poor.

In his book, *Gross National Happiness*, Arthur Brooks reports, "People who give money to charity are 43 percent more likely than non-givers to say they are very happy." In addition, he notes that those who do not give are more likely to experience sadness and depression, "Those who don't give money were nearly twice as likely as givers to say they felt worthless."

Brooks explains the findings, "People are happier when they feel in control of their lives, and charity is one way to achieve a measure of control in a chaotic world." His advice for a life of purpose and meaning is basic: "So give – write a check, volunteer, donate the things you no longer need or even better, things you still do need."

One effective tool to this end is the use of a family trust. You can establish a trust in your name; for example, the "John and Joan Smith Family Trust," and it can receive contributions on a tax-favored basis. Trustees (either you or your adult children) have the responsibility of distributing a certain amount each year (six percent, for example). You can establish criteria for the use of the funds. The trustees have the benefit of sifting through the requests that come in over the course of a year to determine which causes or persons to support. This kind of giving is a great way to keep ourselves from becoming self-centered and to keep in touch with the needs of people around us.

Planned giving can help us make better spending decisions by helping us avoid spending on frivolous or unnecessary things so we can provide for others with genuine needs. Seeing the benefit our giving brings to people increases the importance and value of our daily work. We become aware that we are not only "working for the weekend" but for people and causes we value. Our job can take on new meaning and importance.

We make a living by what we get; we make a life by what we give.

Winston Churchill, statesman & author

Putting money in the hands of those with expertise and influence extends our reach exponentially. Giving to people with talents and skills different from our own multiplies the effectiveness of our resources. For example, suppose we donate money to a group that helps children born with cleft palates in developing countries. Even though we are not medical professionals ourselves, our gift empowers surgeons to perform life-changing miracles far beyond our personal ability.

There's great satisfaction at all levels of giving – from helping *globally* (like supporting the Red Cross or Compassion International) to helping *locally* (like fixing a broken appliance for the single mom next door). If you're a parent, you can help your kids set up a lemonade stand and give the proceeds to the poor. If you're an employer, you can help your staff contribute to a worthy cause as a team. Both can be unifying, transforming events.

○　　○　　○

The French have an expression, "*Noblesse oblige.*" It means those in nobility are obligated to be honorable and generous. The Bible has similar advice, "To whom much is given, much is required." So if you're lucky enough to have a fancy title or a fat bank account, using your position and assets for the greater good is quintessential. I'm all in favor of that. But if you're like me, you're pretty sure the *government* is not the best way to get our charitable resources to those who need it most. In fact, the way the Feds take from the rich to give to the poor is a crime.

Please hear me on this. When a family is unable to provide for themselves because of illness, disability or natural disaster, we who are blessed with resources should take care of them generously and cheerfully. We must provide a safety net so that no one is left without essential care in times of extreme need.

People who want to earn a living but cannot – for whatever reason – deserve our compassion and support. But when someone who is able to work sits back and collects government checks, it defeats the purpose of charity. Worse yet, it feeds a federal bureaucracy that makes an obscene profit by perpetuating what detractors dub "the poverty industry."

For example, welfare recipients who go to work lose their benefits as their income rises. So they're rewarded for staying unemployed.

Does that make any sense to you?

I'm a big believer in the *law of unintended consequences*. And the so-called War on Poverty is a shining example. In 1964, President Lyndon Johnson kicked off his Great Society program to "eradicate poverty and racism." In size and scope it was rivaled only by the disastrous New Deal agenda of Franklin D. Roosevelt back in 1933.

How much did this social experiment cost taxpayers?

The War on Poverty began with a $1 billion appropriation and spent another $2 billion over the next 24 months. Today, federal and state spending on social welfare is nearly $1 trillion a year – $17 trillion since the Great Society was launched. And that's on top of private charity.

Johnson and his social engineers promised an end to poverty.

But what actually happened? Instead of helping, the welfare state did irreparable damage to the basic building blocks of society. By financially incentivizing unmarried women to have children, it institutionalized the fatherless home, turning irresponsibility into a lucrative business. The result? Half of all babies born to women under 30 in America are illegitimate. A staggering 53 percent of Hispanic babies and 73 percent of African-American babies are born out of wedlock.

Black economist Thomas Sowell calls the well-intended Great Society a curse on African-American families: "The black family, which had survived centuries of slavery and discrimination, began rapidly disintegrating in the liberal welfare state that subsidized unwed pregnancy and changed welfare from an emergency rescue to a way of life."

As illegitimacy and unemployment were bankrolled, there was a corresponding boost in the crime rate, the dropout rate, the illiteracy rate, the incarceration rate – all of which (surprise!) necessitated a larger and larger government with more and more bureaucrats to fund and distribute the entitlements. And so the cycle continues, with top-heavy programs that reward failure and indolence.

To even touch on the waste, fraud, and abuse – by donors and recipients alike – could fill ten more books. But suffice to say, private nonprofits and faith-based groups have been proven to help the needy with much greater efficiency and much greater power to transform (rather than perpetuate) societal ills.

The government's goal was to help the poor. The outcome was generational poverty. We now have *millions* more receiving *billions* more from SSI, SSD, WIC, SNAP, CACFP, AFDC, TANF and the other 185 overlapping Federal assistance programs.

Is there a better way?

As I said, if you're blessed with resources, you're morally obligated to help the disadvantaged. We who are successful should treat others – especially those less fortunate – with justice, mercy, and direct help. Providing care for people that Jesus called "the least of these" is the hallmark of civilized society. But I also believe that assistance should be temporary – with a pathway that leads to training, job-seeking, and self-sufficiency.

How to turn the bloated ship around?

I agree with Ronald Reagan: "The best social program is a job." So maybe government's main role in fighting poverty should be to create a climate for job creation. To stop over-regulation and over-taxation. To step out of the way and let the free market rock and roll itself into maximum productivity and profit. Jobs – *real* jobs, private sector jobs – can only come from economic growth. And only a real job gives a person dignity, self-respect and self-reliance. Anything less is insulting. Anything less is addictive. Anything less is condescending, counterproductive and just plain weird – like a nanny spoon-feeding a 35-year-old man in a highchair.

o   o   o

None of us will live forever.

We all have an expiration date.

Often the key to making a significant difference during our short time on this earth is *our outlook*.

Do we see the limitations of our present resources? Or do we see the potential beyond our current reach? Do we operate from an "abundance mentality" or from a "scarcity mentality?"

As my business partner Joe often reminds me, if we focus on what we *don't* have, we're likely to lose what we *do* have. How is this seeming contradiction possible? Because when we focus on what *is* (by being grateful and generous), our resources expand. When we focus on what *isn't* (by being discontent and greedy), they contract.

It just works that way.

When you let go of trying to get more of what you don't need, it frees up oceans of energy to make a difference with what you have. When you make a difference with what you have, it expands.

Lynne Twist, founder, Soul of Money Institute

It's no coincidence that the most prosperous nation on earth (the United States) is also the most generous nation on earth. We spend over $25 billion a year on foreign aid alone. Whether that's too much or too little can be argued, but what's certain is that no other country even comes close to Uncle Sam's openhandedness.

Are you generous and openhanded? Or are you stingy and closefisted? How you answer that question makes a huge difference in the amount of joy you're going to experience when it comes to making, growing, keeping, and distributing your money.

Sometimes we don't realize how much we could easily give away (and how much joy it would bring us) until we take the plunge and actually give it a try. If you've never been a giver, start small. Try doing what Dr. Leo

Marvin (played by Richard Dreyfuss in *What About Bob?*) recommends, and take "baby steps."

It's hard to steer a canoe until you start paddling!

○   ○   ○

Let me close with a challenge.

True wealth is everything you possess that money cannot buy – like peace, joy, love, hope, and contentment.

Complete wealth is true wealth plus everything you own – like your bank accounts, brokerage assets, houses, cars, etc.

Create a plan to identify and grow both your *true* and *complete* wealth, then leverage them toward the things that matter most to you – the things that will outlive our here-today gone-tomorrow lifespan.

If you do, you will improve the corner of the world you live in.

You will experience abundant living.

The great use of life is to spend it for something that will outlast it.

William James, philosopher & psychologist

7F ACTION STEPS: FINANCES

- Know where your money is being spent and who is spending it. For one month, track every purchase you (and your family members) make. Enter that information into the 7F Life Cash Flow Tracker in the Appendix of this book. For each item, check off whether it is fixed or variable. Start by looking at the variable expenses. Do any seem out of line? Which areas would you like to allocate more or less resources to?

- For a simple but effective way of controlling your spending, create an "envelope system." Each month, decide in advance what you're going to spend on various areas – food, gas, clothing, entertainment, etc. Create an envelope for each. Each month, put only the amount of cash you want to spend into each envelope. When you run out of cash in a particular envelope, you're done for that month. The physical act of handing over a $20 bill touches us emotionally in a way that using a debit or credit card does not. If you have money left over in any envelope at the end of the month it will feel like an unexpected gift. Save it, have fun with it, or boost one of the goals you're accumulating assets for. Remember, if you slip and fail, each month is a fresh shot at getting on budget!

• If you feel you lack the time, skill or discipline to build and stick to a budget, consider the services of *Mint.com*. They can automate things like bill payments, expense tracking, savings, and help you develop a cash flow plan. Go to *www.mint.com* for a simple, streamlined way to stay on top of your finances.

• Got kids? Go to *FamilyMint.com* for a simple, step-by-step program that teaches children all facets of money management. Award-winning site combines virtual and real-world experiences to enhance learning (for children 10-years and up). I wish this had been around for my generation!

• Set up a "Thrill Others" fund. Set aside a few dollars each pay period so that when you see or hear of a need you can do something about it. When possible, give the gift anonymously – like the "Secret Santa." Both you and the recipient will get a thrill.

• Seek the assistance of an experienced professional financial advisor. Let's face it, the financial markets are complex. We live in a global economy where an incident on the other side of the planet can affect the value of our portfolios the same day. Get a financial advisor or a wealth coach who can help you navigate the economic cycles.

It's not how much money you make, but how much money you keep, how hard it works for you, and how many generations you keep it for.

Robert Kiyosaki, author of *Rich Dad, Poor Dad*

7F FIRM AND FINANCES

The Firm (your work) and Finances (your money) make up the *Vocational* component of the 7F Life. They're about using our abilities and resources to make a difference in the lives of those we love and serve. Mastering this vocational component helps us strike a healthy balance with the "give and take" of life. Too much taking can leave us fat and sassy – but incomplete and unfulfilled. Too much giving, well… there really isn't a downside to that!

By generously sharing our talents and resources, we express *Personal* leadership and enhance the *Relational* aspect of our lives.

CHAPTER 9

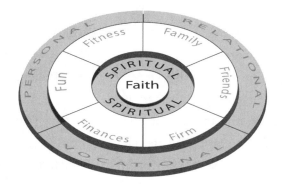

Faith

I live and love in God's peculiar light.

Michelangelo, sculptor

"Everyone has inside of him a piece of good news. The good news is that you don't know how great you can be! How much you can love! What you can accomplish! And what your potential is!"

The optimistic author of that empowering quote was named by *Time* magazine as one of "The 100 Most Important People of the Century." Sadly, she didn't live to receive the award. She died at the age of 15 in a Nazi concentration camp.

Anne Frank was among the over one-million Jewish children who died in the Holocaust. When the Nazis occupied Amsterdam, the well-to-do Frank family received orders to relocate to a work camp in Hitler's Germany. Instead, the family went into hiding in a secret compartment built into the back of the father's office building. Anne and her family spent two years hiding in the cramped, dark space without ever setting foot outside.

To pass the time, the remarkable teenage girl recorded her deepest thoughts in a handwritten diary.

In 1944, the family was betrayed by a collaborator and their makeshift refuge was raided by the *Gestapo*. They were shipped to the Auschwitz death camp in Poland. Because they were young, Anne and her sister were transferred to the Bergen-Belsen work camp. There were no gas chambers there, but starvation and disease were nearly as efficient as the Zyklon B used elsewhere. The emaciated sisters were forced to carry heavy stones in bitter cold. After several months of hard labor, both died of typhus – just three weeks before the camp was liberated by the Allies.

The girls' father was the only member of the family to survive the war and eventually returned to Amsterdam. There he learned that Anne's diary had been discovered in the secret chambers and rescued by friends. Otto Frank made it his life's work to get it published, and her entries have inspired the world for decades.

Anne's courage in the midst of horrific inhumanity has motivated leaders from John F. Kennedy to Nelson Mandela. The teenager's dream still resonates with those of us who embrace her hope "that everything will change for the better, that cruelty will end, that peace and tranquility will return once more."

Before being captured, Anne wrote something at age 13 that I think sums up the human condition: "I am longing – so longing for everything … I feel as if I am going to burst … I'm restless, I go from room to room, breathe through the crack of a closed window, feel my heart beating, as if it is saying, 'Can you satisfy my longing at last?' … I feel utterly confused. I don't know what to read, what to write, what to do, I only know that I am longing."

This longing, this profound, unexplainable feeling that *something is missing*, can be very disturbing. Which is why most of us try to push it out of our minds.

Like Anne, we can't give this "empty feeling" a name. We can't put it into words or pin it down. It's been called a yearning, an aching, a hole in the soul.

THE GOD-SHAPED HOLE

The seventeenth-century French mathematician, Blaise Pascal, described this nagging void: "There is a God-shaped hole in the heart of every man which cannot be filled by any created thing, but only by God the Creator."

The famous scientist born in 1623 has a famous admirer born in 1960. He's the lead singer of the world's biggest rock band, and he's struggled with the same emptiness the Frenchman wrote about. In the book, *U2 by U2*, Bono says, "Pascal called it the God-shaped hole. Everyone's got one, but some are blacker and wider than others. It's a feeling of being abandoned, cut adrift in space and time."

Ever felt like that?

If having fame or money or influence could quench this ennui, certainly Bono would know. He's a multimillionaire. He's recognized worldwide. He's met with presidents and popes. But the hole remains. The Irish rocker continues, "I don't think you can ever completely fill it in this life. You can try to fill it up with songs, family, by living a full life, but when things are silent you can still hear the hissing of what's missing."

What if the pop icon in the tinted glasses is right? What if what's missing can't be replaced by anything *created,* but only by the Creator?

One thing's for sure – this soulful longing goes back a long way.

LOOKING FOR GOD IN ALL THE WRONG PLACES

On a sunny day in 51 AD, the Apostle Paul was preparing to unveil his message to a crowd of highly-sophisticated, highly-educated thinkers in ancient Athens. On his way to the forum at Mars Hill, he walked by countless statues and altars paying homage to the vast number of Greek gods and goddesses. He saw images of Zeus, Apollo, Atlas, Poseidon and Athena. He even saw one that was oddly inscribed "TO AN UNKNOWN

GOD." Apparently, this generic object of worship was an attempt by the Greeks to avoid offending any deity they had inadvertently left out.

When Paul rose to speak to this skeptical crowd, he surprised them by boldly declaring, "I know who the 'unknown' God is. I know who it is you're searching for – he's the God who made the entire world and everything in it."

Paul shocked the greatest intellectuals of his day. How? By telling them that the God who created them was also the God who placed a yearning to find him into their hearts, "So that men would seek him and perhaps reach out for him and find him" (Acts 17:27).

Paul was saying that the void within their hearts – that aching desire to appease an unknown preternatural being – was indeed a God-shaped hole.

The Greeks of that era tried to fill the hole with art, mythology, and philosophical discourses legendary for their brilliance. Today, some people try to quench this longing by jumping into marriage or plunging into work. Others try to cure their restlessness with possessions or accolades or sexual conquests. Some try to silence the "hissing" that Bono mentions by drowning it out with pills, pleasure, or in my case, blue chip portfolios.

But take it from me, even achieving the American Dream – right down to the nice home in the 'burbs with a white picket fence and a perfectly manicured lawn – won't fill the hole. Comedian George Carlin satirized this false hope, "The reason they call it the American Dream is that you have to be asleep to believe it."

○ ○ ○

In my work, I deal with very successful people. People of great net worth and notable achievement. Early in my financial career, a client surprised me with his candor: "Mike, I've been feeling for a while now that something's missing. I've got a great career, great family. I've hit all the goals I set for myself, but I feel like my life isn't complete."

I was floored. From my perspective, he had it all – trophy wife, 2.4 exceptional children and a second home overlooking the ocean. Money to burn, year-round tan, ski trips to Vail, the whole package.

As years went on, I discovered he wasn't the only "winner" in the game of life who felt frustrated and dissatisfied.

During a recent consultation, an auto executive unexpectedly shared his heart: "I know this sounds crazy, but I woke up last night feeling kind of like empty inside, hollow. So I did a mental inventory – money, real estate, good health, and freedom to do whatever I want… it's all there. So why aren't I happy? Why isn't this enough?"

He didn't know it, but my client was beginning to realize that our accomplishments and resources will never solve the happiness problem. Like many of the success stories I meet, he was asking the BIG questions that mankind has been asking since the discovery of fire: *Why am I here? What am I supposed to be doing? What is the meaning of life?*

Like most of us, he had grown up thinking that meaning, purpose and satisfaction could be found by working hard, acquiring possessions, and pursuing pleasure.

But he was wrong.

If you don't believe me, take it from the wisest man in history, King Solomon. Ruling Israel after his father David, Solomon was the ultimate plutocrat, with staggering wealth based on international trading and military might. Solomon was absolute ruler over his kingdom; whatever he said was law. No nation could withstand his armies or his intellect. He was an architect, scientist, songwriter, business baron, and scholar. On top of that, he had 900 beautiful wives and concubines at his personal disposal.

It's safe to say that this man had more money, more power, and more sexual opportunities than anyone who has ever lived.

If that's true, there's only one question that matters: Did his achievements or pursuits ever satisfy the deepest longing of his soul?

Apparently not.

And that's according to the king himself: "I denied myself nothing my eyes desired; I refused my heart no pleasure. My heart took delight in all my labor, and this was the reward for all my toil. Yet when I surveyed all that my hands had done and what I had toiled to achieve, everything was meaningless, a chasing after the wind; nothing was gained under the sun" (Ecclesiastes 2:10, 11 NIV).

Solomon's warning is so gut wrenching that I checked it out in another translation. Let me warn you in advance, if you're consumed with climbing the corporate ladder, this is *not* what you want to hear: "Oh, how I prospered! Everything I wanted I took – I never said no to myself. I gave in to every impulse, held back nothing. I sucked the marrow of pleasure out of every task – my reward to myself for a hard day's work! Then I took a good look at everything I'd done, looked at all the sweat and hard work. But when I looked, I saw nothing but smoke. Smoke and spitting into the wind. There was nothing to any of it. Nothing" (Ecclesiastes 2:10, 11 MSG).

Looking out over his palaces and storehouses and harems, Solomon realized that something huge was missing. That's the God-shaped hole. The hole within the heart that nothing else will fill, no matter how hard we try.

And boy, do we try to cram stuff in!

OUR OWN PRIVATE BOTTOMLESS PIT

Earlier we looked at the "disease of affluence" and how we self-medicate by buying things we don't need. We also saw how materialistic indulgence only makes matters worse. Now, psychologists have actually proven that people living in poorer countries have far lower levels of depression than people living in industrialized comfort. In his book, *Spontaneous Happiness*, Dr. Andrew Weil says the rate of depression among the religious sect known as the Old Order Amish (a group who shuns modernity and rejects materialism) is only ten percent the rate of other Americans.

If that ever catches on, Prozac will be obsolete.

In an effort to fill the hole, many people turn to debilitating, *negative* behaviors like substance abuse or codependencies. That's why Hollywood's elite and pop's glitterati bounce in and out of rehab. But others try to cope by pursuing *positive* things. Things like popularity, achievements, golf, politics, education, golf, hobbies, wait – did I mention golf?

We try everything, but in the end, we are drawn back, sometimes painfully, sometimes eagerly, to the final "F" of this book which is *faith*. Back to the place where the God-shaped hole can be filled and our hearts completed.

Need proof?

On September 11, 2001, millions of us rushed to our local churches and synagogues. Houses of worship could hardly contain the overflow crowds that came to try and make sense of the tragedy and fill the gaping hole that so many of us – religious or not – suddenly felt within our hearts. On the Sunday immediately following the terrorist attacks, "roughly half of the adult population in the United States attended a religious service." That's found in a Fox News report from September 2002 that looked back on the post 9/11 spike in church attendance: "A surge of spirituality occurred as Americans examined just how fragile life was and evaluated what was really important. Answers were hard to come by, and many sought solace in a higher power."

The article also quotes Texas pastor, Ed Young, "When we are riddled with fear, when things fall apart around us… people suddenly respond and they're turning to God and asking those deep questions… and want to get right with him and attend church."

And it's not just acts of war that get our spiritual attention. Economist Daniel Hungerman from the University of Notre Dame has been measuring America's gross domestic product since 1972. In a *Newsweek* story called "No Atheists in Foxholes," Hungerman says the religiosity of Americans runs in almost exact inverse correlation to our economy. "You can see as clear as day a negative relationship in this picture. When the business cycle goes up, religious attendance goes down, and vice versa."

I doubt this survey result made you fall off your chair with surprise.

It's no secret that our spiritual hunger is often strongest in times of calamity or intense stress (serious illness, job loss, family turmoil, whatever). We tend to seek comfort from faith in time of crisis – national or personal. But here's the kicker: Our need for faith *is no less real* when skies are blue and things are humming along merrily. The God-shaped hole that each of us carries within needs to be filled … and filled again and again.

Whether we admit it out loud or not, we're all yearning for purpose. We want our life to matter, to count for something. Something significant that will outlive us. Something big enough to fill the hole.

In 1969, Patti Page made a fortune singing about a person who is disillusioned with life. Her smash hit "Is That All There Is?" captured the longing of a confused and pampered generation. Its existential lyrics reveal how both good and bad experiences in life leave the world-weary singer unimpressed and disappointed with, well… everything.

Page cheerlessly concludes, "If that's all there is my friends, then let's keep dancing. Let's break out the booze and have a ball, if that's all there is."

Thankfully, that is *not* all there is…

OKAY, SO I'M NO PAUL BUNYAN

It was dead.

At least, it looked dead. There wasn't a green needle in sight. Every branch was bare. It was an eyesore and needed to be removed from our backyard. Surveying the rotting trunk and broken branches, I came up with a plan that didn't involve tools or toil. I would simply lean my powerful, perfectly-sculpted six-foot three-inch body against this spindly pine and it would snap off at the base.

I might as well have tried to push over a telephone pole.

It seems this ugly, decrepit tree had developed an extensive root system. When I pushed, it didn't budge. When my veins bulged and my heart raced, it stayed put. Even though the branches were brittle and easy to snap off, the roots had weaved themselves into the soil and the surrounding vegetation.

This old pine wasn't going anywhere without a fight.

I went to my garage, grabbed a pickaxe and started hacking away at the soil around the base of the tree, exposing some of the roots. The ones I encountered ran parallel to the surface, stretching several feet out from the trunk. Each time I uncovered a root I would take a big whack with the axe and sever it. After an hour of picking and sweating and chopping roots, the 16-foot tree seemed cut off from all support. Now I could just shove it over and haul it away. Approaching my adversary, I thought about having my wife capture a short heroic video of man triumphing over nature.

As it turned out, I didn't post the encounter on YouTube.

I huffed and puffed, and while it tilted slightly, it refused to fall over. I couldn't believe it! With the look of dumb disbelief that only males can muster, I stared at the base of the tree, looking at all the roots I had cut off. There wasn't a single survivor around the entire circumference of the tree. And yet it was still standing tall and strong and maybe even chuckling at me if that's possible.

Undaunted, I started digging more dirt out from around the base of the tree. I had to see for myself what was holding it so firmly in place. To my surprise, there was one major root extending straight down from the middle of the trunk into the soil below. This main pipeline was clearly the source of its strength. After hacking away at this core root – twice as thick and strong as the others – I finally severed it. The tree tottered, succumbed to gravity, and fell with an audible whoosh.

Covered in pine sap and dirt, I relished the victory. But I was curious about the tree's hidden source of strength. Later that day, I did a little research and discovered that horticulturists call my hidden nemesis the "tap root" or "striker root." This dominant root is the lifeline for the plant or tree. It draws up water and other nutrients necessary to keep the plant or tree alive and growing.

Cut the tap root and eventually you'll see a dead plant or tree. Even if it still *appears* to be alive for a while above the ground.

Same is true for humans.

o   o   o

Does your life have a hidden root that's the source of your inner strength? Do you have a lifeline that carries essential, life-sustaining ingredients like love, joy, peace, patience, kindness, goodness, and self-control?

If so, that "tap root" is your faith.

If you're not absolutely sure you have one (or if it seems weak), you're not functioning at your full potential; you're not living a balanced, thriving 7F Life.

Maybe you think this chapter doesn't apply to you. The famous theologian Bob Dylan begs to differ. He says *everyone* believes in something or someone. Back in 1979, the shaggy poet sang that whether we're rich or poor, we all put our faith in someone: "It may be the devil, or it may be the Lord, but you're going to have to serve somebody."

In other words, everyone sinks a tap root into something. Is yours connected to a reliable underground stream that you can depend on to refresh your spirit? Or is it dipping into a shallow puddle that's going to dry up in tough times?

Is your faith in your accomplishments? In your bank account? In your family name, your diplomas, your position, your physique? If so, you may fall over like my old pine tree when the winds of adversity blow against you. Personal strength and ingenuity are not enough. Willpower and mind-over-matter won't work. Even good intentions fail. Most of us have tried relying on our own resources and we inevitably come up short.

Any tree that gets disconnected from its *physical* tap root – its life source –will die. Dittoes for us. That's why evaluating the quality of our *spiritual* tap root (our faith in God or some other belief system) is so essential.

Ask yourself: "Does my life source affirm that I am deeply cared for? Does it assure me that I'll never be abandoned? Does it challenge me to be a better person? Does following it bring fulfillment and peace? Has my range of possibilities expanded as a result of being connected to this life source?"

Our beliefs determine our behavior. Or to put it another way, our convictions determine our conduct. But that's not all – they also control our *outcomes*. Beliefs can control our actions, behavior and potential. Positive and negative expectations have the power to alter outcomes in clinical tests and in real life. If you believe the bottom could drop out at any second and all you see are potential pitfalls, you're likely to live with fear and hesitation. On the contrary, if you possess a positive outlook that things will turn out well because you're committed to doing the right thing, they usually will. Even better, if you believe "someone up there" loves you and cares for you and has the power to change people and circumstances, *you will get through –* even in your darkest days.

The stubborn tree in my backyard went from green to gray because something hindered the flow of nutrients from its life source to its limbs. In its weakened state, it was vulnerable to predators like beetles, moths and aphids. Like that pine, we need a constant, daily connection to our spiritual nutrients. Otherwise, the "bugs" of worry, fear, jealousy, envy, malice, and greed may creep in and cause internal rot.

And if we cut ourselves off completely, we'll dry up, weaken, and eventually fall.

Faith is a knowledge within the heart, beyond the reach of proof.

Khalil Gibran, Lebanese-American author

YOU GOTTA HAVE FAITH

Ever lose your car keys?

It's frustrating. Your car is sitting there ready and willing to take you anywhere, but if you can't turn the ignition, it's just two tons of worthless metal. Faith is like that. You face a universe of possibilities, but without faith, you'll just sit there in the driveway. Faith is the ignition switch that triggers the essential *energies* (like initiative and perseverance) and positive *emotions* (like hope and courage) that get us moving! Faith gives birth and fruition to dreams we would otherwise think impossible. Faith takes ordinary endeavors out of the realm of mere human experience and adds a divine, supernatural element to life.

Your faith – regardless of whom or what you place it in – influences every waking moment of every single day.

Your faith – whether you're aware of it or not – is up and running and affecting every choice you make.

When you decided to sit down and read this book, you had faith that the chair you're in would support your weight. You had faith that it wouldn't collapse. When you hit a light switch or turn a water faucet you're unconsciously exercising faith that something good is going to happen. When you direct that kind of childlike faith toward an all-powerful, all-loving God, it brings inner peace and unspeakable joy to daily life.

Disclaimer: I am not trying to convert you to any particular belief system (including mine). But it is critical that your life source – whoever or whatever you have faith in – be sufficient to meet the challenges of the here and now… and for whatever lies on the *other side* of this brief life on earth. I wish you a long and healthy life, but we do need to confront our own mortality. And although we'd rather not think about death, we'll all experience it firsthand – travelling to what Hamlet called "the undiscovered country, from whose border no traveler returns."

The Four Steps to Understanding Faith

Faith is hard to grasp. It's personal; it's transcendent. It's universal to every culture; it's unique to each individual. For now, let's just agree that faith is a primary component of spiritual fitness. Meanwhile, I'll take a swing at defining what it is, explaining why it's essential, and helping you find a version that works for you. The answers lie in what I've found to be four helpful steps on our spiritual journey:

1. DEFRAG YOUR LIFE

If you own a computer you likely know two things about defragging. First, remember to defrag and your hard drive runs faster and more efficiently. Second, *forget* to defrag and you'll want to back a full-size SUV over your sluggish laptop.

Think of it this way – having a fragmented file is like having the pages of a huge Stephen King novel randomly scattered all over your house. Each time you finished reading a page you'd have to search every room for the next one. Defragging gets them back in correct order and next to each other by reorganizing your clusters of data for maximum speed.

When we defrag our *life*, we also improve efficiency.

Here's what I mean. Do you ever feel fragmented, scattered, multi-brained? Does it feel like your life is running smoothly one day, but falling apart the next? Do you behave like Dr. Jekyll with a particular friend, and then an hour later act like Mr. Hyde with someone else? Does your life lack cohesiveness and seem out of sync? If you're like me, you sometimes feel disjointed, confused, and unsure about which direction to take.

To avoid spinning out of control, we need to defrag our lives regularly. But how?

An effective faith provides a framework for organizing (defragging) our thoughts. It's the grid to see the pros and cons of each day's decisions. It's also the power to harness areas of your life that want to wander off or wobble out of orbit.

If you've ever had braces on your teeth you know that when they finally come off the fun's not over. The orthodontist will suggest you wear a retainer to make sure the (expensive) work your braces did to straighten your teeth is maintained. I have a tooth that wants to stray and "fragment" from the others. I have to put my retainer back in regularly to keep that tooth in its place.

Faith is like that. It keeps good things in place and restricts unwelcome movement that would otherwise ruin what we've accomplished.

Faith focuses and directs our thoughts, like a laser focuses random light rays into one powerful and useful beam. Ordinary light scatters and diminishes rapidly, but the concentrated, coherent light of a laser can be seen for miles or be used to cut through steel. Likewise, faith helps us focus *our* energy effectively without dispersion. Do you ever feel like you've used up all your strength without accomplishing your goal? A boxer who swings his arms wildly will wear himself out – and never defeat his opponent. We've got to make sure we're landing our punches accurately if we're going to win in life.

If lack of faith has allowed your best efforts to be dispersed and randomized, your path is probably unclear and your energy is drained. Faith can defrag your mind, recharge your soul, and get you back on track.

Living without faith is like driving in a fog.

Anonymous

2. GOOGLE YOUR LIFE

Did you know the word "google" has made it into our dictionaries?

Google is a verb defined as "to search for information about a person or thing." Have you googled your life lately? I don't mean literally using the famous search engine (although it's not a bad idea to see what's out there). I mean searching your mind, probing your memory, analyzing your thoughts.

Why is this critical? Napoleon Hill observed that only man has the power to transform his thoughts into physical reality. So in a way, you are what you think – your mind is shaping your future. Someone way smarter than me (okay, that doesn't narrow the field dramatically) once said "Watch your thoughts, for they become words. Watch your words because they become actions. Actions become habits, habits become character, and character becomes your destiny."

Have you taken an inventory of what's there? Of what's *not* there?

Here's a simple exercise that will provide insight. Grab some paper. Ask yourself these questions and write down the first thing that comes to mind:

- What do you spend most of your day thinking about?
- What is your greatest concern?
- How do you feel about the way you're allocating your time, money and abilities?
- Describe the depth and breadth of your relationships. Do you have friends you could call at 3:00 a.m. to share a deep concern with? Would they come over to be with you despite the hour?
- When did you last help someone with no expectation of a favor in return?
- What important causes or movements have you recently supported to expand their reach?
- How do you describe the influence you have on people you live and work with?
- What brings peace and restfulness to your soul?
- What makes you feel most like a complete person?

Okay, pencils down. Do you like what you see? Do you feel like you are more loving, aware, generous, and caring than you were a year ago? If you're not sure, ask your spouse or a close friend. They'll tell you the truth.

Begin challenging your own assumptions. Your assumptions are your windows on the world. Scrub them off every once in a while, or the light won't come in.

Alan Alda, actor

3. EVALUATE YOUR OPERATING SYSTEM

If you don't like your answers to the questions in Step 2, ask yourself this: "Am I actually ready to change?" Maybe you secretly want things to stay the same, or you're hoping someone else will make the change for you, or that you'll just wake up someday from a bad dream and everything will be better.

Sorry. Not gonna happen. If you don't *want* change, you won't *get* it – plain and simple. Change only occurs when the pain of staying the same becomes greater than the pain it takes to climb out of the cycle.

Assuming you *do* want to improve your life, let's take a look at your current "operating system." The purpose of a computer's OS is to organize and control hardware and software so your device behaves in a flexible but predictable way. Without an operating system any computer is useless. Without a real and functional faith (a personal operating system) we are severely hampered in our day-to-day activities.

Call me a geek, but I notice a lot of similarities here. A computer's operating system enables the machine to serve a variety of purposes, to interact with users in complex ways, and to keep up with needs that change over time. That's exactly what a vibrant and living faith provides. In fact, it *gives* us purpose and then helps us *serve* that purpose. It enables us to interact with others in complex ways and it meets our needs as they change over time.

If you're not living an abundant life, could it be you're using "operating system" 1.0 when version 8.0 is available for upgrade? (I am resisting all lame jokes about free heavenly downloads.)

To move forward, let's first look backward: When and how was your current OS installed? Was it a system you designed or one that someone else created? Did your parents, teachers, or friends install it? Have you found it adequate, or does your system "crash" when faced with challenging situations?

If you're in need of a more robust, stable, dependable belief system, where can you find it?

There are basically only two places you can look:

A. LOOK INSIDE YOURSELF.

We've been taught to trust our instincts, go with our gut, follow our hunches.

But really, how's that working out for you?

Has your "inner guide" earned you a place at the Mensa picnic? Have your homespun ideas led to consistently great results? Has your intrinsic logic always been clever enough to handle complex situations?

(If you answered "yes" to all of the above, you might have some honesty issues.)

Personally, I've found that my self-generated strategies are not always sufficient to address the complicated situations I face (sometimes, not even the routine ones!). Somebody has rightly said that "the problem with a self-made man is poor building materials." Ouch. We are living in the most narcissistic generation in history. In our lifetimes, magazine titles went from *Life* to *People* to *Self.* Any product or reality show that appeals to ego and self-image seems to become a runaway success.

It's no wonder that most self-help gurus preach that everything you need is *already inside of you* and all we need to "self-actualize" is seek enlightenment from within. Virtually every website, blog and book I researched on improving your life or seeking truth repeated the same clichéd advice – "look within."

And that goes double for the entertainment crowd.

In her hit "The Voice Within," Christina Aguilera sings, "Look inside yourself. Like your oldest friend just trust the voice within, then you'll find the strength that will guide your way."

In their tune "Look Inside Yourself," the band Hear Say suggests, "Way deep down somewhere you've got all the answers... Close your eyes and you'll hear the voice inside you. Once you give it a chance it's gonna guide you."

Well, excuse me, but if the answers are "inside me," does that mean

I possess all the wisdom I'll ever need? Not likely! Trust me, I've created my share of problems and I've had plenty more dumped on me – and I invariably need *outside* help to solve them.

In 1967 a blockbuster book on transactional analysis hit the markets and earned a place in pop culture forever. The author, Dr. Thomas Harris, gave it a title that struck gold with the "me generation" and helped it go on to sell 15 million copies. The moniker was *I'm OK, You're OK*, and it became a mantra for the self-help movement. Trouble is, I'm not OK. And I'm pretty sure you're not, either. At my core, I'm broken and flawed. In my deepest psyche, I'm messed up like everyone else.

I don't know about you, but my track record when relying solely on my own intuition isn't what you'd call stellar. When I finally realized (begrudgingly) that I didn't personally possess 100 percent of the brainpower and insight needed for life's demanding situations, I stopped gazing at my navel and started networking.

Granted, there's a mile-high stack of self-help books that insist we can discover the meaning and purpose of life by looking within ourselves – but what if that's the wrong place to start?

A man wrapped up in himself makes a very small package.

Confucius

B. LOOK OUTSIDE YOURSELF.

I know, I know. This concept flies in the face of pop psychology and motivational speakers and New Age thinking and probably the stylist who cuts your hair. But it's true anyway – the best way to grow as a person is by asking *other* people questions. Preferably people who are smarter (or more skilled, or more generous, or more successful, or more anything) than you.

We are limited by gaps in our knowledge, our experience, and our own cognitive biases. To say otherwise is the height of arrogance.

Of course, you do need to know yourself, you do need to search your own mind, and you do need to look inside – if only to see what a mess you are (teasing). But the vast majority of the world's collected knowledge lies *outside* that three-pound lump of grey matter between your ears. Why not tap into it?

One key to successfully "looking outside" for guidance – and one that's often overlooked – is being intentional about who we associate with.

Why is that important? Because your attitudes, decisions and choices are influenced by the attitudes, decisions and choices of the people you spend your time with. The people around you can be your "true north" or make you veer off course, depending on their character (operating system).

Smart people learn to investigate before they invest money in something. How much more critical when we're choosing who to invest our *time* with! To get the best return on your relationship investment, ask yourself: Who do I know that seems to have their life together? Whose lifestyle do I admire? Who do I know that didn't crash and burn when hit with hard times? Who faces tough issues calmly and with resolve and sees them through? Who do I know that's secure enough to admit their shortcomings and mistakes? Who is successful, but still walks with humility?

In my business I surprise newer investors by telling them, "You don't have to be *rich* to prepare a plan for financial independence, all you have to be is *smart*."

How smart? Just smart enough to say, "I'll look outside myself and outside my current ideas for someone with a better plan."

That principle of looking *outside* – of looking to others for wisdom, encouragement and guidance – applies to every facet of life. Whether it's a trusted friend, experienced mentor, or higher power, consult someone outside your own head space if you want to live a truly abundant life.

When people tell me they've learned from experience, I tell them the trick is to learn from other people's experience.

Warren Buffett, billionaire investor

○   ○   ○

My mom always warned me, "Don't hang out with a bad crowd, they'll rub off on you." She was right. And it works both ways. Spend your quality time with quality people to achieve quality results. We all get the same amount of time per week – 10,080 minutes. As you choose ways to fill your weekly allotment, first ask yourself: "Who do I know that lives with purpose and makes decisions based on it? Who do I know that uses their speech to build others up rather than tear them down? Who do I know that, regardless of circumstances, has an underlying peace and inner strength?"

Ask that person what operating system they're using. Then shadow them until you learn the secret of life or get arrested for stalking, whichever comes first.

Legendary football coach, Vince Lombardi, said, "The quality of a person's life is in direct proportion to their commitment to excellence, regardless of their chosen field of endeavor." Surround yourself with people committed to excellence and investigate their personal operating system.

During this journey of discovery, ask yourself these questions about the OS you are currently using. Does your system…

- Offer profound insight and practical wisdom?

- Motivate through love rather than guilt?

- Come to you as a free gift? (Or depend on doing good deeds?)

- Include others and encourage unity? (Or promote exclusivity?)

- Lead to genuine freedom? (Or bondage to a set of rules?)

- Help you think clearly and passionately about what really matters?

- Inspire you to take worthwhile risks?

- Give you reason to hope in the midst of pain, suffering or loss?

- Stir up a sense of awe and wonder about life and its possibilities?

- Give you courage to tackle difficult tasks and carve new paths?

- Provide proven principles to base your life on?
- Inspire self-expression? (Or conformity to a group standard?)

Remember, *everybody everywhere* has an operating system. Even if they deny it. Even if they're not aware of it. Atheists, skeptics, believers, everybody. The only difference is how efficient, trustworthy and reliable it is!

Here are some more questions to help you evaluate your OS…

- Does it help you discern truth from falsehood and make prudent decisions?
- Has it steered you away from pitfalls and hazardous situations in the past?
- Does it inspire you to look beyond your needs to a greater common good?
- Has the system's designer walked where you've walked?
- Have millions of satisfied users proven it to be trustworthy and effective?
- Does your current system lighten your burdens?
- Does it give you peace in this life and confidence for whatever awaits beyond the grave?

Thanks for being honest and authentic with this self-evaluation.

How did your current operating system stack up? If you answered "No" or "Not sure" to some of the questions, I encourage you to explore other belief systems or faith options by using the same set of questions.

Life's too short and eternity is too long not to be confident about the path you are on.

Faith is not trying to believe something regardless of the evidence; faith is daring something regardless of the consequences.

Sherwood Eddy, missionary & author

4. Tweet Your Life

With apologies to James Taylor, I recently sent my wife a romantic note, "How tweet it is to be loved by you."

Why not? It was under the 140-character limit and it made her smile. When I hit "send," it connected our hearts in a nanosecond even though I was miles away.

As we all know, Twitter is an instant, cut-to-the-chase form of communication. While it can be used to pass along frivolous information like what Lindsay Lohan is wearing to court or Mark Cuban's reaction to a referee's call while his Dallas Mavericks are on the court, it can also be used to share meaningful and heartfelt thoughts. I think one of the reasons "tweeting" has become so popular is that people enjoy the feeling of *being connected*.

I don't think that's an accident.

We were not designed to live in isolation. Communication – regular and meaningful conversation – is necessary to establish and maintain healthy relationships, both vertically and horizontally:

A. HORIZONTALLY. By this I mean "sideways" – with the human beings in your life, like family and co-workers. Without intentional communication, we miss out on the blessings that friendship can bring, and the richness of life can be reduced to monotony. Someone has said that "a friend is someone who knows the song in your heart and can sing it to you when you've forgotten the words." Back in Chapter 5, we learned the advantages of keeping *friends* front and center in our lives.

Not good at conversation? Don't know what to tweet? Please don't worry about what to say – Joseph Addison said "talking with a friend is nothing more than thinking out loud." So do it often.

B. VERTICALLY. By this I mean "upwards" – with the designer of your operating system. The strength of your faith will be determined by how well you "tweet" your life with your system's designer. If someone wrote the instruction manual on how to live, and you're attempting to follow it, doesn't it make sense to talk with the author regularly? One way to communicate with your designer is through prayer. If that seems too religious or mystical for you, don't worry. It doesn't have to be fancy to be effective. Jonathon Edwards said, "Prayer is as natural an expression of faith as breathing is of life."

You could say prayer is just talking (and listening) to God; telling him in our own words that we desire to please him and then asking what he wants us to do on any given day. Prayer is not a shopping list we present to a cosmic Santa, but a thank-you note to a loving parent. It's something we can do while we work, shower, jog, eat, wait for appointments, and yes, even drive (safer than texting).

Doing it can provide us with guidance, encouragement and connection.

Don't have time to pray? Think you're too busy? An English vicar named M.E. Andross put it in perspective, "The great freight and passenger trains are never too busy to stop for fuel. No matter how congested the yards may be, no matter how crowded the schedules are, no matter how many things demand the attention of the engineer, those trains always stop for fuel."

And so should we.

He who has faith has an inward reservoir of courage, hope, confidence, calmness, and assuring trust that all will come out well – even though to the world it may appear to come out badly.

B.C. Forbes, founder, *Forbes* magazine

YOUR ARMS TOO SHORT TO BOX WITH GOD

Muslims, Buddhists, Christians, Jews, and Hindus have at least one thing in common: They've all been persecuted at some time in their history.

Sometimes victimized by hostile governments, sometimes alienated by prejudice, people of faith have long been criticized by the academic and scientific communities for believing in anything that can't be proven empirically.

Even in America – a land founded on religious freedom – people of faith are routinely vilified by intellectuals and mischaracterized by media. In Hollywood, fictional believers are generally portrayed as one of three cartoonish stereotypes – pathetic (a naïve troglodyte to be pitied), hypocritical (a devious schemer to be avoided), or maniacal (a dangerous psychopath to be restrained).

Does that sound paranoid? A 2012 report by the Family Research Council verified a rising pattern of hostility toward religious people and faith-based institutions. Their 140-page "Survey of Religious Hostility in America" listed 600 examples of religious animosity shown by judges, government officials, and secular humanists – aimed at making everyone "check their faith at the door of the public square."

The FRC findings were shocking. Federal mandates are forcing hospitals, business owners and faith-based institutions to violate their religious principles or face closure. Meanwhile, school boards waste time and taxpayer money by expelling honor students for wearing religious symbols or praying before football games. Attacks target Boy Scout troops, Salvation Army bell ringers, even senior citizen centers – like the Texas group that banned elderly patrons from bowing their heads before eating their meals.

If you're a veteran, I thank you for your service, and I warn you to brace yourself: Picture the American Cemetery in Colleville-sur-Mer, France, overlooking Omaha Beach, one of the sites of the D-Day invasion. The graves of U.S. servicemen and women interred there are marked by row after row of white crosses – 9,837 crosses in all. Now picture the Veteran's Memorial in San Diego – where the single cross adorning the site *was forcibly removed* after the U.S. Court of Appeals held it was "unconstitutional."

If that didn't turn your stomach, this will: Remember the cross-shaped steel beam found in the wreckage of the World Trade Center? This 17-foot totem inspired thousands of survivors and workers during the clean-up at ground zero. It is the best know artifact of the 2001 attack on America. Yet the group calling itself American Atheists has sued to block the display of this famous relic at the National September 11 Memorial and Museum in New York.

No longer content to co-exist with religious folk, activists work to eliminate every vestige of faith from public discourse. They litigate to ban public nativities and menorahs, campaign to end the Pledge of Allegiance, and press to delete "In God We Trust" from our currency. In towns across the country, they sue to have The Ten Commandments removed from courtrooms and city halls.

What would replace the time-honored tablets? A sign installed inside the Wisconsin State Capital by the petulant group calling itself Freedom From Religion gives a clue: "There are no gods, no devils, no angels, no heaven or hell. Religion is but myth and superstition that hardens hearts and enslaves minds."

Sorry, Moses.

o   o   o

These attacks against faith have intensified recently with the rise of what's been dubbed the "new atheism." The different camps bicker about policies and jargon, but their common conjecture is that religion – *any* religion – is intrinsically malevolent and toxic. In the words of the late atheist Christopher Hitchens, it "poisons everything."

This angry gang doesn't stop by asserting there is no God, or that intelligent design is laughable, or that scriptures like the Quran or the Bible are a hoax. They go on to assert that all religion is a curse that condemns humanity to endless conflict, ignorance and extremism. As evidence, they cherry-pick negative examples like the Crusades or suicide bombers seeking heavenly harems – while conveniently ignoring religion's majority role in abolition, civil rights, charitable works, disaster relief, etc.

The undisputed godfather (no pun intended) of this movement is

Richard Dawkins, an evolutionary biologist and outspoken critic of religion. In his 2006 book *The God Delusion*, Dawkins contends that a supernatural Creator almost certainly does not exist and that religion is a delusion, "a fixed false belief." According to Dawkins, faith – defined as any belief that is not based on evidence – is one of the world's great evils. He regards it as analogous to the "smallpox virus, though more difficult to eradicate." In his essay, *Viruses of the Mind*, Dawkins explains how he moved from thinking that religion was a "harmless crutch for consolation" to believing it is "lethally dangerous nonsense."

Another stalwart is Daniel Dennett, whose *Breaking The Spell* begins by comparing religion to a deadly parasite that invades the brains of ants. He studies religion because "it does so much harm it's worth trying to figure out how to control it."

From college campuses to Hollywood blockbusters, this relentless skewering of God makes for good box office and lots of headlines. Bookstores and blogs are flush with atheist speakers and authors trying to erase "God" from our social vocabulary.

How much damage has the campaign to stamp out faith inflicted?

Virtually none.

Despite ridicule and persecution, the overwhelming majority of the world still embraces some form of religious belief in a universal spirit, deity, or higher power.

Even in postmodern America, the score is belief over nonbelief by a landslide. According to a 2011 Gallup poll, over 9 in 10 Americans still say "Yes" to the question "Do you believe in God?"

The results are far too consistent to be a fluke. American's self-reported belief in God has been unwaveringly high and surprisingly consistent over the last 65 years; at 92 percent, it's just a few points lower now than it was in the 1940s!

In 1882, Nietzsche declared "God is dead."

But there's plenty of evidence he's alive and well. A Pew Forum survey on religion found nearly 80 percent of Americans think miracles occur, and that angels and demons are real. In a *Newsweek* poll, 93 percent of Americans believe Jesus Christ actually lived, and 82 percent think he was the Son of God. Other surveys show that nearly 3 out of 4 Americans pray on a daily or weekly basis.

BETTER THAN VITAMINS

According to new medical studies, our insistence on clinging to faith and prayer is doing us some unexpected good. In an article titled "47 Health Benefits of Prayer," researchers say those who pray regularly and attend any kind of religious services enjoy a decidedly longer and healthier life span than those who don't.

Dr. Andrew Newberg is founder of a new discipline called "neurotheology," the study of relationships between spiritual phenomena and the human brain. Newberg says "Religious beliefs and activities can have a profound impact on our mental and physical well-being by reducing stress, improving resistance to diseases, enhancing memory and mental function, and helping us to lead longer lives."

Sound like wishful thinking?

Maybe. But it comes with impressive credentials. Dr. Newberg is Director of Research for Integrative Medicine at Thomas Jefferson University Hospital and Medical College, and Professor of Religious Studies at the University of Pennsylvania. In his book, *Why God Won't Go Away*, he writes, "So impressive are the health benefits of religion ... that after reviewing more than a thousand studies on the impact of religion upon health, Dr. Koenig of Duke University recently told *The New Republic*, that 'Lack of religious involvement has an effect on mortality that is equivalent to forty years of smoking one pack of cigarettes per day.'"

And having faith doesn't result in just *more* years, but *better* years.

Certain areas of the brain are distinctly affected by prayer and other religious experiences. The result is an improvement in brain function and well-being, plus an increase in our capacity to connect with others. If a person prays for 12 minutes daily, it may slow the age-related decline of the frontal lobe (the brain's "rational part") and stimulate the anterior cingulate (the brain's "compassion part"). The latter is considered the area of the brain that most clearly sets human beings apart from animals – it's activated when we feel compassion or empathize with the emotions of others.

Do all prayers produce the same benefits? Actually, no. Dr. Newberg says, "Prayer that focuses on gratitude, celebration or a positive vision of the future (as well as rejecting anger and resentment) will reduce depression and anxiety, relieve stress, lower blood pressure and heart rate, and eventually extend life."

No matter what our personal beliefs, or what name we use for God, surely we can all say "Amen" to that!

The very fact that this world is so challenging is exactly why you sometimes must reach out of its jurisdiction for help, appealing to a higher authority to find your comfort.

Elizabeth Gilbert, author of *Eat, Pray, Love*

OPTIONAL. READ AT YOUR OWN RISK.

Disclaimer: I'm not a pastor, priest, rabbi, or imam. I've never even played one on TV. So you don't have to take my spiritual advice. You can skip this section. But here's my two cents' worth. Yesterday I saw a bumper sticker that read "Life is hard and then you die." Wow. What an encouraging, uplifting message.

Thankfully, most of us are a bit more optimistic. Although plenty of Americans have turned away from organized religion, a recent study by Trinity College confirmed Gallup's findings – 93 percent of us believe in God or a higher power.

And the vast majority of us *also* believe things will get better in the end.

Somebody once said that fairy tales ruin us.

I agree. Real life is seldom the "happy ever after" scenario that's promised in fables. But if we open ourselves up to the possibility that maybe there is a God out there who created us and cares about us, then maybe there *can* be a happy ending to our story. If this God exists, and we look to him for guidance and direction, maybe we can stop spinning our wheels, chasing our tails, or whatever metaphor for going nowhere we come up with.

My friend Steve Norman once asked, "What if happiness is not about getting something good or getting rid of something bad, but about growing into somebody different?" That's what I'm suggesting. Seek out the God who I contend loves you unconditionally, and ask him to change you from the inside out. You won't see a bolt of lightning or feel radically different, but when you invite God to reveal himself, something profound begins. Life doesn't instantly become a bed of roses. Your doubts and questions don't disappear. But even a teetering, uncertain baby-step toward God can give you a sense of hope and purpose that nothing else can.

The God who I believe created the oceans and mountains and galaxies is aware of the smallest details of our daily lives. The Bible says he even knows the exact number of hairs on our heads (and presumably in the sink). That's mind-boggling. But he doesn't just sit back and watch. He promises to personally stick with us through every adversity we could ever face. I couldn't get my brain around that until back in December 2011, when a Utah policeman demonstrated it to the world. When a city bus ran over a pedestrian, officer Kevin Peck crawled underneath the five-ton vehicle to assist a badly-injured woman wedged under the wheels. In a much publicized photo, we see Peck's blue-gloved hands clutching the hands of Aryann Smith. "She was afraid she was going to die," said Peck. "I was just praying the bus didn't move, trying to reassure her and calm her. She was very scared, she asked me not to leave."

I loved Peck's response, "I told her I would stay with her until we got her out."

That sounds a lot like Jesus to me: "I will never leave you or forsake you." God never promises we won't get hit by a bus. Bad things do happen to good people. But he pledges to be there with us when it happens, holding our hands.

Only God can bring us joy that's not dependent on our mutual funds, our medical check-up, the annoying driver in front of us, or even the bus on top of us. With faith in him, the restless longing that Anne Frank wrote about in her diary can be replaced by the "peace of God that passes human understanding" (Philippians 4:7).

○　○　○

As a believer, it's not my job to *judge* people.

It's not my job to *fix* people.

It's my job to point them to God.

Someone in a developing country described this process as "one beggar showing another beggar where the bread is." That's me. I'm not the owner of the bakery so I can't brag about my kindness or generosity. Nope. I'm a beggar like everyone else, but I've been shown where to get the free bread that gives life.

So I share that good news with people I meet.

I do it because God's forgiven my past and called me to a new future.

I do it because I know from experience that all my plans and ambitions were dead ends until I found the one goal that matters most and fills the hole in my soul. It's found in the old Westminster Catechism and it answers a lifetime of questions in just 12 words: "Man's chief end is to glorify God and to enjoy him forever."

All my other hopes and dreams and aspirations fall under that overarching objective. With that mission in mind, let me close with my hope for you. Back in 315 AD, a devout man named Cyril, Bishop of Jerusalem, said: "God is fishing for you. Allow yourself to be caught, don't try to escape. Jesus is fishing for you, not to kill you, but to give you life."

Here's to life!

I believe in Christianity as I believe that the sun has risen; not only because I see it, but because by it I see everything else.

C.S. Lewis, author of the *Narnia Chronicles*

7F ACTION STEPS: FAITH

There are countless reasons why I encourage you to pursue and explore your faith; here's a summation: First, it helps you live a life based more on love and less on ego. Second, it helps you align your goals with your values. Third, it can have a positive impact on your mental and physical well-being.

Here's a caveat: Who or what you put your faith in will determine *what you focus* your attention on. And what you choose to dwell on will have profound influence on your life trajectory. That's brought out in a tale handed down by Native Americans...

An old Cherokee chief told his young grandson: "My son, there is a battle between two wolves inside us all. One wolf is evil. It is anger, greed, jealousy, resentment, lies and hatred. The other wolf is good. It is love, joy, hope, peace, humility, kindness, empathy and truth." The boy thought about it, and asked, "Grandfather, which wolf wins?" The old man quietly replied, "The one you feed."

This beautiful story makes me pause and do a gut check – which wolf am I feeding? Am I making good choices based on my operating system? If I focus inwardly on myself (and why my needs are not being met), I can become envious, angry, or depressed. But if I focus outwardly on others (and give my time to something worthy), I'm going to be content, happy, and productive. It's my *faith* – the operating system I base my life on – that nudges me to feed the right inner wolf!

Make sure your faith (your tap root, your life source, your OS) is worth basing your life on. Investigate it, question it and evaluate it so you can have absolute confidence in it. When you have that assurance you will live boldly – and abundantly. Here are some books I strongly recommend and some next steps...

- Read *Reasons for God: Belief in an Age of Skepticism* by Tim Keller. Using literature, philosophy, anthropology, pop culture, and intellectual reasoning, Keller explains how the belief in a Christian God is, in fact, a sound and rational one.

- Read *The Case For Faith: A Journalist Investigates the Toughest Objections to Christianity* by Lee Strobel. Retracing his own journey from atheism to faith, this former legal editor of the *Chicago Tribune* cross-examines the experts.

- Read *The Purpose Driven Life* by Rick Warren. Before the universe was created, did God have us in mind? Does he have plans for us that extend beyond our few years on earth? Warren says knowing this can give new meaning to life.

- Read *Mere Christianity* by C.S. Lewis. Arguably the twentieth century's most influential Christian intellectual, Lewis explains and defends the basic beliefs that nearly all Christians in all denominations hold in common. His simple (yet profound) classic was originally delivered as a series of WWII radio broadcasts.

- Read *Prodigal God* by Tim Keller. With clarity and intelligence, Keller uncovers unexpected hope in the often misunderstood parable of the prodigal son. The father who unhesitatingly receives his wayward son back into the family is a picture of the God who generously reconciles estranged humans back home.

○   ○   ○

- Go to a quiet place where you won't be disturbed. Take several deep breaths. Slow down the RPMs of your mind. Be still. Reflect on what you know to be true. What is your heart telling you about your faith system? Is it solid? Dependable? Need modifying? Be a seeker; pursue truth wherever it takes you.

• This isn't a religious book and I'm not proselytizing. But if you're interested, you can view a brief video about my personal spiritual journey at *www.7FLife.com*.

7F FAITH

Faith has a *Spiritual* focus, and it's the Gorilla Glue that holds the *Personal*, *Relational* and *Vocational* areas of the 7F Life together. This aspect gives meaning and purpose to all of our other activities. It helps us keep each component of the 7F Life in proper perspective and integrates them in a healthy way. The more we keep faith at the center of our lives, the more peace, joy and fulfillment we'll likely experience.

There are only two ways to live: either nothing is a miracle or everything is a miracle.

Albert Einstein, physicist & philosopher

Applications

Commencement

He was only a baby when his great-grandfather died.

Yet he's patterned his entire life after the man.

"My great-grandfather, Karl Wallenda, was my biggest hero, the biggest inspiration behind everything I do," says 32-year-old performer, Nik Wallenda.

In the Preface to this book, we looked at the courage and tenacity of Karl Wallenda, patriarch of the acrobat family that still bears his name. We learned about his philosophy of laying it all on the line, of pursuing his passion and taking risks. True to his own creed, he died in 1978 while doing what he loved most.

Now fast forward to June, 2011. On a damp morning in San Juan, Puerto Rico, Nik Wallenda is walking slowly toward his mother, Delilah. She is 300 feet away. She carries a 25-pound balancing pole. Nik is carrying a 45-pounder. Both are wearing soft moccasin style shoes. Both are balancing on a steel cable no wider than the nickel in your pocket. They meet in the middle on the same wire strung between the same towers of the Conrad Plaza Hotel where Karl Wallenda plunged to his death 33 years earlier.

"I've seen the video of my great-grandfather falling hundreds of times. It replays in my head constantly. To walk in his exact footsteps is an extremely huge honor."

Poised 100-feet above the ground, Nik and Delilah face each other.

While the crowd below gasps, the mother sits down on the wire as her son steps over her in slow motion. There is no safety net. No options. The move seems to take an eternity. Delilah struggles for a moment to get up and then both make it across to safety.

Nik said the heart-stopping tribute was a lifelong goal. "I started walking the wire at age two, and this has been a dream of mine to re-create his walk."

The takeaway for us who prefer to keep our feet on the ground is clear: "My great-grandfather always said, 'Never give up,' and that's something we'll never do."

As we strive for a better life, let's make that *our* motto also.

Will it be easy? No way. I've studied the 7F Life for years, and there are still times when I'm tempted to quit and settle for less. To compromise. To cut corners. Sometimes when I slip and fall, I'm tempted to throw in the towel and opt out of the program. But I've resisted. I've hung in there.

And so can you. But it will be a constant battle.

As you complete this book, you'll have three options: You can quit right now and surrender without a fight. Or you can jump in, give it a test drive and bail out when things get tough. Or you can commit to the program with unflinching tenacity come hell or high water. If you're in that last category, welcome aboard. Make no mistake, you will blow it now and then. That's inevitable. But when you do, I urge you to get back on the wire, grab your balance pole, and keep pursuing your dreams.

The secret of life is to fall seven times and get up eight times.

Paulo Coelho, from the *Alchemist*

GRADUATION DAY

At this point I'd like to congratulate you. You've stuck with it. You've read the texts, hopefully did the homework. Now it's time to matriculate.

But before you start planning the party, note that this will be a different kind of graduation. There'll be no cap and gown. No "Pomp and Circumstance." No student loans to pay back.

You're almost ready (insert drumroll) to receive an advanced degree in what I call "getting it all together." Almost ready to experience life at an uncommon level.

By now you have a basic understanding of each individual element of the 7F Life. We studied them one at a time, like separate ingredients on a kitchen shelf. But what do you get when you *blend* these seven elements together in single dish? What kind of life comes out of the oven when you integrate them in a healthy and meaningful way?

Let me first tell you what you *don't* get. You don't get a perfect life. You don't get a free pass to "champagne wishes and caviar dreams." The 7F Life is not void of heartache or hardship or struggle. It's not a hypothetical life that exists only on paper, or a vicarious experience played out in a sim game.

In fact, it's just the opposite – a life deeply engaged with reality, experiencing all that life brings our way: excitement, disappointment, achievement, set-backs.

There's an old Irish saying, "Into every life a little rain must fall." Emphasis on "every." We all get wet. None of us stay dry. The only difference between an ordinary life and a 7F Life is how we *respond* to that rain – to the problems that can sprinkle us, soak us, or wash us away in a flash flood.

I wish I had better news, but here's the unvarnished reality about being human:

PROBLEMS ARE INEVITABLE. They barge in whether we're ready or not. No matter who we are in the world, or where we are in life, problems will come. No matter if we're rich or poor, young or old, smart as a Rhodes scholar or dumb as a bag of hammers, problems will come – family feuds, gas prices, clogged drains, terrorism, the boss from hell, the neighbor from crazyville, tension with your spouse, letters from the IRS, your dog eating your remote, a gator eating your dog, whatever.

PROBLEMS ARE UNPREDICTABLE. Sometimes *we* invite them in (like credit card debt or sunburn or speeding tickets). Sometimes they invite *themselves* in (like a medical emergency or flat tire or hail storm). Either way, they catch us off guard. The great philosopher, Forrest Gump, said it best: "Life is like a box of chocolates, you never know what you are going to get." We can't anticipate the particular problems we're going to face in life, but we can be absolutely sure that nobody gets off Scot free.

Bad things do happen; how I respond to them defines my character and the quality of my life. I can choose to sit in perpetual sadness, immobilized by the gravity of my loss, or I can choose to rise from the pain and treasure the most precious gift I have – life itself.

Walter Anderson, German author

Okay, that was a pretty big reality check. Now let's move on to much happier news. Here's what you *do* get by following the 7F principles: a deeply meaningful, playfully adventurous, unusually exhilarating life!

Few people are willing to make the tough calls and put in the daily effort it takes to experience this kind of confident, creative life. But those who do will give themselves a tremendous gift – an abundant life that's purposeful, principled, and influential.

Instead of being a burden, they'll be a delight to the people they come in contact with. Instead of being an emotional drag, they'll be a pleasure to be around.

Remember, if you *do* what everybody else does, you'll *get* what everybody else gets – an average, mediocre life. You won't experience the extraordinary by doing the ordinary. So don't follow the lemmings. Don't copy the masses. Swim upstream, run against the wind, march to a different drummer (are you seeing a trend here?).

Don't be normal!

Seven Cool Things about Your New Life

1. THE 7F LIFE IS A PURPOSEFUL LIFE.

It helps answer the question, "Why do I exist?" It is a life with a target – a great big reason for living that goes way beyond just pleasing ourselves. It seeks to harness and aim all of our activities, energies and resources toward that target. It knows what is truly important in life and is in hot pursuit. Once you've identified the "why," the "how" will become clear. Friedrich Nietzsche once wrote, "He who has a *why* to live can bear almost any *how*."

2. THE 7F LIFE IS A FREE LIFE.

When all seven elements are functioning, you're free to be exactly who you were designed to be. You can stop worrying about trying to please everyone. You can be comfortable saying "no" to certain requests because you know you can't be all things to all people. It's a life that's lived with arms wide open, free to explore new paths, free to fail, free to laugh and learn from your mistakes, free to start over in a fresh, better-informed way.

3. THE 7F LIFE IS A PRINCIPLED LIFE.

It encourages us to live in a manner that's consistent with our beliefs. It knows the difference between right and wrong, and the self-control necessary for protecting and nurturing the quality of our lives. Our faith system gives meaning and purpose to the other Fs, and helps define the standards we live by. These principles recognize the value and contributions of all people and seek to promote respect and dignity for everyone.

4. THE 7F LIFE IS A CREATIVE LIFE.

It's a life that generates new ideas, imagines fresh possibilities and dreams of what could be. It's a life that produces new works of art and literature, invents new products and services, and re-creates itself by being in a continual state of learning and exploration. It's here that we are more relaxed, more receptive, more open to new ideas. This playful form of mental aerobics is the opposite of bureaucracy, rigidity, tunnel vision and staleness.

5. THE 7F LIFE IS A RELATIONAL LIFE.

It recognizes that living a solitary existence pales in comparison to living in healthy relationships with others. It understands that people cannot reach their full potential without pursuing social interaction and welcoming honest feedback from friends and family. It recognizes that 1 + 1 can equal 3 or 5 or 100 when we work together with others who share similar goals and values.

6. THE 7F LIFE IS A TRULY HUMAN LIFE.

It seeks primarily to collect life experiences rather than stuff. It realizes that "we can't take it with us" and invests time, talent, and resources into human beings rather than material things. It focuses our energy on what really matters in the long run. It regards pursuing profit and creating wealth as a tool – a self-reinforcing value loop that creates opportunities and lifts people out of poverty into the mainstream. We live deliberately and intentionally to improve our life *and* impact the lives of people around us.

7. THE 7F LIFE IS AN INTEGRATED LIFE.

Life is not a static thing we can "fix" once and relax; it is perpetual motion. It requires continual reflection, evaluation and recalibration. It regularly asks, "Am I satisfied with how I'm spending my time, energy and money? Are the people I care about in agreement with how I'm using my resources?" When we behave in ways that match what we believe and value, *then* we are living an integrated life. We can live without apology – not in arrogance, but in quiet confidence that we are on the right path.

GETTING IN BALANCE

If you spent your entire paycheck on the day you got paid, could you survive the month? If you ate a week's worth of groceries on the day you bought them, could you feed your family? Of course not. The key to good budgeting is appropriate *allocation*.

The same is true in life. How do you divide your time, energy and resources? For instance, if you're allocating 80 percent of your time and energy to work, realize there's only 20 percent of "you" left over to allocate to the other six Fs.

In a *Newsweek* article titled, "What Matters Most," Dr. Dean Ornish said, "We often spend our time and energy on things that, if we were to ask ourselves, 'Is this really important to me?' the answer would be, 'Not very.'"

But as creatures of habit, we seldom – if ever – ask ourselves that *most obvious of all questions!* As a result, says Ornish, "We're not living our lives closest to what has meaning and passion and value for us."

If that's your present situation, "You've got issues, mate." That's an unsustainable model. You have to develop a healthier pattern of allocating yourself to all seven key areas. Check out the 7F Allocation chart below on a regular basis. Each of us has limited hours, dollars and assets. Where are you going to use yours?

THE 7F ALLOCATION

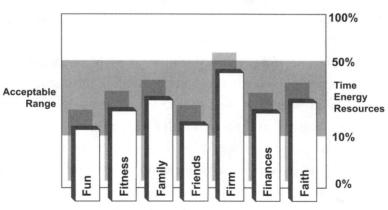

As I stated earlier, you can't possibly allocate equal amounts of time, energy and resources to each area all the time – that's unrealistic (and probably not even appropriate). But you can keep them in a healthy range.

Remember the movie *Big*? Tom Hanks made cinematic history by playing footsy piano on the giant floor keyboard at FAO Schwartz. With the innocence of a child he jumped from key to key in perfect rhythm. Maybe the movie brainwashed me, but sometimes I imagine the 7Fs as keys on that enormous piano. Don't laugh. In any given week, you'll need to decide which "keys" you're going to play, how hard you'll press down, how long you'll hold each note, and what other keys you'll need to play simultaneously to make a harmonious chord.

Do it wrong and all you get is discordant noise. Do it right and you get, well, "Heart and Soul."

And that's a life worth singing about.

○   ○   ○

Ever sit with a pilot in the cockpit of a plane? Do you like movies about gladiators? (Ooops, uncalled for reference to *Airplane.*) To stay on course, a pilot (even Peter Graves as "Captain Oveur") must make continual adjustments in his flight pattern because of crosswinds, fuel consumption, weather changes and other air traffic. Likewise, to arrive at our destination we must adjust our life path as we go.

The key is knowing where you're at in each 7F area and making frequent adjustments. Socrates' admonition that "the unexamined life is not worth living" rings especially true in today's hyper-busy world of distractions. We can never predict what the winds of life are going to blow our way. But by committing to a predetermined flight plan – an intentional allocation of our intellectual horsepower, creative juices, and all-around capabilities – we can make prudent decisions as we go along and arrive in good shape.

Even if our luggage was shipped to Cleveland by mistake.

The methods people use to integrate the 7Fs into their lives are as unique as the individuals themselves. It's not a one-size-fits-all plan. Each of us has a different way of engaging with our environment based on our personality type and internal wiring. For example, some will implement a sequential, systematic program, like designating the specific days and times they're going to play golf or have friends over. They'll predetermine the number of hours they're going to devote to work in a week (if they have that flexibility) and so on.

Others will prefer a less structured, more organic approach. They'll incorporate the 7Fs in an experiential, spontaneous way by creating situations that "automatically" address various vital areas. For example, let's say you choose to join a casual tennis league comprised of players with similar skills. This one strategic move could easily hit multiple Fs – making new "friends," improving your physical "fitness," having "fun," and creating a "family" group to engage with.

Use whichever method seems natural to you, and do it consistently.

THE HEART OF A LEADER

In his classic book, *The 21 Irrefutable Laws of Leadership*, John Maxwell says, "Leadership is influence – nothing more, nothing less." If you're not able to influence others, they won't follow you. If nobody's following you, you're not a leader – no matter what the title on your door or the diploma on your wall may say.

The 7F Life is an influential life. If you're firing on all 7F cylinders, you'll likely be respected, trusted and loved by others. Why? Because you're not a hypocrite. Your words and your actions are congruent. Because you have a clear vision of what's worth doing. Your goal is paramount and your actions are consistent with it. And when you're enjoying this kind of respect and trust, your words are going to carry some weight. People are going to be interested in what you have to say and what you're all about.

You will have opportunities to be an influence for positive change. You will make choices that matter and influence other decision makers.

AN ABUNDANCE MENTALITY

Back in 1989, Steven Covey debuted his watershed work, *The Seven Habits of Highly Effective People*. In it, he coined the phrase "abundance mentality." It's the mindset of a person who believes there are more than enough resources and opportunities to go around. This person can celebrate when others win or prosper or get promoted. He doesn't feel threatened by the success of others because he knows life is not a zero sum game. Sadly, much of the world operates out of the opposite spirit, the "scarcity mentality." These folks (and we all know plenty of them) think that if someone else wins it means they must lose. They don't play for win-win outcomes, so they struggle to maintain control any way possible. This fear of failure nurtures our psyche's most self-destructive twins – comparing and competing.

It's no accident that my two-word definition for the 7F experience is "abundant living." It's a lifestyle of sharing that allows you to relax and loosen your grip, knowing that if you miss out on something, there's an infinite supply of new chances and opportunities.

The scarcity mentality says: "I must make every sale, win every argument, score every point, close every deal."

The abundant life says: "Win some, lose some. There's plenty more to go around."

The scarcity mentality is always selfish and one-sided: "It's a dog eat dog world. Every man for himself."

The abundant life can share ideas, resources, and rewards: "Let's create a mutually beneficial relationship where we both win."

When the pressure to always be top dog is removed, you're "free to fail" – and that means you're also free to experiment and take risks that can produce amazing benefits. In many corporate cultures, employees are scared of doing the wrong thing. But truly great companies encourage their workers to "think out of the box" and reward them for risk-taking. Companies known for creativity like Pixar and Google create open, playful work spaces that encourage impromptu collaborations and informal brain-storming sessions.

When the pressure to compete and compare is gone, you're free to collaborate and reach consensus.

> *It's amazing what you can accomplish when you don't care who gets the credit.*
>
> Harry S. Truman, 33rd U.S. president

I can almost hear some of you asking, "Is there a place for competition and individual achievement?"

Yes, absolutely! Competition improves the breed. Competing for profit and market share not only fuels capitalism, it drives innovation and fosters excellence. That's the beauty of a free market economy. If you build a better mousetrap, you will outsell your competitors. If you invent a more efficient artificial heart, or a higher-mileage engine, or a faster microchip processor, you will profit financially. That's what keeps inventors and entrepreneurs busy – and we all reap the rewards.

If my company was the only financial consulting firm in America, I might tend to get lazy and sloppy. But our aggressive competitors keep us on our A-game at all times. And our clients benefit! That's why I'm all for "healthy competition."

What does that mean? If you're in a sports event or a sales contest or a political election, it's good and natural to want to be the winner. Rivalries between schools, teams, and companies are fun. The Gran Prix is thrilling to watch because of the intense competition between drivers. Without it, you might as well watch traffic go by on the freeway. But there's an "unhealthy competition" also. Let's compare the two...

HEALTHY competition brings out the best in people. It motivates you to push yourself (or your business) harder and farther than you would without someone to compete against. To win a prize, you willingly discipline yourself physically and mentally. And here's the bonus – whether you win, lose, or draw, you still achieve personal and professional growth because you expanded the limits of what you thought was possible. If a competition is healthy, you should be able to congratulate the person who "beat" you.

Their victory should inspire you to try again and do better – not inspire a plot to hold them back or destroy them.

UNHEALTHY competition brings out the worst in people. When your happiness and self-esteem depend entirely on winning, you're dysfunctional. When your reaction to losing is so negative that you're depressed, jealous, or emotionally unstable, you're dangerous. Remember Nancy Kerrigan? In 1994, the Olympic skater was attacked while training for the U.S. Figure Skating Championships. The assailant struck her in the knee with a metal pipe, knocking her out of the competition – and allowing archrival Tonya Harding to win. Conspiracy, hostility, and irrational behavior are the dark side of competition, and they can topple families, teams, and organizations.

When it comes to competing, I subscribe to the Lexus motto, "In pursuit of perfection" because it inspires me to try harder and think smarter to stay ahead of the competition. But even while I'm competing (playing golf, coaching basketball, or pitching a new client) I always wish the best for my competitors. My staff (and my foursomes) will tell you I'm a very tough competitor, but not at the expense of my integrity or 7F lifestyle. I want to win, but I never feel shame, guilt, or anger when I lose – only the urge to come back stronger!

o   o   o

Three Keys to a "No Regrets" Life

1. THE 7F LIFE MEANS TAPPING INTO YOUR HUMAN POTENTIAL.

Psychologist Abraham Maslow was the first to validate the existence of universal human needs in a work published in 1943. Maslow's famous "hierarchy of needs" is often portrayed in the shape of a pyramid, with the most fundamental needs – like breathing, food, water, sex, sleep, and really good pizza – at the bottom. At the top of the pyramid is the need for self-actualization. Maslow defined that top-ranked desire as the yearning to discover what your full potential is and reaching it. That's what the 7F Life taps into – your desire to become more and more of what you were created to be, to become everything you are capable of becoming. Writing about this innate hunger to reach our potential, Maslow declared, "What a man can be, he must be."

2. THE 7F LIFE MEANS BEING FULLY PRESENT AND ENGAGED.

Maslow said the ability to be in the present moment is a major component of mental wellness. Which explains why so many of us are unbalanced – we live regretting the past and worrying about the future. The seventeenth-century French essayist Jean de la Bruyere concluded, "Children have neither past nor future; they enjoy the present, which few of us do." Like kids, we need to find the magic in each day, the silver lining in each cloud, the good in each person. If that sounds pollyannish, I apologize. But is it better to live with a sense of childlike wonder or a sour, cynical view? I prefer to follow Einstein's advice: "Learn from yesterday, live for today, and hope for tomorrow."

3. THE 7F LIFE MEANS REFUSING TO STAGNATE.

A person living the 7Fs is always striving to become more engaging, interesting, relational, confident, and productive. We try to live from a perspective that doesn't settle for mind-numbing routine or servile complacency just to chase a buck. Do you admire the Apple business empire? My favorite (and most troubling) quote from their late great founder, Steve Jobs, is: "For the past 33 years, I have looked in the mirror every morning and asked myself: 'If today were the last day of my life, would I want to do what I am about to do today?' And whenever the answer has been 'No' for too many days in a row, I know I need to change something."

What would *you* change?

SIMPLE, BUT NOT EASY

Some of life's most powerful and complex concepts can be expressed briefly.

Like $E=mc^2$ for example.

If you recall your college physics (or a recent episode of *Big Bang Theory*), you know the formula for taking the mass of an object and multiplying it by the speed of light to calculate the amount of energy released means that... uh, well, it means that subatomic particles... oh, never mind.

With apologies to readers with enormous frontal lobes, let's switch to another brief but less demanding maxim: "Practice what you preach."

Simple to grasp. Easy to remember. Very succinct.

In fact, most helpful advice is *usually* packaged up short and sweet. Like Bobby McFerrin's musical admonition, "Don't worry, be happy."

An entire philosophy of life in just four little words.

But brevity doesn't make a concept any less true – or easier to master. If your goal was to lose 50 pounds, I might advise you "Eat less, move more." To help you retire wealthy I could tell you "Spend less than you earn."

Both instructions are easy to understand, but not exactly easy to pull off. Which helps explain our staggering rates of obesity and consumer debt. So please understand that the simplistic equation that follows could take a lifetime of effort and prayer and willpower and sacrifice to implement.

With that caveat, I present what I believe is the formula for a life well lived:

Knowing **WHO** you are

\+ Knowing **WHY** you are

\+ Having the **RESOURCES** to do what matters most

———————————————————————

= **Abundant Living**

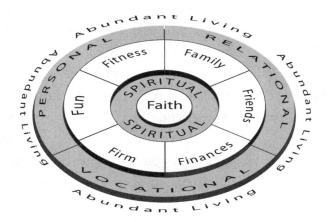

GETTING IN SYNCH

As you take steps toward integrating the 7Fs, you'll start to see new doors of opportunity opening up and new relationships forming that may enrich your life in surprising ways. Previously unknown resources will become available, and you'll discover new stores of energy and focus to apply to things that matter most. You will experience a quality of life few ever do.

At this point, I'd like to ask you a ten-megaton question about your future, based on an idea developed by Dan Sullivan of The Strategic Coach, Inc. Please get some paper and write down everything that comes to mind when I ask the following question. Don't limit the areas of your life that this question may apply to, and use the 7Fs as a filter to think about your responses:

> If you want to be truly happy with where you're at in three years, what will you need to do between now and then to achieve it?

Please re-read the question. Give yourself permission to think freely and courageously, then write down whatever comes to mind. Don't dismiss any idea, thinking "that could never happen." Write it down anyway.

Surprised by what surfaced? Excited?

Now arrange your list in order of priority. Which goal matters most?

Least? Hint: Some leaders prioritize projects in three categories – *urgent, important*, and *nice to have*. Next, look at each item and ask, "Realistically, when can I begin taking action on this item? Six months from today, a year from now?" Write your time frame next to each item.

Let me give you a "high five!" You've just set some important targets for your life. Commit to experiencing these wonderful things in the time frame you identified. Then write down what you need to do for these dreams to become reality. What steps must you take for each one to materialize? Lastly, tell a close friend or advisor about your plans. Ask this person to hold you accountable.

Decide in advance how you'll celebrate when you achieve each of your targets. When you do achieve them, go ahead and party! You'll be inspired to keep growing, to keep reaching.

o   o   o

Make a commitment to yourself to accept full responsibility for whatever comes of your life. What matters is what *you* decide to make of your time on earth, not what others decide for you. So no excuses, no explanations, no blaming. Just take the plunge.

Your plan won't be 100 percent perfect (nothing ever is), but write it down anyway and work it like a dog on a bone.

If you wait to do everything until you're sure it's right, you'll probably never do much of anything.

Win Borden, writer & farmer

WHAT SHAKESPEARE KNEW

What are the two saddest words in the English language? Some might nominate weepy pairs like "needless tragedy" or "broken hearts" or even

"good bye." Personally, I think the two saddest words are "what" and "if."
You know, as in…

"*What if* I hadn't lost track of my high school sweetheart?"
"*What if* I'd taken that trip to Africa I always promised myself?"
"*What if* I'd started my own business when I had the chance?"
"*What if* I didn't sell my shares of Apple back in 2002?"

Shakespeare said, "Of all the words of tongue and pen, the saddest are, 'it might have been.'" In all of human existence, nothing brings more regret than missed opportunities. And nothing brings more joy than rejecting passivity and fear to follow your heart into uncharted waters!

Someone once said, "Tragedies are when we put off living." And that's what we do. We don't *reject* opportunities outright; we just *delay* them until some future time.

Meanwhile, life goes by at triple digits and we never cash in that IOU we've written to ourselves.

In my line of financial work, timing is critical. So people ask me about timing in other areas, too. I get questions like, "When's the best time to start a business?" Or my favorite, "When's the best time to get married?" (Not joking.) Sorry, folks, *there is no best time.* Some times are likely more favorable than others. But the reality is that we will *never* know enough, have enough, or feel secure enough to begin living the way we envision – if we wait for perfect conditions.

So do it now. Don't be paralyzed by your analysis of all the things that might possibly go wrong. Take a step – even if it's a baby step.

The best time to plant a tree is 20 years ago. The second best time is now.

Chinese proverb

CHANGE FOR THE BETTER

Not many of us get excited by the notion of change. In fact, most people would rather walk barefoot over broken glass than change their ways. Woodrow Wilson said, "If you want to make enemies try changing something." Yet we know change is necessary for growth. Those opposed to change risk becoming like a pond cut off from its source of fresh water – it stagnates, gets covered in scum and eventually stinks.

Don't let your life stink.

Reaching our dreams and aspirations requires us to change. Period.

If you keep doing what you're doing right now, you'll keep getting the results you're getting right now. But don't take my word for it. A pretty smart guy named Einstein defined insanity as "doing the same thing over and over again and expecting different results." Something has to change if you want your life to improve. In fact, change is the only real scientific evidence of an organism being alive. It's the difference between you and a pet rock.

Historian and philosopher Will Durant rightly stated, "The future never 'just happened' – it was created." And at the root of creating a better future is change.

Perhaps you've heard someone say, "I'm open to change." Sounds good, rolls off the tongue, but it's not enough. It's too passive. We must eagerly *pursue* change. Just being "open" to it is a lazy, weak position – you responding to someone else's initiatives. Eagerly pursuing change (or a dream or a goal) means being proactive, pushing your own initiatives. As a result, you operate from a position of strength.

○   ○   ○

One type of change that's especially daunting is pulling the plug on a personal relationship or a career path. While "endings" are an everyday part of nature and standard business procedure, we often approach them with feelings of fear, sadness, even dread. But we shouldn't. Dr. Henry Cloud, author of *Necessary Endings*, writes, "Getting to the next level always requires ending something, leaving it behind, and moving on. Growth itself demands that we move on."

Cloud argues that our personal and professional lives can't really improve much until we can see endings as a strategic step to something better: "Without the ability to end things, people stay stuck, never becoming who they are meant to be, never accomplishing all that their talents and abilities should afford them."

So sometimes we have to cut our losses. Sell a losing stock. Break off an engagement. Quit a dead-end job. Leave a toxic relationship. Transfer to another department. Pull our kid out of a school. Shut down a plant. Cut the quarterback. Change barbers. Change churches. Sell our house. Say *adios* to that old clunker that's leaking oil in the driveway. Whatever.

If we can't see endings in a positive light, growth will never come in either our business or our personal lives. It's like pruning the bad and broken branches of a bush so new growth can take place. Except that when it involves people instead of shrubs, it has to be done with utmost sensitivity, honesty and compassion – or both parties can suffer pain for years to come.

How to Ace Your ACT

Ideally, change opens the door of your life to a new world of experiences and opportunities. But as George Carlin once noted, it doesn't always work: "I put a dollar in one of those change machines. Nothing changed."

Isn't that how life feels sometimes?

We think we're doing the right things to bring about change, but nothing happens. To help out, I offer three keys to making significant and lasting change. They're found in the acronym ACT…

"A" IS FOR AFFECTION

A marriage without love is not likely to last. It takes an emotional attraction to stay connected 'til death do us part. Similarly, you can't make life changes based merely on willpower and logic. If reaching a goal is only an intellectual exercise, it's not likely to amount to much. Your goal must stir you emotionally. You must have a genuine *affection* for what you're doing.

Author John Maxwell says, "You can make a sudden decision, but you cannot make a sudden change." To change a habit takes an average of 21 days. To make a change stick, we need to understand how our minds work. The three components of personality are emotion, intellect, and will. With your will, you can make a decision in a moment. But to sustain that decision, you must fully engage your intellect *and* emotions. A decision to change must be accompanied by looking forward (delayed gratification) to the positive emotions you'll experience when you finally reach your goal.

We will inevitably encounter difficulties on our quest. The best way to get past them is to anticipate the feelings of accomplishment we'll experience on the other side. Looking beyond our challenging circumstances (the present) and focusing on the future can get us through trying times. A great example of keeping our "eyes on the prize" is a mother-to-be in labor – it's painful, it's exhausting, but focusing on the joy the newborn will bring pulls her through.

Obstacles are those frightful things you see when you take your eyes off your goal.

Henry Ford, founder, Ford Motor Company

The desire for significant life change needs to become a conviction – an obsession, really – before you can hope to live it out long-term. Gauge your passion with these questions: *Are you (deeply) dissatisfied with your present life? Are you (totally) fed up with just getting by? Are you (extremely) tired of your days all blurring together?*

We often start off with the right mental attitude. Positive emotions permeate and influence our intellect as we first make plans. But over time, feelings can fade. So once you're moving in the right direction, continually go back and reconnect to the original affection and stirrings you felt when you first envisioned making a change.

Your brain can kick-start a dream, but only your heart can sustain it!

"C" IS FOR CONFIDING

Ever travel to a foreign city for the first time? Necessities like hotels, transportation, and currency are a total mystery. You feel lost and helpless. But with an experienced companion, your journey is totally different. No matter where you want to go in life you're more likely to arrive successfully if you connect with someone who's already been there. Common sense, right? Talking to somebody who's walked the path you're about to embark on (an overseas trip, a medical operation, a complex project, etc.) is invaluable.

Every pro golfer has a mentor. Every pro baseball player has a batting coach. The greatest athletes in the world keep one or more experts within their inner circle. Why? We can get so close to our circumstances that we lose objectivity. We lose perspective. We can get off track (and not be aware of it) unless we get a "second opinion."

Seek out the assistance of a mentor or life coach and confide your dreams in that person. They'll see what you can't. They'll improve your swing. They'll point out bad habits before your blind spots derail you. (Warning: Potential coaches are likely to have full schedules and demands on their time. But that doesn't mean they're not willing to assist you. It just means they won't seek *you* out. Pursue them anyway.)

Where do you find these individuals?

Evaluate the people around you from the standpoint of experience, talents, and strengths. Evaluate how well their personality fits with yours, and determine who's best qualified to mentor you. Briefly share your life vision with this person, then ask if they'll meet with you for coffee or over the phone regularly.

When we share our vision for life with someone we trust (and who cares about us), we take a *big* step toward making that dream a reality. Once you speak it out loud to someone else, it becomes more real, more cut in stone. Someone who shares your dream can guide you and hold you accountable along the way. Including another person in your process will strengthen your resolve and energize you. For example, I'm a busy guy. Taking on a project like writing this book was daunting. But during my regular conversations with friend and mentor Dr. Loren Siffring, I was encouraged to go for it.

Coaching can come from an individual or a small group of close friends. Being part of a mini-community of people who know you and love you can be a great source of inspiration, guidance, and encouragement.

If one falls down, his friend can help him up. But pity the man who falls and has no one to help him up!

King Solomon, Book of Ecclesiastes

"T" IS FOR TARGETING

People living the 7F Life are motivated to get a little better each day. But progress and growth don't happen by accident. Progress is intentional. With no *measurement* there's no *movement*. The sad fact is that human beings often take the path of least resistance. We act on a whim; we do whatever we feel like doing at any given moment. Without motivation, we do as little as we can get away with. But living continuously in our comfort zone will result in a life of mediocrity. Like muscles, our brain atrophies without exercise. We need to be stretched and challenged.

Basically, we need a bright red bullseye target that excites and rejuvenates us whenever we think about it. For Microsoft founder, Bill Gates, the target is stamping out malaria. For Habit for Humanity founder, Jimmy Carter, it's housing the poor. For Charity Water founder, Scott Harrison, it's digging wells. Whatever yours is, follow Stephen Covey's advice, "Begin with the end in mind."

Smart target. Smart tactics.

You've probably heard it said that if you aim at nothing you're sure to hit it every time. To avoid that mistake, make sure your target is SMART.

OMG, that's another annoying acronym. Sorry. Please don't LOL, but your GR8 target needs to be Specific, Measurable, Attainable, Realistic and Timely.

For decades, the SMART system has inspired individuals and companies to reach remarkable goals – even the kind that initially appear unattainable. Using the SMART criteria will make targets that seem out of range move closer – not because your goals shrink but because your confidence and skills expand. Ready?

"S" IS FOR SPECIFIC

Begin creating your target by identifying one of the 7Fs in your life that you think needs the most attention. Then answer these six questions:

- WHO is involved?
- WHAT do you want to accomplish?
- WHERE is it going to be accomplished?
- WHY is this important to you?
- WHEN is it going to happen?
- HOW are you going to pull it off?

For example, a general target could be "I gotta get in shape." But a *specific* target would be, "I'm going to join Rock Body Fitness Club and work out four days a week, first thing in the morning, to increase my energy and improve my appearance."

"M" IS FOR MEASURABLE

Pick a time frame – for example, three days a week – for giving attention to your target. As I stated earlier, without measurement there's no movement. How can you tell if you're improving or declining if there's no grid in place? That's why a runner training for a marathon keeps a logbook of his workouts and timed events. Ask yourself these questions about your goal: "How often? How many? How much?"

"A" IS FOR ATTAINABLE

You've heard the old joke, "How do you eat an elephant? One bite at a time." Implementing the 7F Life is like that. It's a gradual process. You're not going to ramp up all seven areas in your first week. Your transformation will occur over time. Don't get down on yourself if you miss your mark. You're not bionic. As you take consistent steps toward your target, you grow and your capacity increases – improving the likelihood of attaining your goal. Keep the target in front of you. Get back in the batter's box and take another swing at it.

Try again. Fail again. Fail better.

Samuel Beckett, avant-garde playwright

"R" IS FOR REALISTIC

Realistic is so overrated. I mean what's realistic about landing on the moon? Or curing polio? Or inventing Facebook? Your target should be high enough to motivate and inspire you. How high? Only you can determine that. You'll know in time if you've set the bar too high. But go ahead. Reach a little higher than you think you can attain.

Confucius said, "Shoot for the stars. If you hit the moon, that's okay. Most people don't shoot at all." You'll never know how high you can go unless you extend your reach. Ironically, it's usually not our limited *abilities* that hold us back, but our limited *thinking* (the scarcity mentality) that hinders our progress.

Here's a classic example: Throughout history, it was believed that running a mile in less than four minutes was not humanly possible.

It seemed too unrealistic to even consider.

Then in 1954, an English runner named Roger Bannister ran a mile in 3 minutes, 59.4 seconds. That was amazing. But even more amazing is that within a few months of Bannister's achievement, many other runners also broke that four-minute barrier. Currently, the world record is an "unrealistic" 3 minutes, 43.13 seconds – almost 17 seconds below what had been deemed impossible!

Recalling his achievement more than 50 years later, Bannister said, "There was a mystique, a belief that it couldn't be done, but I think it was more a psychological barrier than a physical barrier." Your target probably won't be a world speed record, but the point is, you're capable of a whole lot more than you think.

Just remember, to have a realistic shot at achieving your target you need to commit time and energy to it and be able to participate in the necessary activities. Bannister ran 52 weeks a year training to smash the record.

"T" IS FOR TIMELY

Without a time frame there's no sense of urgency. When do you want to lose ten pounds – someday? Not good enough. When do you want to learn a second language – someday? *Excusez-moi.* Not gonna happen. You may have good intentions, but the trouble with "someday" is that it never arrives. Anchor your target to a deadline or due date and you'll activate the focus and energy it takes to succeed.

Don't let others distract you. There are plenty of people who haven't a clue where they are going with their life and they would like to take you with them down their random road. Know what you are about. Stay on target. Stay on your timeline.

Speaking of time, be aware that it flies by. Live like that king of *carpe diem*, Ferris Bueller: "Life moves pretty fast. If you don't stop and look around once and a while, you could miss it."

I can't argue with that. So work hard, but every so often, play hooky, call in sick, and take somebody's Ferrari out for a joy ride!

GET SMART, GET MOVING

Your SMART target needs to be written down, shared with others, and kept in front of you as a constant reminder. Maybe a tattoo on your hand. Okay, maybe not. But when you establish a SMART target, you stimulate a powerful part of the body called the "reticular activating system." This is a network of cells at the base of your skull that works like a radar system. As soon as you set a goal, your reticular activating system goes to work screening out information not related to your target. It helps you focus on the topics and issues most critical in helping achieve your vision.

All of us have experienced our reticular activating system at work – we just weren't conscious of it. For example, have you ever thought about buying a certain car – say, a Mustang convertible – and wondered how it looked on the road? All of a sudden you start seeing Mustang convertibles all over the place! It's not that they weren't there before; it's just that you created a target – an image in your brain – and your reticular activating system was subconsciously focusing on it.

o   o   o

Don't procrastinate. You don't have to have all the pieces figured out. But you do have to *start*. Really. Once you've established an exciting SMART target and you begin to ACT, you'll be amazed how the resources you need start falling into place. For example, my family considered having a professional woman from Japan stay at our home for a week (through Rotary's Friendship Exchange program). My wife and I often talked hypothetically about what a fun experience that would be. But we were concerned about the language barrier and worried about how to occupy her time.

It wasn't until we actually agreed to host someone and had an actual date on the calendar that resources started surfacing. Just a few weeks before our visitor arrived, a man from Japan who works in my building heard about our exchange. Since we don't speak Japanese (I can't even order sushi), he suggested we bring our guest by his office to spend some time. That was an enormous help. We discovered that our overseas guest enjoyed art. When a friend of mine who's an award-winning artist heard about her interest in art, he invited us to bring our guest to his studio for a lesson. There, he helped her create a painting she could take back to Japan. Soon, we learned of a local presentation called "A Glimpse of Japan" put on by a local Asian-based corporation. It featured Ikebana floral art, live Koto and Shamisen music, much to her delight.

Seemingly out of nowhere, people began stepping forward and offering to take our visitor on tours of the Detroit Art Institute, the Chrysler Museum, area shopping malls and more. In addition, we met three students of Japanese culture who helped us with translation issues and came to our house for lively international discussions. Without these "surprise helpers," the visit would have been challenging to say the least. But we didn't meet any of them until *after* we'd committed to the visit. If we'd not taken the risk, we would have missed out on a priceless friendship and the invaluable experience of learning about Japan and its customs.

Here's my point: Once you set a target, the resources will begin to reveal themselves. Establish your target; make it SMART. Set your beginning date and start taking action. The results? The Japanese word *kaizen* sums it up – "continuous change for the better."

The most valuable result of all education is the ability to make yourself do the thing you have to do when it ought to be done.

Thomas Henry Huxley, biologist

PUTTING IT ALL TOGETHER:
THINK BIG, START SMALL

When the Dalai Lama was asked what surprised him most about humanity, he answered, "Man. Because he sacrifices his health in order to make money, then he sacrifices his money to recuperate his health. And then he is so anxious about the future that he does not enjoy the present; the result being that he does not live in the present or the future; he lives as if he's never going to die, and then he dies having never really lived."

That's sobering.

Surely nobody wants to live that way on purpose. Then how *do* we get stuck in that awful cycle the Dalai Lama described?

The difference between someone experiencing a dynamic, vibrant life and someone experiencing a 75-year snooze is often in the little things they *choose to do or not do.*

Notice I didn't write "say or not say," but rather "do or not do."

Despite inflation, talk is still cheap.

A 7F person doesn't just *talk* about the changes they're going to make. They actually take steps, carve out time and reorganize their life to allow them to occur. The difference between dreaming and doing is "execution." Lots of NFL football players can memorize a playbook, watch team videos, and even do well at practice. But only the players who can execute plays on game day, at crunch time, can become stars.

In sports and life, everything depends on execution.

A dream is just a dream. A goal is a dream with a plan and a deadline. And that goal will remain a dream unless you create and execute a plan of action to accomplish it.

Harvey Mackay, business writer & speaker

o   o   o

CHAPTER 10: COMMENCEMENT

When I was in high school, one of my teachers showed a short film about a man in his fifties who was diagnosed with terminal cancer. Doctors told him he had just six months to live – tops. Approximately three months after getting the bad news, he was interviewed by a reporter. He was asked how his life had changed since receiving the diagnosis. He responded enthusiastically about how he had traveled to places he'd always dreamed of visiting, mended broken relationships, talked with family members he hadn't spoken to in years, gone sailing, etc.

It was like the movie *Bucket List*, but it wasn't fiction.

When the film was over I remember feeling so sad for this man. It was as if he hadn't begun living until he got word that he was going to die in a few months. When we get near the end of life everything seems to come into clear focus – we see what's important and what's not. Sitting in class, I thought to myself, *What a waste. He allowed so many years to evaporate without doing the things that really mattered to him.*

The fact is we're *all* dying. Nobody gets out of here alive. It's just that some people know their expiration date and some don't. Please don't wait until you know you're circling the drain before you look intensely at your life.

Dr. Ornish has worked with many patients suffering from late-stage cancer. In the same *Newsweek* article, "What Matters Most," he talks about the courage it takes to let go of what is insignificant: "There is a moment of clarity when you know what's important to you... the view from the edge of life is a lot clearer than most of us have. In all those years, nobody ever said to me, 'If I die of this disease, I'm going to miss my Mercedes. What matters is who you've touched on your way through life."

Live today like you knew you were going to be gone tomorrow. Don't wait until you're diagnosed with an illness before you start living a 7F Life.

Many people take no care of their money till they come nearly to the end of it, and others do just the same with their time.

Johann Goethe, German novelist

You will never fully respect yourself when you live or perform below the potential you know is inside you. So go for it. Think big. Start small. Don't let others hold you back. Writer and speaker Zig Ziglar gave us all a good kick in the pants, "You don't have to be great to start, but you have to start to be great."

Don't be afraid of failure.

Don't be afraid of success.

Just unleash your greatness.

That's the liberating message from *A Return to Love* by Marianne Williamson. Her advice is to shirk false modesty and be all you can be:

> Our deepest fear is not that we are inadequate. Our deepest fear is that we are powerful beyond measure. It is our light, not our darkness, that most frightens us. We ask ourselves: "Who am *I* to be brilliant, gorgeous, talented and fabulous?" Actually, who are you *not* to be? You are a child of God. Your playing small doesn't serve the world. There is nothing enlightened about shrinking, so that other people won't feel insecure around you. We were born to manifest the glory of God that is within us. It's not just in some of us; it's in everyone. And as we let our own light shine, we unconsciously give other people permission to do the same. As we are liberated from our own fear, our presence automatically liberates others.

WHERE THE RUBBER MEETS THE ROAD

Now that you know what's possible, why be satisfied with a 2F or 3F Life when you can step up to a full-blown 7F Life? It's there for the taking. It doesn't matter where you've been; it matters where you're going. So don't let anyone dissuade you. Don't let anyone get behind the wheel of your life but you.

This is such an exciting time to be alive. Don't just take up space, make a difference. Put your fingerprints on your corner of the world. Be fit, fulfilled, and influential. Live every moment to the fullest; don't look back, don't close your eyes, and whatever you do... *don't look down.*

While I was writing this book, Nik Wallenda became the first person to ever walk across Niagara Falls on a high wire. To honor his great-grandfather's legacy and to fulfill a lifelong dream, Nik walked the length of four football fields over raging waters and into history. Over 130,000 spectators gathered at the Falls on June 15, 2012 as millions more watched the 30-minute crossing on live television. When he stepped off the wire and onto Canadian soil, a uniformed customs agent asked, "What is the purpose of your trip, sir?"

Wallenda replied, "To inspire people around the world."

Be an inspiration.

Keep battling your natural tendency to play it safe. Keep challenging your preconceived notions, perceptions, and assumptions. Keep seeking truth, exploring new ideas, expanding your boundaries, giving more than you take, maximizing your capabilities.

In short, live life close to the bone, where it's most tender and savory.

In the end, when all is said and done, people are going to take one of two approaches to life: Some will *live* and some will *exist*. Those who choose to enjoy life will have more happiness and satisfaction than those who merely endure it – guaranteed.

I hope you will choose to truly live by joining me on the 7F Life adventure.

One day your life will flash before your eyes. Make sure it's worth watching.

Gerard Way, musician

ACTION STEPS: LIVING THE 7F LIFE™

- Use the 7F framework as a filter to make daily decisions. When you encounter an opportunity, ask yourself: "Which of the 7Fs will this affect? Will it have a positive or negative impact?" If that "F" is a weakness in your life, you might say "Yes" to the opportunity in order to strengthen that area.

• Turn to the 7F Life Balance Assessments in Appendix A. Read the questions below the grid corresponding to each of the 7Fs. Circle the appropriate numbers in the chart. If you have a spouse or partner, copy the page and have them do the assessments separately. The "Current" assessment is a snapshot of your status today. The "Desired" assessment is a goal-setter for where you'd like to be by a future date. Complete both the Current and Desired assessments. Use this newfound clarity to begin making changes in your life.

• Check out *www.7FLife.com* for additional resources to inspire and assist you in your adventure...

>> Use "My Dashboard" to help identify the 7F activities you want to focus on in any given week. This quick, easy tool also helps monitor your progress and calibrate the time, energy, and resources you're giving to each of these vital areas.

>> Join "My Community" to interact with other 7F Life implementers. You'll receive ideas and encouragement while living the 7F Life.

>> Learn about historical figures and current achievers who've lived by 7F principles and created great opportunities for themselves and others. Get to know people like pioneer TV personality Art Linkletter, former Secretary of State, Condoleeza Rice, and Nobel Prize winner, Mother Teresa.

CHAPTER 10: COMMENCEMENT

The words of the Rascal Flatts' song "My Wish" (from the 2006 Platinum album, *Me and My Gang*) express my desire for you to experience the 7F Life. If you haven't heard it yet, grab the CD – it will get your adrenaline pumping!

"My wish for you is that this life becomes all that you want it to...

Your dreams stay big, and your worries stay small...

You never need to carry more than you can hold...

And while you're out there getting where you're getting to,

I hope you know somebody loves you, and wants the same things too."

By Karl Nilsson

Words

Remember the Bee Gees? Wait, you *do*? Wow, you're like, ancient. Or maybe your parents kept disco alive during your formative years. Either way, my condolences. Now, focus your remaining brain cells on a tune the Gibbs' brothers wrote called "Words." Ink and paper cannot convey their warbling vibrato, but the lyrics were "It's only words, but words are all I ha-have to steal your heart away-ay-ay."

Or something like tha-at-at.

When I first heard this ballad, I wanted to find Barry, Robin, and Maurice and slap them. Okay, an exaggeration. What I really wanted to tell the trio was, "Words may be all you have, but that's cool because words are all you need."

Think about it. Words can have such power: *I pronounce you man and wife… I'm leaving… You're hired… We're downsizing.*

A few syllables can change everything: *I'm pregnant… I regret to inform you.*

One thing's for sure. When it comes to words, it's not the quantity, but the quality that counts. The Lord's Prayer is just 66 words. The Ten Commandments are a mere 179 words. Lincoln's Gettysburg Address is 286. By contrast, the current U.S. tax code is 3.8 million words. That's nearly five times longer than the entire Bible (and almost half as long as this book. Kidding).

Mike Komara and I tried really, really hard to choose words that would encourage change. But we knew it would be an uphill battle. I doubt that anyone reading this thinks that chain smoking or eating gravy on French fries is helpful. By now, we all know the dangers of obesity and the downside of carcinogens. But we suck smoke and gobble greasy food anyway. By now, we know about workaholism and overspending and not flossing regularly. But we still keep screwing up.

We don't need more information, we need more motivation.

We need to make like Nike and *just do it.*

(That ubiquitous phrase, incidentally, is one of the most recognizable ad slogans ever penned, and took – wait, let me count – a whopping three whole words.)

We hope that our 108,059 words inspire *action.* That they make you look at life differently, make you zoom out and see the big picture.

I'm pretty sure motivational speaker, Charlie "Tremendous" Jones, was right when he said, "You'll be the same person in five years that you are now, except for the people you meet and the books you read."

So seek out inspiring people to learn from and inspiring words to live by.

But don't wait to get started.

A cheetah goes from 0-to-60 mph in about 3 seconds. If they don't go flat out they go hungry. If they put off the chase while they analyze the data they go hungry. If they wait for perfect conditions they go hungry. People, too. Making a difference now, using what we know today, using the tools we have in our hands instead of waiting for some fuzzy, far-off future date is the key. The founder of Talking Heads, David Byrne, titled one of his albums *Everything That Happens is Going to Happen Today.*

Perfectly stated.

Another rock star (in my estimation) named Mother Teresa, put it like this, "Yesterday is gone. Tomorrow has not yet come. We only have today. Let us begin."

EPILOGUE

We only have today...

○   ○   ○

In July 2012, a masked gunman burst into a crowded movie theater and killed twelve people at the midnight premier of *Dark Knight Rises*. One of the victims of the Colorado massacre was 24-year-old Jessica Ghawi. Ironically, Ghawi had escaped death just one month earlier during a deadly shooting spree that occurred in a Toronto shopping mall. The Denver resident was eating dinner in the same food court where the killer opened fire, but for some unknown reason, felt compelled to step outside – less than two minutes before shots rang out.

The aspiring sportscaster's last blog entry was a first-person account of the Eaton Shopping Center shootings: "I was shown how fragile life was on Saturday. I saw terror on bystander's faces. I saw the victims of a senseless crime. I saw lives change. I was reminded that we don't know when or where our time on earth will end. When or where we will breathe our last breath."

Her prophetic words came terribly true as she sat with a friend in the darkened movie theater. She was hit twice. Her final blog entry contains advice that I want to live by and suggest you consider doing the same: "I say all the time that every moment we have to live our life is a blessing. So often I have found myself taking it for granted. Every hug from a family member. Every laugh we share with friends. Every second of every day is a gift."

Enjoy the gift.

Share the gift.

And above all, thank the Giver.

7F Life™ Balance:
Current Assessment

_____ / /
NAME   DATE

Circle the number that best describes your *current* reality in each of the seven vital areas of life (1 is low and 10 is high). Before beginning, please read the questions below the chart to help you determine your responses. Be truthful (even if it hurts). This isn't a test; it's just a way to establish a baseline to compare your progress against.

VITAL AREAS OF LIFE (WHERE I AM TODAY)

1. **Fun**	1	2	3	4	5	6	7	8	9	10
2. **Fitness**	1	2	3	4	5	6	7	8	9	10
3. **Family**	1	2	3	4	5	6	7	8	9	10
4. **Friends**	1	2	3	4	5	6	7	8	9	10
5. **Firm** (work)	1	2	3	4	5	6	7	8	9	10
6. **Finances**	1	2	3	4	5	6	7	8	9	10
7. **Faith**	1	2	3	4	5	6	7	8	9	10

FUN – To what extent are laughter, pleasure, and enjoyment present in your life? Do you build in time for playfulness, recreation, and goofing off?

FITNESS – How emotionally, physically, intellectually, and spiritually fit are you? How robust and resilient do you feel in these areas, overall?

FAMILY – How connected do you feel to members of your family – whether you're related by bloodlines (siblings, parents, cousins, etc.) or by other ties (teammates, co-workers, board members, etc.)?

FRIENDS – To what extent can you be transparent and real with your friends about the things that concern you? Can they be transparent and authentic with you? How would you describe the quality and health of these relationships?

FIRM – Is the time and effort you put into work commensurate with the satisfaction and fulfillment it brings? Does your job fill you up or drain you? How does it affect your ability to be present emotionally and physically with the people who matter to you?

FINANCES – How well do the pursuit and usage of your financial resources align with your personal mission, vision, values, and goals?

FAITH – To what extent do your beliefs inspire, strengthen, and guide you in your daily life? Do you pursue spirituality, either privately or within a group?

7F Life™ Balance:
Desired Assessment

_____   /   /   ____
NAME   DATE

Circle the number that best describes your *future desire* for each of the seven vital areas of life (1 is low and 10 is high). Before beginning, please read the questions below the chart to help you determine your responses.

BE REALISTIC. No one can shoot for a 10 in all seven areas. Don't worry about perfection, focus on growth. For example, to move from a current 2 to a desired 10 is probably unrealistic, depending on the time frame you choose.

SET A DATE. To make your desire concrete, choose a specific time frame (from six months to three years) that makes sense to you and works with your circumstances.

Time frame for my goals: _____

VITAL AREAS OF LIFE (WHERE I WANT TO BE)

1. **Fun**	1	2	3	4	5	6	7	8	9	10
2. **Fitness**	1	2	3	4	5	6	7	8	9	10
3. **Family**	1	2	3	4	5	6	7	8	9	10
4. **Friends**	1	2	3	4	5	6	7	8	9	10
5. **Firm** (work)	1	2	3	4	5	6	7	8	9	10
6. **Finances**	1	2	3	4	5	6	7	8	9	10
7. **Faith**	1	2	3	4	5	6	7	8	9	10

FUN – To what extent will laughter, pleasure, and enjoyment be present in your makeover plan? How large a role will recreation play?

FITNESS – How emotionally, physically, intellectually, and spiritually fit do you hope to become? How robust and resilient do you plan on being?

FAMILY – How connected do you desire to be to other members of your family, whether related by bloodlines (siblings, parents, cousins, etc.) or other ties (teammates, co-workers, board members, etc.)?

FRIENDS – To what extent do you desire to be transparent and real with your friends about the things that concern you? How much stronger do you want these friendships to be?

FIRM – How much more will your time and effort at work match the satisfaction and fulfillment you wish to derive from it? How much will it positively affect your relationships with people who matter to you?

FINANCES – How will the pursuit and usage of your financial resources align more closely with your personal vision, values, and goals?

FAITH – In your time frame, how much more do you want your beliefs to inspire, strengthen, and guide you in your daily life?

7F Life™ Balance:
Working the Plan

Comparing your Current and Desired assessment charts, identify the Fs with the greatest gaps between where *you are now* and where *you want to be*. Then write two specific action steps you'll use to close those gaps. Refer back to SMART planning (on page 341) and structure your growth goals to be: Specific, Measurable, Attainable, Realistic, and Timely. Here are a couple of examples and lots of room to jot down your ideas…

GROWTH AREA: _FITNESS — lose 25 pounds_

    Action Step A _Dust off treadmill, walk at least 4 times /week_

    Action Step B _Buy a juicer – no snacks after 7 – more veggies_

GROWTH AREA: _FIRM — cut my stress level_

    Action Step A _Delegate more to my staff – don't work Saturdays_

    Action Step B _Use up my vacation time – book the cruise today!_

GROWTH AREA: _____

    Action Step A _____

    Action Step B _____

GROWTH AREA: _____

    Action Step A _____

    Action Step B _____

GROWTH AREA: _____

    Action Step A _____

    Action Step B _____

GROWTH AREA: _____

    Action Step A _____

    Action Step B _____

GROWTH AREA: _____

    Action Step A _____

    Action Step B _____

GROWTH AREA: _____

    Action Step A _____

    Action Step B _____

GROWTH AREA: _____

    Action Step A _____

    Action Step B _____

GROWTH AREA: _____

    Action Step A _____

    Action Step B _____

GROWTH AREA: _____

    Action Step A _____

    Action Step B _____

GROWTH AREA: _____

    Action Step A _____

    Action Step B _____

GROWTH AREA: _____

    Action Step A _____

    Action Step B _____

GROWTH AREA: _____

    Action Step A _____

    Action Step B _____

GROWTH AREA: _____

    Action Step A _____

    Action Step B _____

GROWTH AREA: _____

    Action Step A _____

    Action Step B _____

7F Life™ Balance:
Cash Flow Tracker

INCOME (INFLOWS)		
Monthly income	You	Your Mate
Salary	$	$
Bonus	$	$
Commissions	$	$
Pension	$	$
Social Security	$	$
Other (e.g. rental income)	$	$
Sub-total income (monthly)	$	$
Investment income (monthly)	You	Your Mate
Taxable	$	$
Non-Taxable	$	$
Total income (monthly)	$	$
Multiply by 12		
Total Annual Income	$	$

(continued)

EXPENSES (OUTFLOWS)		
Monthly expenses	You	Your Mate
Mortgage/Rent	$	$
Utilities	$	$
Food	$	$
Telephone/Internet	$	$
Tuition/Education	$	$
Child Care	$	$
Insurance (life, health, home, auto, etc.)	$	$
Personal Care	$	$
Entertainment	$	$
Medical/Dental	$	$
Alimony Support	$	$
Gifts (birthdays, holidays, etc.)	$	$
Charity	$	$
Student Loans	$	$
Dues and Subscriptions (club membership, etc.)	$	$
Debt Maintenance (credit cards, etc.)	$	$
Car Payment(s)	$	$
Clothing	$	$
Recreation	$	$
Home Repair	$	$
Vacation	$	$
Property Taxes	$	$
Savings/Investing	$	$
Total Expenses (monthly)	$	$
Multiply by 12		
Total Annual Expenses	$	$
Discretionary Subtract annual outflows from annual inflows	$	$

ABOUT THE AUTHORS

MICHAEL KOMARA

The future belongs to those who prepare for it.

That brief advice from Ralph Waldo Emerson sums up the mission that drives Michael Komara's personal and professional life.

This unusually well-prepared guy describes himself as an educator, business owner, sports mentor, and public speaker. He's also a "wealth coach" and partner at a successful financial consulting firm in southeast Michigan. In addition, Komara serves on the board of two nonprofit organizations with global footprints – Leader Dogs for the Blind and the multi-site Kensington Church.

Michael is also a board member at the Financial & Estate Planning Council of Metropolitan Detroit, the Boy Scouts of America Great Lakes Council, and the Athletics Advisory Council at Oakland University. Komara has started two successful businesses, pastored three growing churches, and coached both boys' and girls' basketball teams to championships.

Always up for adventure, Michael has taken his globetrotting family to 17 countries. He's enjoyed flying a glider in New Zealand, snorkeling in Australia's Great Barrier Reef, and sailing in the Mediterranean. On any given day, you might find him on a golf course, basketball court, hockey rink, ski slope, tennis court – did we mention *golf course?*

An avid reader and lifelong learner, Michael earned his Bachelor of Science degree in education from Central Michigan University, a Master

LIFE IN THE BALANCE

of Theology degree from Dallas Theological Seminary, and the Chartered Financial Consultant designation from The American College.

Why the book? Komara saw that many of his daily contacts and clients were living unfulfilled, fragmented lives – despite their wealth and success. Through trial and error, he developed the 7F Life™ system specifically to help them. As a speaker and author, he can now offer his hard-earned insights to a wider audience.

Michael and his wife Mary Ann have been ecstatically married for over 30 years. Their son Drew is an aspiring entrepreneur who loves life and people.

KARL NILSSON

You can't postpone sorrow, so why postpone happiness?

That quote by essayist Robert Brault is taped on the doorway of Karl Nilsson's messy office. And it captures the heart of this self-described "recovering existentialist."

A Michigan native, Nilsson is managing editor of Elk Lake Publishing. He co-founded Elk Lake with the group's president, Jeff Petherick, back in 2007 to "publish the positive." True to that mission statement, Karl has collaborated with Petherick on three ELP books: *Wavelength, Bigger than the Sky*, and *Grace Like Rain*.

He describes his work with Michael Komara: "Working on *Life in the Balance* has been a great learning experience. I'm the worst guy on the planet when it comes to grown-up things like handling money and planning for the future. My idea of getting organized was to order Post-it notes in bulk. Working around Mike is like plugging into the most optimistic, entrepreneurial, and energizing person you'll ever meet. Which is pretty annoying. I'm teasing. Mike lives to encourage others and is always ready to share his unique insights. And he didn't pay me to say that."

For two decades Nilsson has worked at Kensington Church in Metro Detroit, specializing in communications. Before leading a team at the burgeoning megachurch, he operated an advertising agency where he was paid big bucks to exaggerate. Prior to his marketing career, he was a syndicated cartoonist, rock & roll magazine editor, and newspaper columnist. He enjoys watching movies, bicycling, and exploring backroads in his increasingly-vintage Mustang convertible.

He is married to his proofreader and best friend, Marie. The couple has two adult children, Britt and Karl.

REFERENCES

The authors gratefully acknowledge material relied upon from numerous literary sources, internet ramblings, hallway conversations, and their own leaky memory banks.

CHAPTER 2 – POWER OF SEVEN

Rawicz, Slavomir. *The Long Walk: The True Story of a Trek to Freedom.* Guilford, CT: Lyons Press, 1956.

Rock, Dr. David. From online resources at *psychologytoday.com/experts/daniel-rock* and his blog at *www.davidrock.net*

CHAPTER 3 – FUN

Marano, Hara Estroff. "Laughter: The Best Medicine." *Psychology Today.* Featuring Dr. Michael Miller, published April 5, 2005.

Bombeck, Erma. *Eat Less Cottage Cheese and More Ice Cream.* Kansas City, MO: Andrews McMeel, 2003.

Dungy, Tony. *Quiet Strength: The Principles, Practices & Priorities of a Winning Life.* Carol Stream, IL: Tyndale House, 2007.

Bettinger, Frank. *How I Raised Myself from Failure to Success in Selling.* Whitby, ON: Fireside, 1992.

Maxwell, John. *The 21 Irrefutable Laws of Leadership.* Nashville, TN: Thomas Nelson, 2007.

Hansel, Tim. *When I Relax I Feel Guilty: Discover the Wonder and Joy of Really Living.* Elgin, IL: Chariot Family, 1979.

Cousins, Norman. *Anatomy of an Illness as Perceived by the Patient.* New York, NY: Norton, 2005.

CHAPTER 4 – FITNESS

Goleman, Daniel. "What Makes A Leader." *Harvard Business Review*, Nov-Dec, 1998.

Goleman, Daniel. *Emotional Intelligence: Why It Could Matter More Than IQ.* New York, NY: Bantam Books, 2005.

McDonald's USA Nutrition Facts for Popular Menu Items, online at *mcdonalds.com* as a downloadable pdf, 2012.

Maas, James B. *Power Sleep: The Revolutionary Program that Prepares Your Mind for Peak Performance.* New York, NY: Harper Paperbacks, 1998.

Robert Fulghum, *All I Really Needed to Know I Learned in Kindergarten.* New York, NY: Ballantine Books, 1986

Maxwell, John. *The 21 Irrefutable Laws of Leadership.* Nashville, TN: Thomas Nelson, 2007.

Ball, Karlene, et al., for the ACTIVE Study Group. "Effects of Cognitive Training Interventions with Older Adults: A Randomized Controlled Trial." *Journal of the American Medical Association* 288 (2002): 2271-81.

Greene, Kelly. "The Latest in Mental Health: Working Out at the Brain Gym." *Wall Street Journal*, Mar. 28, 2009.

Meier, Paul D., Frank B. Minrith, Frank B. Wichern, and Donald E. Ratcliff. *Introduction to Psychology and Counseling: Christian Perspectives and Applications.* 2nd ed. Ada, MI: Baker Academic, 1991.

Wilson, R. S., P. A. Scherr, J. A. Schneider, Y. Tang, and D. A. Bennett. "Relation of Cognitive Activity to Risk of Developing Alzheimer Disease." *Neurology* 69 (2007):1911-20.

CHAPTER 5 – FAMILY

Doherty, William J., comp. "Over-Scheduled Kids, Under-Connected Families: The Research Evidence." *University of Minnesota Institute for Social Research Center Survey*, Jan. 1999.

Godin, Seth. *Tribes.* New York, NY: The Penguin Group US, 2008.

McGraw, Dr. Phil. *Family First: Your Step-By-Step Plan for Creating a Phenomenal Family.* New York, NY: Free Press / Simon & Schuster, 2004.

REFERENCES

Greene, Melissa Fay. *No Biking In the House Without A Helmet*. New York, NY: Farrar, Straus and Giroux, 2011.

Lieberman, Susan A. *New Traditions: Redefining Celebrations for Today's Family*. Vancouver, CAN: Douglas & McIntyre, 1991.

Moore, General Harold. *We Were Soldiers Once... And Young*. New York, NY: Ballantine Books, 2004.

Albom, Mitch. *Five People You Meet In Heaven*. New York, NY: Hyperion Books, 2003.

Albom, Mitch. *For One More Day*. New York, NY: Hyperion Books, 2008

CHAPTER 6 – FRIENDS

Turkle, Sherry. *Alone Together*. New York, NY: Basic Books, 2011.

Pausch, Randy. *The Last Lecture*. New York, NY: Hyperion Books, 2008.

Zaslow, Jeffery. *The Girls from Ames: A Story of Women & a Forty-Year Friendship*. New York, NY: Gotham Books, 2010.

Maxwell, John. *The 21 Irrefutable Laws of Leadership*. Nashville, TN: Thomas Nelson, 2007.

CHAPTER 7 – FIRM (YOUR WORK)

Warren, Rick. *Daily Hope Blog*. Online motivational material free at *purposedriven.com/blogs*.

Rath, Tom. *StrengthsFinder 2.0*. New York, NY: Gallup Press, 2007.

Truett, Cathy, S. *How Did You Do It Truett? A Recipe for Success*. Decatur, GA: Looking Glass, 2007.

Clifton, Donald, and Paula Nelson. *Soar with Your Strengths: A Simple yet Revolutionary Philosophy of Business and Management*. New York, NY: Dell, 1995.

Colavito, Joe. "Job Track to Joyride: Re-launching Your View of Work." *Highlands Forum*, April 2010.

CHAPTER 8 – FINANCES

Chilton, Dave. *The Wealthy Barber*. New York, NY: Prima Publishing, 1989.

Lindstrom, Martin. *Brandwashed: Tricks Companies Use to Manipulate Our Minds*. New York, NY: Crown Publishing, 2011.

Chilton, Dave. *The Wealthy Barber Returns*. New York, NY: Prima Publishing, 2011.

McInerney, Jay. *The Good Life*. New York, NY: Vintage Books, 2007.

Crompton, Simon. *All About Me: Loving a Narcissist*. New York, NY: Harper Collins, 2008.

Alcorn, Randy. *The Treasure Principle: Discovering the Secret of Joyful Giving*. Sisters, OR: Multnomah, 2001

Weil, Bonnie. *Financial Infidelity*. New York, NY: Plume, 2009.

Brooks, Arthur. *Gross National Happiness*. New York, NY: Basic Books, 2008.

Sowell, Thomas. "War on Poverty Revisited." *Capitalism Magazine*, August 2004.

CHAPTER 9 – FAITH

Dawkins, Richard. *The God Delusion*, New York, NY: Mariner Books, Houghton Mifflin Company, 2008.

Dennett, Daniel. *Breaking the Spell: Religion as a Natural Phenomenon*, New York, NY: Penguin Books, 2006.

Frank, Otto. *Anne Frank: The Diary of a Young Girl*. New York, NY: Doubleday, 1952.

McCormick, Neil. *U2 by U2*. New York, NY: Harper Collins, 2006.

Weil, Andrew. *Spontaneous Happiness*. New York, NY: Little, Brown and Company, 2011.

Miller, Lisa. "No Atheists in Foxholes." *Newsweek Magazine*. July 22, 2010.

Newberg, Andrew. *Why God Won't Go Away*. New York, NY: Random House, 2001.

REFERENCES

CHAPTER 10 – COMMENCEMENT

Coto, Danica. "Acrobat, Mom Reenact Fatal Wire Walk." Associated Press Wire Story, San Juan, Puerto Rico, June 4, 2011.

Ornish, Dr. Dean. "What Matters Most?" *Newsweek Magazine*. Feb. 26, 2008.

Maxwell, John. *The 21 Irrefutable Laws of Leadership.* Nashville, TN: Thomas Nelson, 2007.

Covey, Steven. *The 7 Habits of Highly Effective People*, New York, NY: Simon & Schuster, 2004.

Isaacson, Walter. *Steve Jobs*, New York, NY: Simon & Schuster, 2011.

Cloud, Dr. Henry. *Necessary Endings: The Employees, Businesses, and Relationships That All of Us Have to Give Up In Order to Move Forward.* New York, NY: Harper Collins, 2010.

Williamson, Marianne. *A Return to Love*, New York, NY: Harper Collins, 1992.

Gomstyn, Alice. "Nik Wallenda Crosses Falls, Fulfills Lifetime Dream." ABC News online at *www.abcnews.go.com*, June 15, 2012.

Other Books from Elk Lake:

WAVELENGTH
TUNING IN TO GOD'S VOICE IN A WORLD OF STATIC

By Jeff Petherick with Karl Nilsson

Did God stop speaking? Or did we stop listening?

> *"A spiritual hearing aid. Your guide for moving from mundane to miraculous."*

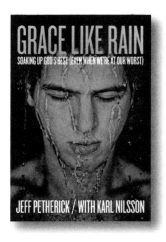

GRACE LIKE RAIN
SOAKING UP GOD'S BEST (EVEN WHEN WE'RE AT OUR WORST)

By Jeff Petherick with Karl Nilsson

True stories of people surprised by grace and changed forever.

> *"Religion is prison. Grace is freedom. Get ready for a spiritual jailbreak."*

BIGGER THAN THE SKY

GROWING UP IS NEVER EASY

By Jeff Petherick with Karl Nilsson

Lavishly illustrated by award-winning artist Bodhi Hill.

"A visual feast. Teaches patience, trust, and the importance of connection."

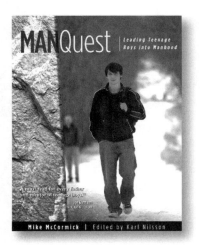

MAN QUEST

LEADING TEENAGE BOYS INTO MANHOOD

By Mike McCormick with Karl Nilsson

How does a boy become a man? And who teaches them?

"Essential playbook. Transforms boys into men of courage, honor and integrity."